Arabic Political Discourse in Transition

Arabic Political Discourse in Transition

El Mustapha Lahlali

EDINBURGH
University Press

Edinburgh University Press is one of the leading university presses in the UK. We publish academic books and journals in our selected subject areas across the humanities and social sciences, combining cutting-edge scholarship with high editorial and production values to produce academic works of lasting importance. For more information visit our website: edinburghuniversitypress.com

© El Mustapha Lahlali, 2022, 2023

Edinburgh University Press Ltd
The Tun – Holyrood Road
12 (2f) Jackson's Entry
Edinburgh EH8 8PJ

First published in hardback by Edinburgh University Press 2022

Typeset in 11/15 Adobe Garamond Pro by
Manila Typesetting Company

A CIP record for this book is available from the British Library

ISBN 978 0 7486 8274 4 (hardback)
ISBN 978 0 7486 9788 5 (paperback)
ISBN 978 0 7486 8273 7 (webready PDF)
ISBN 978 0 7486 8275 1 (epub)

The right of El Mustapha Lahlali to be identified as author of this work has been asserted in accordance with the Copyright, Designs and Patents Act 1988 and the Copyright and Related Rights Regulations 2003 (SI No. 2498).

Contents

Figures	vii
Guide to the Arabic Transliteration System	viii
Acknowledgements	xi
Introduction	1
1 Discourse and Social Change: A Theoretical Framework	6
What is Discourse?	6
Approaches to Discourse	10
Conclusion	34
2 Discourse, Framing and Representational Strategies	35
Representational Strategies in Discourse	35
Discourse Representation	41
Discourse of Revolutions	56
Arab Spring: Transnational Arab Media versus Social Media	65
Social Media and the Arab Spring	67
Conclusion	73
3 Framing, Representation and Conflict in Arabic Discourse	74
Theoretical Background	75
Arab Public Discourse: Positive-Self and Negative-Other	87

	Positive Self and Negative Other in Arabic Political Discourse	94
	Discussion	107
	Conclusion	110
4	Doing Arabic Discourse: Micro-Analysis of Arabic Political Discourse	111
	Micro-Analysis of Arabic Political Discourse	111
	Conclusion	135
5	Macro-Analysis of Arabic Political Discourse: The Discourse of Enforcement and Persuasion	137
	Argumentation and Persuasion: Who is to Blame for the Uprising?	137
	Cognition in Arabic Political Discourse	181
	Conclusion	186
6	Arabic Political Discourse and Politeness Strategies	187
	Politeness and Arabic Discourse	187
	Politeness in Multilingual Slogans	192
	Politeness in Leaders' Speeches	196
	Politeness and the Tribe	199
	Antonyms and Politeness in Leaders' Speeches	201
	Conclusion	203
7	Arabic Islamic Political Discourse	204
	The Arab Spring and Islamic Parties	205
	The Arab Spring: Al-Nahda Discursive Practices	207
	Ḥizb al-Ḥurriyya wa al-'Adāla, Freedom and Justice Party (FJP), Egypt	233
	A New Approach to Studying Shifts in the Discourse of Islamic Parties	257
	Conclusion	259
Conclusion and Findings		261
References		265
Additional References		276
Index		282

Figures

1.1	Dimensions of discourse analysis	18
3.1	Hosni Murabak's face crossed out	102
3.2	Gaddafi's face crossed out and torn into two pieces	104
3.3	'Dégage' (leave) and 'wanted'	105
3.4	Protesters holding national flags	106
3.5	Multilingual slogans	109
5.1	Arab leaders' strategy shift	144
5.2	Discourse of concession: types and degrees of concession	173
5.3	Shifts in discourse in relation to the stages of the Arab Spring	178
5.4	The shift in discourse strategies of Arab leaders and the Arab public during the Arab Spring	179
6.1	Protester holding image of Gaddafi demanding his departure	191
6.2	Yemeni protesters calling for the departure of the president	192
6.3	Multilingual call for the departure of Mubarak	193
7.1	Shifts in the discourse of Islamic parties	258

Guide to the Arabic Transliteration System

The transliteration system adopted is The Library of Congress Transliteration system.* The following tables will firstly list Arabic consonants and vowels.

Arabic Letters

Arabic	Transliteration	Arabic	Transliteration
أ	a	ض	ḍ
ء	ʾ	ط	ṭ
ب	b	ظ	ẓ
ت	t	ع	ʿ
ث	th	غ	gh
ج	j	ف	f
ح	ḥ	ق	q
خ	kh	ك	k
د	d	ل	l
ذ	dh	م	m
ر	r	ن	n

* The full version of the Library of Congress Transliteration system for Arabic consonants and vowels is available at <http://www.loc.gov/catdir/cpso/romanization/arabic.pdf>

Arabic	Transliteration	Arabic	Transliteration
ز	z	ه	h
س	s	و	w
ش	sh	ي	y
ص	ṣ		

Arabic Short-Long Vowels and Case Endings

Arabic	Transliteration
ا	ā
َ	a
ي	ī
ِ	i
و	ū
ُ	u
ً	an
ٍ	in
ٌ	un

Acknowledgements

This book could not have been written without the support and encouragement of many people. I wish to express my sincere gratitude to them all.

I am indebted to Professor Wafa Abu Hatab for her positive and constructive feedback on a draft of the book. I am also very grateful to Christine Barton for all her very positive and constructive remarks. Sincere thanks also go to Nicola Ramsey at Edinburgh University Press for initially supporting the project.

My sincere thanks also go to my PhD students for showing genuine interest in the project, and for all their comments and support.

I wish also to express my gratitude to the anonymous reviewers for their positive and constructive feedback on the proposed project.

Last but not least, this book would not have seen light without the inspiring wisdom of my beloved mother, who continued to be a source of encouragement and inspiration, particularly after the passing away of my adored father.

In memory of my late father

Introduction

In 2011 the Arab world woke up to an eruption of protests and demonstrations, in what has become known as the Arab Spring. These waves of protests took everyone by surprise inside and outside the region. Such unprecedented uprisings across the Arab world have heralded a new era of social and political change, evidenced by the cacophony of voices and interruption to the structure of governance, paving the way for a new social and political order, where Arab citizens have been empowered to call for change. This change has been manifested in the discourse employed by both citizens and leaders of these countries.

The study of discourse in this regard will be vital to determining the social, cultural and political contexts in which it has been generated. Most of the publications in the field have dealt with the discourse of hegemony in the Arab world, but little attention has been given to the discourse of conflict in this region. Ten years since the eruption of the Arab Spring, this book will explore the dialectical relationship between discourse and social change during and post the conflict. It will in particular inspect how Arabic discourse shapes and is shaped by the social, cultural and political changes. It will analyse a wide range of discourses of different actors and stakeholders to identify discourse strategies and key features used to deliver key messages. The main focus will be on the discourse of the Arab public and officials to examine how they represent, frame and position themselves vis-à-vis each other. To examine this change, this book will be considering the following:

1. The notion of framing in the Arab public discourse. Attention will be centred on the discourse employed by the Tunisians, Egyptians and Libyans in naming and labelling each other. A thorough analysis of the genre and type of discourse used would offer an insight into the social and political landscape in these countries during and post the Arab Spring.
2. Another dichotomy that will help us examine this change in discourse is the notion of Us vs Them. This will enable us to examine how the Arab public position themselves in relation to their governments, and how the latter are being portrayed. The book will also look at the way some Arab officials position themselves in relation to their citizens, focusing therefore on the concept of framing and representation in discourse.
3. The other aim of this book is to examine politeness strategies used by the Arab public, and whether they reflect a change in discourse. The focus will be on inspecting the genre of politeness used (i.e. negative politeness, positive politeness, off record . . .) and its purpose.
4. Another aim of this book is to examine the discourse of Islamic parties during and post revolution. The analysis of the discourse of these parties will enable us to gain a good understanding of the type of discourse employed by Islamic parties, notably Al-Nahda and the Freedom and Justice Party in Tunisia and Egypt respectively. The book will also offer a detailed analysis of the strategic shifts in discourse throughout the course of the uprising in Egypt, Libya and Tunisia.

The analysis of the data will be conducted through the prism of Critical Discourse Analysis (CDA), where different layers of analysis will be adopted to account for different objectives. Fairclough's (1995a) framework of social change, amongst others, will be implemented in this book. A micro and macro analysis will be carried out to examine textual and thematic aspects of discourse. This will not only enable us to understand the substance and linguistic features of discourse, but will allow us to examine any shift in discourse.

However, in order to account for the shifts in Arabic discourse, the book will aim to offer a framework for analysis in the context of conflict.

It accommodates different actors and stakeholders as well as minority voices that have often been marginalised. This model will allow a careful examination of shifts and transition of discourse during different stages of its production and consumption. It could be applied to different genres of discourses, where different viewpoints have been expressed during a particular period of time.

Apart from the introduction and conclusion, this book will comprise seven chapters, each of which will contribute to the main theme of transition of discourse in the Arab world.

Chapter 1: Discourse and Social Change: A Theoretical Framework
This chapter will provide the reader with an insight into key approaches to discourse analysis, which are deemed vital to this book. Although other approaches and frameworks will be introduced and discussed, the main focus will be on CDA, particularly Fairclough's (1995a) approach. As this book deals with the transition of Arabic discourse, CDA has been chosen as the main discipline here because it offers adequate tools and mechanisms for the analysis of discourse and social change. It will enable us to examine this transition by adopting a textual and social analysis of the data.

Chapter 2: Discourse, Framing and Representational Strategies
This chapter will introduce the reader to key approaches and concepts on framing and representational strategies in discourse. It will provide the reader with a review of some of the approaches that deal with framing and positioning. This is particularly relevant to this book as it intends to cover the positioning of Arab leaders and protesters vis-à-vis each other. This will allow us to examine the dichotomy of Us vs Them, as well as the representation of different voices and actors in the discourse of conflict. It will also give us an insight into the type and nature of strategies and ideological orientation of discourse.

Chapter 3: Framing, Representation and Conflict in Arabic Discourse
This chapter will consolidate the previous two chapters by examining the notion of Us vs Them in the context of Arabic conflict. It will look at how the Arab public present and position themselves vis-à-vis their officials during

the Arab Spring. In our analysis of the notion of Us vs Them we will identify the discursive construal of an Us/Them binary and how it is presented through language. This chapter will also offer a textual analysis of a set of speeches and slogans of the Arab public during the Arab Spring. The focus will be mainly on the Arab public's use of particular labels in describing and representing their leaders. By examining this representation, it is hoped that more light will be shed on the changes in discourse, and further insight into the type and genre of the relationship governing the Arab public and their officials will be offered.

Chapter 4: Doing Arabic Discourse: Micro-Analysis of Arabic Political Discourse
This chapter will offer a practical analysis of extracts from both Arabic political speeches and public discourse in the context of the Arab Spring. It will offer a step-by-step guide into the application of key discourse analysis concepts and tools that are deemed relevant to understanding different dynamics of Arabic discourse. Some of these concepts include, but are not limited to, presupposition, foregrounding and backgrounding, overlexicalisation, grammatical positioning, nominalisation, cohesion and coherence, use of pronouns, etc. It will in particular highlight and contextualise key textual features in relation to the context of their production.

Chapter 5: Macro-Analysis of Arabic Political Discourse: The Discourse of Enforcement and Persuasion
In this chapter, the discursive practices of two main actors will be examined and analysed. Arab leaders' strategies and discourses in response to the Arab Spring and uprising will be carefully examined to identify the type and nature of discourses used and the shift in their discursive practices. It will demonstrate how shifts in discourse shape and are shaped by the social and political changes. This chapter will also offer an insight into the discursive practices and strategies of the Arabic public (protesters) during the Arab Spring. It is designed to capture their response to officials' discourses and strategies. While the analysis of these discursive practices will enable us to understand the nature of discourse generated, it will also offer an insight into

the argumentation strategies employed by leaders and the Arab public. These strategies will be analysed in relation to the linguistic features used.

Chapter 6: Arabic Political Discourse and Politeness Strategies
This chapter will examine the concept of politeness in the context of the Arab Spring. It will look at politeness strategies in different speeches, statements and slogans, examining therefore any shift in these strategies and discourses. The chapter will explain and contextualise these changes in their wider social, political and cultural contexts.

Chapter 7: Arabic Islamic Political Discourse
This chapter will examine the Islamic parties discourse during and post Arab Spring. The landslide victory of most Islamic parties in post Arab Spring elections in Egypt and Tunisia took many observers by surprise and revealed the popularity of the parties in these countries. The study of their discourse will offer a good understanding of the dialectical relationship between these parties and the wider public. It will also enable us to examine their discourses in the context of conflict and social change. The chapter focuses on Al-Nahda and the Freedom and Justice Party (FJP) in Tunisia and Egypt respectively. A CDA approach, mainly Fairclough's (1995a) framework of language and social change, has been adopted for the analysis of the data, which has been collected from speeches, statements and slogans made by leaders of the two parties.

1

Discourse and Social Change: A Theoretical Framework

This chapter will seek to review the main approaches to discourse analysis in order to give the reader a clearer insight into the main development of discourse and the main approaches and frameworks that deal with discourse and social change, which are of direct relevance to this research. Although other approaches and frameworks will be introduced and discussed, the main focus will be on CDA, particularly Fairclough's (1995a) approach. CDA has been chosen as the main discipline here because it offers, in my view, adequate tools and mechanisms for the analysis of discourse and social change. It offers a variety of approaches and frameworks, some of which allow us to closely study the development of discourse and its link to the wider social, cultural and political contexts. As this book is about the transition of Arabic political discourse, CDA will enable us to examine this transition by adopting a textual and social analysis.

Discourse has become multidisciplinary, with rich and diverse approaches. This chapter will not attempt to cover all approaches related to discourse analysis, but will be selective and only cover those that deal with language in its social context.

What is Discourse?

Defining discourse remains one of the most intricate issues in the field of linguistics. This is due to the diversity of viewpoints and approaches to discourse.

Schiffrin (1994: 20), for instance, defined it in two ways: 'a particular unit of language (above the sentence), and a particular focus (on language use)'. Schiffrin's definition of discourse reflects the existing divide between the formalists and functionalists. Historically, this divide is manifested in the way discourse is approached, and where language was considered as the main grammatical element in the clause or sentence, as opposed to the function language performs in a certain context. Leech (1983: 46) attributed this distinction between the formalists and functionalists to the fact that formalists consider language to be a mental phenomenon while functionalists regard it as a social one. In other words, formalists study language as an autonomous system, while functionalists study it in relation to its social function. The function of language can therefore be explained in relation to two main assumptions, as Schiffrin (1994: 22) outlines: (1) 'language performs a function outside the linguistic system'; (2) 'The organisation of texts can be influenced by external variables.'

Formalists, on the other hand, argue that external factors do not impinge upon the internal organisation of the language. Newmeyer (1983: 2) lucidly points out:

> the grammar of a language is characterized by a formal autonomous system. That is, the phonology, syntax, and those aspects of meaning determined by syntactic configuration form a structural system whose primitive terms are not artifacts of a system that encompasses both human language and other human facilities or abilities.

As clearly pointed out in the above quotation, formalists consider language to be an autonomous system where the meaning is determined by the internal syntactic configuration. The assumption here is that elements of grammar come together to form a unit, which conveys its own meaning away from any external factors that could influence it. Any attempt to explain meaning in relation to external factors is considered irrelevant to the understanding of meaning.

While formalists strongly defend the autonomous system of language, discourse practitioners, however, have considered external factors central to the understanding of meaning. For instance, Stubbs defined discourse as a 'language above the sentence or above the clause' (Stubbs 1983: 1). Similarly,

Van Dijk (1985: 4) observes 'structural descriptions characterise discourse at several levels or dimensions of analysis and in terms of many different units, categories, schematic patterns, or relations'. The common point here is that the functionalists shared the formalists' focus on how units function in relation to each other, although the latter disregard 'the functional relations with the context of which discourse is a part' (Van Dijk 1985: 4).

Central to the definition of discourse is the notion of context. In this respect, Van Dijk (2011a: xvii) asserts that 'discourse is no longer just conceived of as verbal text and talk, but also encompasses the nature of contexts as models of communicative events pragmatically controlling such discourse'. In the same vein, Kress et al. refer to the 'resources for constructing and interpreting the content of texts and communicative events' (Kress et al. 2011: 113), suggesting that discourses are not mere utterances but a true reflection of the cognitive process which generates this discourse and knowledge.

While the cognitive process remains one of the resources for 'constructing content of texts', Van Dijk (2009) highlights the complexity of discourse and refers to it as a 'multidimentional social phenomenon', which brings different elements together. In Van Dijk's words, it is

> a linguistic (verbal, grammatical) object (meaningful sequences or words or sentences), an action (such as an assertion or a threat), a form of social interaction (like a conversation), a social practice (such as a lecture), a mental representation (a meaning, a mental model, an opinion, knowledge), an interactional or communicative event or activity (like a parliamentary debate), a cultural product (like a telenovela) or even like an economic commodity that is being sold and bought (like a novel). (Van Dijk 2009: 67)

Van Dijk's above definition of discourse involves various dimensional aspects that consist of internal aspects of the text as well as social, cultural and cognitive variables that govern the production of discourse, which in turn require careful understanding and examination. As apparent from Van Dijk's definition, discourse is a complex phenomenon and its definition ought to reflect this complexity, which emanates from the multidimensional process which governs the definition of discourse.

By the same token, discourse is taken to refer to authentic texts used in multilayered contexts to perform social functions. In order to understand such social functions, the analysis of any discourse ought to, as Mautner (2009) puts it, 'look beyond the text proper in order to unearth socially meaningful interpretations that can then be enlisted to do socially transformative work' (Mautner 2009: 124). By this, Mautner considers discourse as an agent of social change. The notion of context, reality and social practice are central to Critical Discourse Analysis. Van Dijk, for instance, argues that discourse and reality are inextricably linked, which entails that discourse shapes and is shaped by realities. 'If discourse withdraws from the reality that has been built on it, or to put it more precisely, if people withdraw from that discourse, this part of reality becomes meaningless in the truest sense of the word. It returns to a blank state' (Van Dijk 2009: 39–40). In his definition of discourse, Van Dijk emphasises the significance of cognition. He regards discourse as 'inherently part of both cognition and situations' (Van Dijk 2009: 81). A discussion of Van Dijk's model is introduced in Chapter 3.

My view of discourse here is that it is constitutive as it contributes to the production, transformation and reproduction of social life. Such transformation and production shape and are shaped by discourse itself, as clearly outlined in Fairclough's (1995a) framework, in which he stipulates that there is a strong link between social theories and language analysis. Such a link is manifested in three main dimensions, which are: text, discourse practice and social practice. These dimensions will be discussed at length in Chapter 2.

Discourse: Language Use

While the formalists and functionalists have different viewpoints on the definition of language and its function, some have defined discourse as a language in use. According to Fasold, 'the study of discourse is the study of any aspect of language use' (1990: 65). Brown and Yule expressed the same view that 'the analysis of discourse is, necessarily, the analysis of language in use. As such, it cannot be restricted to the description of linguistic forms independent of the purposes or functions which these forms are designed to serve in human affairs' (1983: 1).

These two quotations make it clear that the analysis of language cannot be divorced from the functions of language in human life. Critical Discourse

Analysts (henceforth CDA) have established such a link by looking at the relationship between language, power and ideology. Fairclough (1989: 23), for instance, advocated the view that there is a dialectical relationship between language and society, which links the daily practice of individuals and groups to the reality they live in; to put it differently, it links language to the context of production, be it the narrow situational or broader contexts. The following section shall be devoted to discussing such a dialectical relationship, highlighting the importance of discourse in communicating social, cultural and political variables that have contributed to generating it. It also examines the process of social change and its impact on discourse, as well as how discourse conveys these changes. In order to understand this process, the following section will review some of the approaches to discourse, in which notions of text, context and social practice are discussed in depth.

Approaches to Discourse

This section will provide a review of the following approaches: Conversational Analysis, Critical Linguistics and Critical Discourse Analysis. These approaches have been selected because of their relevance to studying discourse in relation to its context of production. It is hoped that this review will acquaint the reader with the main tenets of each approach, underlining therefore the similarities and differences between these approaches, as well as providing a clear rationale for the relevance of some of them to this research.

Conversation Analysis

Conversation analysis (CA) is regarded as an approach of discourse analysis, which was developed by Harvey Sacks, Emanuel Schegloff and Gail Jefferson, a group of 'ethnomethodologists', in the 1960s and 70s. Their work was inspired by Harold Garfinkel who first introduced in 1950 the notion of ethnomethodology, defined as 'a label to capture a range of phenomena associated with the use of mundane knowledge and reasoning procedures by ordinary members of society' (Heritage 1984: 4). Garfinkel's concept of ethnomethodology inspired Sacks, Schegloff and Jefferson in the late 1960s and early 1970s, who introduced a system that was 'directed at describing and explicating the competences which ordinary speakers use and rely on when they engage in intelligible, conversational interaction' (Heritage 1984: 241).

This system was based on the observation of various aspects of conversation: conversational opening and closing; the selection of topics; turn-taking; rationale behind the formulation of topics, etc. Some of these aspects will be examined in considerable detail in order to untangle essential information needed for understanding the major tenets of CA.

Turn-taking rules are one of the main aspects of CA, which are introduced to regulate and ensure the flow of conversation, where speakers are fully engaged in the process. In order to ensure the flow and continuity of conversations, Sacks et al. (1974) proposed the following rules: (1) the current speaker may select the next speaker; (2) if not, the next speaker may 'self-select' by starting to produce a turn; (3) if not, the current speaker may continue. These rules are designed to ensure continuation of the conversation with minimal overlap and lapses in conversations. While these rules are established to ensure smooth transition in conversations, CA laid significant focus on the 'sequential implicativeness' of conversation. This entails that any sequence of conversation is linked to what precedes or follows it. 'Adjacency pairs' such as question-and-answer are good examples of this. For instance, answers are generated by a sequence of questions, which implicate answers by the recipient.

Although these rules in most cases ensure that participants are engaged in conversations in a systematic manner, CA's critics often highlight how CA fell short of considering the social and political relationship between participants, and how this implicates their turns and contributions to conversations. They have in particular underlined the issue of power as a major factor in conversation, particularly when conversations take place between participants who have different social rankings. Take for instance, a conversation between a doctor and a patient; such a conversation would be asymmetrically dominated by the doctor, whose social and structural role allows him or her to dominate the process. This, according to Fairclough (1992: 19), is clear evidence 'that producing discourse is part of wider processes of producing social life, social relationships, and social identities'.

However, CA practitioners argue that it does take power relations into consideration when examining utterances. They, for instance, refer to CA studies on interruption in conversations, and how CA practitioners have demonstrated that these acts have been used to dominate conversations. They give the example of Hutchby (1992) who studied conversations on radio talk shows and concluded that interruption was used by the host to dominate the conversation, and in other cases to exert power, especially in cases where callers exhibited different viewpoints to the host.

Sacks (1992) focused on the turn-taking, displaying how the first participant can be in a weaker position, compared to the second participant who is in a much stronger position, as he or she has the chance to comment on the first participant's opinions. This puts the second participant in a powerful position (Sacks 1992). While CA has been criticised for paying little attention to the issue of power in conversations, other approaches have devoted time and space to examine the relationship between language and society, including power. Amongst these approaches is Critical Linguistics, which will be introduced in the following section.

Critical Linguistics

In 1970 a group from the University of East Anglia developed Critical Linguistics (CLS). Drawing on systematic linguistics, they sought to marry text linguistics with social theory, to examine the function of language in its social and political context, taking into account the political and ideological processes in the interpretation and explanation of discourse (Fairclough 1992: 26). Text linguistics could be said to have put a rupture between the Chomskyan paradigm and sociolinguistics. This rupture is visible in its rejection of the argument that language systems are autonomous and somehow independent from the language use which has a 'function in social structure' (Halliday 1973: 65). Indeed, language can be very revealing of the social position of speakers, who 'make "selections" according to social circumstances' (Fairclough 1992: 26).

Critical Linguists' main interest is establishing the dialectic relationship between language and society. CLS starts from the assumption that language shapes and is shaped by society. To borrow Fowler's words, 'language serves to confirm and consolidate the organisations which shape it' (Fowler et al. 1979: 190).

In order to unearth social meanings expressed in texts, Fowler et al. proposed 'analysing the linguistic structures in the light of their interactional and wider social context' (Fowler et al. 1979: 195–6). Drawing on Halliday's work in 'systemic grammar', CLS combines textual and social analysis; Critical Linguists' approach to text is different from other approaches as they focus on grammar and vocabulary and their occurrences in contexts. Further emphasis is on aspects of grammar which have interpersonal meanings, that is, the focus on how social relations and identities are marked in clauses (Fairclough 1992: 28). Critical Linguists' approach to vocabulary is based on the assumption that the choice of lexis may not be done at random, but it could carry ideological connotations, regarding the text as a product; however, Fairclough criticises this approach as it pays little attention to the process of text production and interpretation. Fairclough went even further to criticise CLS for what he considers 'one-sided emphasis upon the effect of discourse in the social reproduction of existing social relations and structures, and correspondingly neglects both discourse as a domain in which social struggles take place, and change in discourse as a dimension of wider social and cultural change' (Fairclough 1992: 28–9). This has led Fairclough to assert that language-ideology interface is narrowly perceived in CLS, asserting that elements of texts beyond grammar and lexis (i.e. overall structure) could be of ideological significance. The second point that Fairclough highlighted is that CLS dealt with written monologue, with little articulation of ideologically important aspects of the organisation of spoken dialogue. His other criticism concerns the narrow focus of CLS on ideology as realised in the text rather than on the process of interpretation, which involves interpreters making assumptions, which have ideological nature but are not present in the text (Fairclough 1992: 29). Such interpretations spring from the interpreter's assumption and interpretation of the text.

These limitations have been observed by CLS practitioners, who have attempted to come up with a developed approach to combine a social theory of discourse with a method of text analysis, with a clear emphasis on political discourse. Pecheux, whose ideas were inspired by Althusser's Marxist theory of ideology, was one of the scholars who attempted to make such a link explicit. He accentuates 'the effects of ideological struggle within the functioning of language, and, conversely, the existence of linguistic materiality within ideology' (Pecheux 1982 in Fairclough 1992: 30).

Critical Discourse Analysis (CDA)

CDA is a newly developed discipline that found its roots in the work of Foucault, whose work inspired CDA researchers such as Fairclough. Foucault approaches discourse from a wider perspective and considers it to be constitutive as it constitutes or constructs society on various social dimensions: 'Discourse constitutes the objects of knowledge, social subjects and forms of 'self', social relations and conceptual frameworks.' The second element in his approach is 'the emphasis on the interdependency of the discourse practices of a society or institution: texts always draw upon and transform other contemporary and historically prior texts' (Fairclough 1992: 39–40). He considers any discourse type to be generated out of combinations of others, and to be defined by its relationship to others. His view of discourse centres on 'the socio-historically variable "discursive formations", system of rules which make it possible for certain statements but not others to occur at particular times, places and institutional locations' (Fairclough 1992: 40).

Before dwelling on the main approaches of CDA, it would be useful first to provide a brief definition and description of CDA. According to Van Dijk, CDA 'is a type of discourse analytical research that primarily studies the way social power abuse, dominance and inequality are enacted, reproduced, and registered by text and talk in the social and political context (2005: 352). Similarly, Chouliaraki and Fairclough have emphasised the interdisciplinary approach of CDA, where linguistic and social theories are married to make sense of a text. They described the eclectic nature of CDA as follows:

> We see CDA as bringing a variety of theories into dialogue, especially social theories on the one hand and linguistic theories on the other, so that its theory is a shifting synthesis of other theories, though what it itself theorises in particular is the mediation between the social and linguistic or the 'order of discourse', the social structuring of semiotic hybridity (interdiscursivity). (Chouliaraki and Fairclough 1999: 16)

Chouliaraki and Fairclough's above definition of discourse emphasises the transdisciplinarity of discourse, where different 'disciplines are brought together into dialogue with one another' (Fairclough 2001: 362). Similarly, Wodack (2009: 34) rejected the claim that there is a 'uniform, common theory formation' for CDA. Meyer (2001: 18) has also reiterated this diversity in CDA, underscoring that there is no 'guiding theoretical viewpoint that is used consistently within CDA'. This indeed underlines the variety of theoretical viewpoints within CDA, some of which will be introduced in the subsequent section.

Van Dijk's 'Social-Cognitive' Model

This model is widely associated with Van Dijk who has developed a framework for analysing news as discourse. Van Dijk's approach has moved beyond the textual analysis into the analysis of practices concerning news production and news comprehension, and which has a social-psychological emphasis on the process of social cognition. Van Dijk's model laid emphasis on how cognitive 'models' and 'schemata' shape production and consumption of discourse (Fairclough 1995b: 29).

Van Dijk's framework has been used in the analysis of news texts, with a focus on the 'structures of news', processes of news production and processes of news comprehension. The framework tends to show the existing relationship between the text and processes of production and comprehension of discourse, and between these and the wider social practices they are embedded within' (Fairclough 1995b: 29). At the textual level, Van Dijk emphasises the importance of the macro and micro levels in interpreting texts through the cognitive model (Van Dijk 1997). The idea of macro-structure is central to the analysis of thematic structure, which refers to the overall organisation in terms of themes or topics (Van Dijk 1997). The microstructure of news discourse, however, is analysed in terms of the semantic relations between propositions. It also examines the syntactic and semantic aspects as well as rhetoric features of news report. Both the macro and microstructures are vital to the analysis of news production and comprehension, as well as the analysis of news structures.

Apart from the text production, Van Dijk's notion of 'mental representation' of texts is constructed by consumers of texts, influenced by their societal beliefs (Kintsch and Van Dijk 1983). This means that readers of media texts interpret the content of texts in relation to their own societal and individual beliefs. Kintsch and Van Dijk regard the mental representation as 'the interface between the social and the personal, between the general and the specific, and between social representations and their enactment in discourse and other social practices' (1978: 27).

Although Van Dijk confidently reassured readers of the sound link of the production of discourse to the cognitive state of mind of the producer, others, including Fairclough (1995b: 31), remained sceptical and asserted that Van Dijk's framework has a number of limitations. They argue that his model pretends to focus on representations, while little attention has been given to social relations and identities in news discourse. His framework has also been criticised for focusing on the linguistics analysis of sentences, where little or no focus has been paid to intertextuality.

Some other limitations of Van Dijk's framework include 'a one-sided emphasis to news-making practices as stable structures which contribute to the production of relations of domination and racist ideologies, which backgrounds the diversity and heterogeneity of practices' (Fairclough 1995b: 31).

Having introduced Van Dijk's cognitive model within CDA, we now turn to Fairclough's social model.

Fairclough's Model: A Social Theory of Discourse
In this section we shall consider Fairclough's framework of discourse as a social practice. A review of language use and function takes us back to De Saussure (1959) who considered language use as an individual activity designed to express individual thoughts. Fairclough, however, believes that language use is a form of a social practice. His view of discourse as a social practice entails that discourse is a mode of social action, where people collectively act upon issues surrounding them. This also implies that there is a 'dialectical relationship' between discourse and social structure, meaning that discourse shapes and is shaped by the sociocultural practices. Drawing on Foucault's view that discourse is socially constitutive, Fairclough has provided three main aspects of the constructive effects of discourse: Discourse contributes to the construction of 'social identities', social relationships between people, and 'system of knowledge and belief' (Fairclough 1992: 64).

According to Fairclough, these three aspects correspond to three functions of language. These functions are: 'identity', 'relational' and 'ideational'. Fairclough further explains this to mean that the identity function is related to the way social identities are represented in discourse; the relational function refers to the way social relations between participants are enacted and represented in discourse; the ideational function refers 'to the ways in which texts signify the world and its processes, identities and relations'(Fairclough 1992: 64). It should be mentioned here that Fairclough drew on Halliday's (1985) metafunctions of grammar (ideational, interpersonal and intertextual).

As mentioned above, Fairclough laid much emphasis on the dialectical relationship between discourse and social structure. According to him, discourse contributes to 'the constitution of all those dimensions of social structure which directly or indirectly shape and constrain it: its own norms and conventions, as well as the relations, identities and institutions which lie behind them' (Fairclough, 1992: 64).

Fairclough regards discourse as a political practice, which establishes, 'sustains and changes power relations'. He argues that 'discourse as a political practice is not only a site of power struggle, but also a stake in power struggle' (Fairclough 1992: 67). His view of discourse and power will be discussed in detail later in this chapter.

The other issue that has attracted Fairclough's attention is the discursive nature of discourse. He believes that discursive practices are manifested in texts, both written and spoken. He also considers discursive practice to be part of the social practice, which in turn is 'wholly constitutive' of the discursive practice. And, therefore, any analysis of discourse as part of discursive practice should consider the 'processes of text production, distribution and consumption' (Fairclough 1992: 71). These processes are vital to the analysis of discourse, with reference to the social, cultural, political and economic institutions within which discourses are generated. Apart from the social and political variables that govern the production of discourse, production and consumption of discourse tend to have a socio-cognitive nature, as discussed in Van Dijk's model.

As stated above, in his analysis of discourse, Fairclough refers to three main dimensions, which are: Text; discourse practice and social practice, as demonstrated in the following diagram (Figure 1.1).

As Figure 1.1 shows, Fairclough's model consists of three main dimensions: text, discourse practice and social practice. These dimensions will be introduced and discussed below.

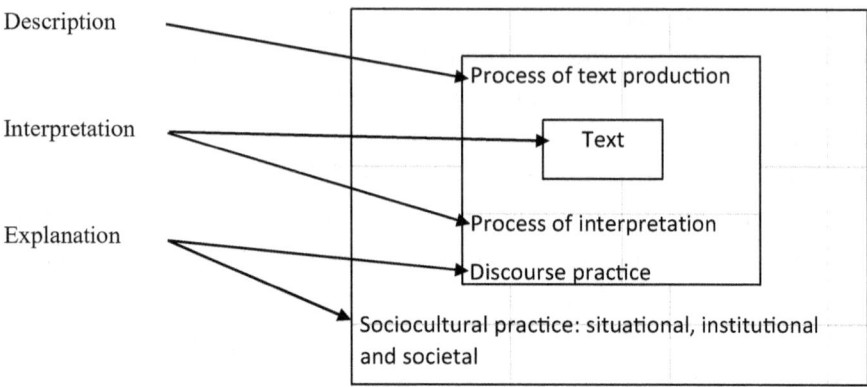

Figure 1.1 Dimensions of discourse analysis

Discourse as Text

This dimension is based on the traditional methods of linguistic analysis, where the focus is mainly on the grammatical and semantic aspects of sentences and other smaller units. The analysis also contains elements beyond the sentences, including the way sentences and paragraphs are linked together, as well as coherent overall structure of the text (Fairclough 1995b: 57). Based on his multifunctional view of discourse, Fairclough asserts that individual clauses and sentences have 'three main categories of function: ideational, interpersonal and textual' (1995b: 58).

Discourse Practice

This dimension involves aspects of text production and text consumption, which have an institutional nature. For instance, the production process would include editorial procedures involved in the production of a piece of discourse.

Fairclough (1995b) has distinguished between what he refers to as conventional discourse practice and creative discourse practice. The former is reflected in the form and content of the text, which are homogeneous. The latter practice is heterogeneous where the textual analysis is combined with the social and cultural analysis (Fairclough 1995b: 60).

Intertextual analysis is another element of discourse practice, which focuses on the text from a discourse practice perspective; that's to say looking at the traces of the discourse practice in the text. In Fairclough's words, 'intertextual analysis aims to unravel the various genres and discourses which [. . .] are articulated together in the text'(Fairclough 1995b: 61). Linking the text analysis to intertextual analysis, as far as Fairclough is concerned, is vital to 'bridging the gap between text and language' (Fairclough 1995b: 62).

Social Practice
The other dimension in the analysis of texts is the sociocultural practice. This includes the immediate situation context, the wider social context as well as the global context.

This dimension allows the analysis of texts in relation to the context of the situation, which includes the interpretations of the totality of the social practice of which discourse is a part; these interpretations, one could argue, inject more clarification and reduce ambiguity of the meaning of texts, as it sheds more light on aspects of the social identity of participants, and their roles and functions in the social context of the text, particularly that 'social practices are socially regulated ways of doing things' (Leeuwen 2008: 6). So the effect of the context on the interpretation of the text depends upon the 'reading of the situation' (Fairclough 1995b: 83). This reading would consider different elements, some of which are structures and social practices, which will be discussed in the subsequent section.

While Fairclough's CDA approach has been welcomed and celebrated by CDA practitioners, it has attracted criticism from other scholars outside the field. Widdowson (1998), for instance, points out that CDA 'still suffers confusion in its theoretical framework' (Lahlali 2007: 61). He describes Fairclough's approach as 'interpretive rather than analytic, descriptive rather than theoretical' (1998: 515). Similarly, Gottlieb (1987: 276) criticised the lack of a unified methodology of research within CDA, and the absence of explicit rules which govern the type of analysis to be conducted. He also criticises CDA practitioners for viewing their work as 'an art achieved through practice' (Gottlieb 1987: 276). Widdowson and Gottlieb are not the only ones who have expressed their concerns about CDA methodology. Gallagher (1998), a CDA practitioner, 'considers CDA methodology inadequate' (Lahlali 2007: 61), expressing her dissatisfaction with the lack of rules and mechanisms of analysis within CDA (Gallagher 1998: 85). She calls for a unified methodology within CDA; however, this call has been rejected by Chouliaraki and Fairclough (1999) who emphasised the importance of transdisciplinary* analysis, pointing out that different questions require different methodologies.

As mentioned above, CDA diverse methodologies emanate from its focus on the relationship between discourse and social structures, which is complex and could be considered as a two-way traffic, meaning that discourse is determined by the social structures, but also has 'effects upon social structures and contributes to the achievement of social continuity or social change' (Fairclough 1989: 37). Social structures are not only a product of discourse, but they are themselves a means to determine discourse. This dialectical relationship between discourse and social structures has been emphasised by scholars such as Fairclough who linked the production of discourse to social structures, pointing out that 'whenever people produce or interpret discourse, they necessarily draw upon orders of discourse and other aspects of social structure'. By being drawn upon, 'the social structures are created anew in discourse and practice generally' (Fairclough 1989: 39). By practice here, Fairclough refers to the social practice which he defines as an 'active relationship to reality, and it changes reality' (Fairclough 1989: 37). This social practice is often determined by the social structure, which in turn is 'a product of social practice' (1989: 37).

This dialectical relationship between the social structure and discourse, as well as social practice, emphasises the importance of discourse in terms of power relationships, power struggle and ideology. The following section will shed some light on the relationship between discourse and ideology.

Political Discourse Analysis (PDA)

Having briefly introduced the notion of discourse, methods and approaches to discourse, which are deemed relevant to this research, we now turn to introducing the notion of political discourse and relevant approaches associated with it.

CDA practitioners consider PDA to be a vital critical enterprise. It deals with 'the analysis of political discourse from a critical perspective,

---

* By transdisciplinary, Fairclough means 'relationship wherein the logic of one theory is put to work with another' (2000: 164).

a perspective which focuses on the reproduction and contestation of political *power* through political discourse' (Fairclough and Fairclough 2013: 17). Political discourse is not confined to politicians only, but attached to political actors, citizens, institutions, organisations, all of which are engaged in political activities and events in particular contexts (Van Dijk 1997). The concept of context remains vital to understanding political discourse. In this regard, Fairclough and Fairclough (2013: 18) pointed out that 'outside political contexts, the discourse of politicians or any "political actors" is not "political"'. The underlying reason for such a claim is that political contexts are 'institutional contexts, i.e. contexts which make it possible for actors to exert their agency and empower them to act on the world in a way that has an impact on matters of common concern' (Fairclough and Fairclough 2013: 18).

They go on to argue that political discourse can contribute to providing tangible answers for political questions, if 'it focuses on features of discourse, which are relevant to "the function of the political process or event whose discursive dimension is being analysed"' (Fairclough and Fairclough 2013: 18).

Fairclough and Fairclough have divided PDA into two main current approaches: Chilton's (2004) approach examines PDA from a cognitive perspective, trying to establish the link between language and politics from a cognitive and evolutionary perspective. It is strongly grounded in cognitive sciences and cognitive linguistics. While Chilton (2004) underlines the cognitive aspects of discourse, his critics have criticised him for paying little attention to the notion of action. Fairclough and Fairclough (2013) consider this to be a shortcoming as it marginalised the notion of action, taken by individuals, groups or institutions, and which could have an impact on the ground.

Chilton and Schäffner (2011: 311) have identified two main problems when dealing with political discourse analysis. The first issue is 'what is political depends on the standpoint of the commentator'. The second point raised is that 'the multiplicity of acts that are performed through language (that is, discourse), can be interpreted as serving many different purposes – not only political but also heuristic, ludic, informative, etc.'

The political notion raised in the first problem is taken to mean 'those actions (linguistic or other) which involve power, or its inverse, resistance' (Chiltern and Schäffner 2011: 331). As for the second issue, Chilton and

Schäffner propose to 'link political situations and processes to discourse types and levels of discourse organization by way of an intermediate level, which we call strategic function' (2011: 311). This strategic function 'enables analysts of text and talk to focus on details and contribute to the phenomena which people intuitively understand as "political", rather than on functions such as the informational, the ludic, etc.' Chilton and Schäffner (2011: 311). For Chilton and Schäffner, syntax and lexis can only be used as 'the means by which speakers and hearers will interactively produce complex and diverse meanings' (2011). They go on to argue that the lexis is often 'given meanings that are consistent with our background knowledge and values' (2011: 313). Indeed, lexis is chosen and selected to conform with individuals and groups' knowledge and beliefs.

Another aspect of political discourse is the notion of argumentation, which Fairclough and Fairclough regard as vital to political discourse as a social activity used by speakers to advance and justify their claims. While stressing the importance of argumentation in political discourse, Fairclough and Fairclough call upon Wodak to consider argumentation in its approach, Discourse-Historical Analysis.

Although Wodak is internationally recognised for her work on political discourse, her approach, according to Fairclough and Fairclough, needs adjusting to accommodate the analytical needs, including the focus on argumentation. 'This is why we have developed a way of representing and evaluating practical argumentation, partly drawing on informal logic and pragma-dialectics, and using concepts such validity, soundness, argument scheme, etc.' (Fairclough and Fairclough 2013: 23).

While Wodak (2001: 46; 2009: 94) considers *argumentation* a 'discursive strategy', Fairclough and Fairclough's approach does not recognise argumentation as a strategy nor as a 'discursive strategy'. The definition of strategy is also a point of difference between Wodak's and Fairclough's. For the latter, a strategy is a 'category within the theories of action, not within theories of discourse' (Fairclough and Fairclough 2013: 24). Strategies, they argue, 'involve goals which are outside and beyond discourse, i.e. they involve desired changes in the world, not in discourse' (2013: 24). Strategies 'have a discursive dimension in the sense that they are devised in processes of practical reasoning, and formulated in language, but the argumentation that corresponds to this reasoning is not itself a strategy' (2013: 250). For them, political action is strategic and not the discourse itself. This supports their view that language is a form of social action, and that action may lead to a change of the world surrounding us.

Although Fairclough and Fairclough (2013) have tried to propose a new framework for the analysis of political discourse, their approach remains very complex and complicated. Their central focus on the argumentation of political discourse has its limitations as it is not broad enough to accommodate different genre of political speeches, for instance. Not all political speeches have an argumentative nature/form. Some could be informative and are designed to convey plain information to citizens.

Mediated Discourse

The term 'mediated discourse' is quite a complicated term to define. According to Scollon (1998) mediated discourse can refer to the discourse of 'the media', both print and audio-visual media. The term has also been used in association with the 'computer-mediated discourse'. This refers to the type of communication that computers serve as a medium of communication between different participants. The third proposed definition of the term involves any mediation in carrying out everyday discourses. This includes both written and oral discourses.

Scollon (1998) draws on CDA (Fairclough 1989, 1992, 1995a, 1995b), mediated action theory (Wertsch 1991, 1994) and situated learning (Lave and Wenger 1991; Chaiklin and Lave 1993) in his analysis of discourse as a social action. The chief aim for these theories and approaches was to develop a social/cultural and historical perspective on the relationship between society, participants and the role of language in this mediation. Scollon argues that mediated 'discourse is best understood as social interaction' (1998: 18). However, he highlighted concerns related to the methodology of conducting such an analysis, especially that mediated discourse is founded in ethnography.

Discourse and Ideology

The dialectical relationship between discourse and social practice, and between the social structure and social practice, discussed in previous sections, allows different interpretations of the discourse practice in relation to the wider social practice; this includes establishing the link between aspects of discourse and ideology. This combination of discourse and ideology is not a new phenomenon, but can be traced back to Althusser (1971) who provided a theoretical framework which highlights the relationship between discourse, ideology and reality, pointing out that ideology does not 'reflect' the real world but 'represents' the 'imaginary relationship of individuals' to the real world. According to Fairclough, discourse has materials embedded in the practice of institutions, which often reflects 'beliefs and values of those institutions, and this encourages investigation of ideology as a social practice' (Fairclough 1992: 87).

Unlike Althusser's configuration of ideology, Fairclough is of the view that ideology resides in both the structure (order of discourse; the outcome of past and current events) and event themselves 'as they reproduce and transform their conditioning structures' (Fairclough 1992: 89). Ideology becomes rooted in our norms and conventions, as well as in our practices. It has become a naturalised process that cannot be avoided, embedded in the discourse we produce, reflected in its content and meaning (Fairclough 1992). Indeed, ideology becomes part of political discourse, where different individual, groups and parties seek to promote their type of discourse and make it the predominant type. This competition or struggle over language 'can manifest itself as a struggle between ideologically diverse discourse types' (Fairclough 1989: 90). The struggle over maintaining a certain type of discourse is an ideological struggle, as the establishment of a particular discourse indicates the dominant nature of this discourse in a certain social context (Fairclough 1989). Take, for instance, political discourse, in which each party or a group seeks to advance their discourse and make it acceptable to citizens, and as a result to promote its ideological thinking. This diversity of discourse types is reflected in the complex structures of institutions and societies, in which different discourse types are used in different situations and contexts. This frequently creates different sets of ideologically competing discourse types, which are generated by different individuals, groups or parties. In this respect, Wodak considers ideology as part of our daily practice, asserting that 'ideology is an unavoidable moment of all thinking and acting' (2007: 2).

Similarly, Van Dijk considers ideology as a set of ideas and beliefs that are practised by social groups, and that these beliefs 'influence their interpretation of social events and situations and control their discourse and other social practices as group members' (Van Dijk 2011b: 380). He reiterated the value of the group in these shared ideas, reinforcing his claim that belief systems are not 'individual, personal beliefs' (Van Dijk 2011b: 382). He goes on to argue that the idea of a shared ideology does not mean all members of the community or a group have identical ideology, nor do they 'apply it in the same way' (2011b: 383). People may choose to apply ideology in ways which reflect their individual beliefs, as well as beliefs of groups which they represent. These ideologies are not inherently born with individuals, but are acquired, created and enhanced in social contexts. They are then reproduced through the mean of discourse. They are 'adapted in many debates, manifests and other forms of in-group discourse, as was the case for liberalism, socialism, feminism, pacifism and environmentalism' (2011b: 384).

Althusser (2014) has divided the notion of ideology into two types: a general theory of ideology, which is detached from any historical or social elements; and a theory of specific ideologies where certain ideological beliefs emanate from political and cultural beliefs of producers (i.e. socialism, capitalism, fascism).

Local Coherence Relations and Ideology
I draw here on Fairclough's definition of local coherence as the relationship between clauses, clause complexes or sentences. They are of three main types: elaboration, extension and enhancement. In elaboration, one clause elaborates on the other by explaining, providing specific information or examples. In extension, one clause 'extends the meaning of another by adding something new to it'. In enhancement, 'one clause enhances the meaning of another by adding something new to it' (Fairclough 1995b: 121).

The coherent relations between clauses and sentences may be either implicit or explicit. They are not often signalled by markers of cohesion such as conjunctions or sentence-linking adverbials (but, accordingly, nevertheless, afterwards, etc.). In their categorisation of cohesion, Halliday and Hasan (1976) distinguish between what they refer to as grammatical cohesion and lexical cohesion. These are categorised into four types of cohesion: conjunction, lexical cohesion, reference and ellipsis.

It should be mentioned here that relations of coherence between clauses and sentences of a text are not objective properties of the text, 'they are relations that have to be established by people interpreting it' (Fairclough 1995b: 122). This is the case for clauses that have no explicit cohesive markers binding them together. Although cohesion relations are largely explicit they can be, at times, implicit and rely on interpreting relations between these clauses and sentences. Interpreters of these relations draw upon other prepositions, which allow them to make sense of the text at hand. Such interpretations are not always impartial and they can embody an individual's thoughts and views on the world.

Discourse and Power

It would be incomplete to talk about CDA without mentioning power and hegemony in discourse, as this is one of the main tenets of CDA. In this section we will explore the relationship between discourse and power from a CDA perspective.

In this respect, Van Dijk states that 'one of the crucial tasks of Critical Discourse Analysis (CDA) is to account for the relationship between discourse and social power' (1996: 84). Like other CDA leaders, Van Dijk (2001: 352) emphasised the role of CDA in exposing relations of power and hegemony, as well as inequality within discourse. Weiss and Wodak assert that 'in texts discursive differences are negotiated; they are governed by differences in power [. . .] determined by discourse and by genre' (2003: 15).

Like Weiss and Wodak (2003), Fairclough acknowledges that discourse reflects implicit power and hegemony practices. He defines hegemony as 'leadership as much as domination across the economic, political, cultural and ideological domains of a society' (1992: 92). This hegemony is exercised in social structures and reflected in discourse. In order to understand how power is reflected in discourse, Van Dijk (2001) proposed that any analysis within CDA should establish the link between the 'micro' level of discourse (i.e. discursive practice) and the 'macro' level (i.e. power relations in society) (Van Dijk 2001: 354). The idea of linking the 'macro' and 'micro' levels of discourse has been reinforced by other CDA leaders such as Fairclough. This linkage serves a tool to reveal the social interpersonal relations constructed in discourse, including power relations.

In order to unearth this power in discourse, Fairclough refers to two types of power relations in discourse: 'power in discourse' and 'power behind discourse'. According to Fairclough, 'power in discourse is concerned with discourse as a place where relations of power are actually exercised and enacted' (1989: 43). Fairclough has given an example of power in a 'face-to-face' discourse where participants are in an *unequal encounter*. Examples of this could include the encounter between doctors and patients, students and teachers, employees and employers, etc.

Fairclough proclaims that power in discourse is to do with 'powerful participants controlling and constraining the contributions of non-powerful participants' (1989: 46). In his analysis of the power in discourse, Fairclough referred to three types of such constraints:

1. Contents: what is said and done.
2. Relations: the social relations people enter into discourse.
3. Subjects: the positions the participants occupy.

In addition to the contextual analysis, a good interpretation of the content of discourse could serve as a clear indication of the relationship between the participants.

Hidden power, on the other hand, entails looking at how orders of discourse, 'as dimensions of the social orders of social institutions or societies, are themselves shaped and constituted by relations of power' (Fairclough 1989: 43). According to Fairclough (1989), power is not something that can be dominated by one person, but it is a social struggle phenomenon. While distinguishing between the power in discourse and behind discourse, Fairclough highlighted the key difference between 'face-to-face' discourse and media discourse. He emphasised the fact that in face-to-face interaction, participants can be producers and interpreters of discourse, while in media discourse there is a big difference between producers and consumers of this type of discourse.

While power in discourse can be explicit and detected through different mechanisms of analysis, 'power behind discourse' is different as 'the whole social order of discourse is put together as a hidden effect of power' (Fairclough 1989: 55).

Fairclough has given the example of the discourse of medical examination in which he focused on how medical staff and patients are positioned in relation to each other, and how this positioning can be revealing as to the power relations and dominance of discourse. He has given the medical encounter and the relationship between the doctor and patient, in which the doctor has full power to control the flow of interaction (Fairclough 1989). This dominance is reflected in the genre of discourse used and its structure, such as turn-taking, opening and closing, order of discourse, etc. However, although the example of a medical encounter embodies this type of power relations, it could be argued that the nature of the doctor's position/job dictates that he or she should ask questions and initiate discussion to be able to gather information pertaining to the patient's well-being, and this will only be realised by asking questions related to the patient's illness.

Another point that was highlighted by Fairclough is that in face-to-face discourse producers design their interaction to correspond to the people they are interacting with. They can change their language and methods based on the feedback of their co-participants. However, this feature is often absent in media discourse as it is produced to a mass audience, and it is difficult to know the audience/recipients or consumers. According to Fairclough (1989), producers generally address an ideal subject, be it viewers, or listeners or readers. Despite this, producers of media discourse continue to exert power over their consumers, as they have the right over what content to include and exclude. Such a distinction underlines that discourse is not a straightforward process, but it is the outcome of the producer's ideological, social and political stance. Discourse, as mentioned above, does not only shape, but is shaped by, various social variables. A good understanding of the dynamics of discourse requires an insight into the producer and the context in which discourse has been produced. This has its challenges and may not be a straightforward process, but relying on the text only without a close examination of its context would not allow greater access to the main elements constituting discourse, and where the dialectical relationship between the discourse and the social context of its production is central. This dialectical relationship between the text and social context is indeed very useful in the interpretation of the main motives and enticements behind the production of discourse. Discourse does not only contribute to the construction of social identities and social relations between people, but shapes and reconstructs ideologies which arise in societies characterised by relations of domination, and this includes gender, class, cultural groups, etc. (Fairclough 1992). These relations of dominance tend to have a detrimental effect on societies, and for this purpose Blommaert (2005: 1) reiterated the role of CDA in considering the 'outcome' of the influence of power on societies. He considered CDA to be a useful tool in unveiling power and hegemony expressed in discourse, and which often reflects the asymmetrical relations in societies (Blommaert 2005: 24–5).

Discursive Change

Discursive change is one of the main aspects that have been examined by Fairclough in relation to social and cultural change. Fairclough's assumption is that any change of the social structure of the society finds its way to discourse. In other words, discourse shapes and is shaped by the social structure of the society. Fairclough's main question pertaining to this has been: What are the main factors that lead to discursive change? Can the social and cultural change lead to a discursive change? In his answer to these questions, Fairclough asserts that any process of change does affect the order of discourse. Any change, irrespective of its scope, does leave 'traces in texts in the form of the co-occurrence of contradictory or inconsistent elements – mixtures of formal and informal styles, technical and non-technical vocabularies, markers of authority and familiarity, more typically written and more typically spoken syntactic forms' (Fairclough 1992: 97).

Another element of discourse that Fairclough has given more attention to is the order of discourse. As highlighted above, a change in the social and political structure infrequently leads to a new order of discourse, which reflects such a change, irrespective of its magnitude. Depending on the nature of discourse, the order of discourse can have a local or societal form (1992: 97).

Discursive change is mostly important in this book because it tends to examine how the change of political structure in some Arab countries, post Arab Spring, has led to a change in discursive practices. For instance, has the new political landscape in Egypt, Libya and Tunisia affected the discursive practices of political parties and civil societies in these three Arab countries? What type of discourse, if any, emerged after the Arab Spring? Answering these questions would require a discursive analysis of the type of discourses that emerged after the eruption of the Arab Spring, as in Chapters 4, 5, 6 and 7.

Intertextuality

Intertextuality 'refers to the linkage of all texts to other texts, both in the past and in the present' (Wodak 2009: 39). Similarly, Fairclough refers to intertextuality as series of texts 'which are transformationally related to each other in the sense that each member of the series is transformed into one or more of the others in regular and predictable ways' (Fairclough 1992: 130). To simplify Wodak and Fairclough's definitions, intertextuality is the link of a text to elements of other events or actions that took place in the past. This is what Fairclough (1992) refers to as 'intertextual chains', which serve to demonstrate the linkage between the text and other previous texts. This will be particularly useful in the context of the Arab Spring, as 'intertextual chains' will allow us to establish the link between certain discourse types pre and post Arab Spring. For instance, it will enable us to establish any intertextual chains in the discourse of political leaders, especially when contextualising the Arab Spring within the wider historical contexts of their respective countries.

The analysis of intertextuality in political discourse in the context of the Arab Spring will not only help in gaining an insight into the type of discourses that emerged post Arab Spring, but will serve as an indicator of the type of political change, or lack of it, that took place in some Arab countries. As mentioned above, the transformation of the political landscape in societies shapes and is shaped by the type of discourse used, and most often traces of this change are visible in texts.

According to Fairclough, 'transformations between text types in an intertextual chain can be of diverse sorts. They may involve forms of manifest intertextuality, such as discourse representation' (1992: 131). Different elements of discourse (vocabulary, grammatical choices, etc.), often offer different interpretations at different levels (Fairclough 1992: 131).

For Fairclough 'intertextual relations are central to the understanding of processes of subject constitution. This is on a biographical time-scale, during the life of an individual, and for the constitution and reconstitution of social groups and communities' (1992: 133). Fairclough's intake on intertextual relations will prove useful in this book, as we intend to examine the change of political discourse pre and post Arab Spring, with a particular focus on the discourse of Arab leaders. Intertextual relations will indeed provide us with the opportunity of examining political leaders' discourse during a certain timescale in the life of political leaders, selected for this study.

Fairclough has commented on how intertextuality 'complicates the process of interpretation' as texts are a reflection of a mixture of a wide range of elements (1992: 135). Fairclough refers to this mixture of different levels of texts within a text: 'metadiscourse is a peculiar form of manifest intertextuality where the text producer distinguishes different levels within her own text, and distances herself from some level of the text, treating the distanced level as if it were another, external, text' (1992: 122). One way of achieving this, according to Fairclough (1992), is through hedging, using expressions such as 'sort of' and 'kind of'.

Discourse, Identity and Culture

In order to understand how social relations between individuals and groups are organised and represented in discourse, it is vital to look at how language serves as a means of communication for such an organisation and representation (Achard 1998: 191). This representation reflects the identity, not the social, political and cultural aspects of the speaker.

Identity
Erikson defines identity as a concept that 'connotes both a persistent sameness within oneself (selfsameness) and a persistent sharing of some kind of essential character with others' (1980: 109). The self here, as De Fina points out, 'is seen as a property of the individual, firmly located in the mind . . . such a connection has been particularly strong in psychology where theories of identity have been consistently linked with theories about the persona and the self" (2011: 265). Butler (1990) regards identity as something not inherent in individuals but as a result of what people do and recreate through continuous interaction and discussion with others. Both De Fina's and Butler's definitions regard identity as something acquired through the daily contact and practice within society and in relation to others. They rule out the claim that identity is inherent in people.

According to Shamul (1996: 9) the formation of identity takes place within two social reality contexts: 'the authority social reality' context which is formed by the people who are positioned in a 'dominant power structure', and 'the everyday-defined social reality' which is directly experienced by people during the course of their daily practices. Shamul's categorisation of identity reinforces the view that identity is not a common uniform concept in a society, but it is a reflection of different contexts and groups. Identity is a hybrid phenomenon, as it is recreated and reconstructed depending on the social and cultural contexts.

In this respect, Holland et al. (1998) studied the notion of identity in relation to 'historically situated, socially enacted, culturally constructed worlds' (Daniels 2007: 96). They draw on the work of Bakhtin and Vygotsky for the development of their theory of identity, and they argue that social identities are organised and 'reproduced in figured Worlds which shape and are shaped by participants and in which social position establishes possibilities for engagement' (1998: 96).

Holland et al. summarised their vision by pointing out that actors are linked to the context of production or what Holland refers to as 'landscape of action', which in turn has been given 'a human voice and a tone'. He also refers to the historical development of identities, stating that 'the identities we gain within figured worlds are thus specifically historical developments, grown through continued participation in the positions defined by the social organisations of those worlds activity' (Holland et al. 1998: 41).

It is apparent from Holland et al. that identity is a hybrid notion that can be reconstructed and enacted through history; its development is directly linked to the development of history, and as identity is not inherent, it is acquired within a time and space. This identity then becomes the guide that governs our action and practice. It shapes our practice and discourse in relation to others. However, this action in relation to others can take various forms. For instance, Bernstein (1990: 13) used the concept of 'social positioning' to describe the position actors take in relation to others. Hasan (2001: 8) regards Bernstein's analysis of how speakers position themselves in relation to the social context of their discourse as valuable analysis in offering an explanation of certain discursive practices. Social positioning can indeed be very revealing of the actors themselves as producers of discourse within social and cultural contexts. It can demonstrate how discourses are not produced from a vacuum, but are a reflection of the producer's identity and social positioning within society.

Types of Identities
Identities are 'plural and complex. Such complexity is [. . .] shown in the fact that the production of identities may involve different kinds of agents and processes of communication' (De Fina 2011: 268). De Fina distinguishes between individual and collective identities, as well as social identities. She has also referred to 'situational identities' which are constructed within 'specific context of interaction such as those of teacher/student or doctor/patient' (2011: 268).

In the context of the Arab Spring, we aim to examine how protesters identify themselves in relation to each other and in relation to their leaders. The question to be answered here is whether these protesters have constructed a collective identity to protect themselves from any threat from the outgoing group and champion their own rights, or have they constructed multiple identities, which reflect their diversity and political as well as social activities? We will also hope to examine 'situational identities' and see whether the uprisings have created a new context for interaction and communication, which engage the public. This will be examined through the analysis of their discourses.

Identity Processes
Identities can be communicated in different ways and manners. 'They may be openly discussed and focused upon, or indirectly and symbolically conveyed' (De Fina 2011: 269). People often choose different ways of conveying their identities, and this is are reflected in the language they employ. When someone describes himself or herself as a 'Green', or a 'liberal', he or she has associated himself or herself with certain ideas and values. 'These, in turn, are related to social groups and categories that can be seen as sharing or representing them in a process of meaning creation that rests on accepted social meanings while continuously modifying them. This process has been called *indexicality*' (De Fina 2011: 269). The term indexicality here means that symbols or texts have a direct link to a social context. De Fina has given the example of 'mate' to illustrate this. The usage of 'mate' is an index of close friendship between individuals. She goes on to say that 'words, accents and expressions may also become associated with aspects of the larger context as when they evoke specific traits, ideas, activities and properties that may be

seen as typical of certain social identities' (2011: 269). Identity is an emerging process generated by continuous contact with the other (2011: 271).

Conclusion

In this chapter we offered a review of some of the approaches to discourse. After the definition of discourse, which has considered different perspectives, the reader has been introduced to different approaches to discourse, notably Conversation Analysis, Critical Linguistics, and Critical Discourse analysis (CDA). These approaches have been introduced because they embody aspects that are deemed important to the analysis of Arabic political discourse. While some of the approaches are discussed in this chapter, full attention has been paid to CDA as it offers the main tools and mechanisms for combining textual and sociocultural analysis. Fairclough's model enables us to apply the three dimensions of discourse, which are: text, discursive practice and social practice, while Van Dijk's approach allows us to look at cognitive aspects of discourse.

This chapter has also outlined the historical development and the main similarities and differences between these approaches. A clear justification of the adoption of CDA has been provided. By applying CDA we aim to unearth the relation between Arabic political discourse and the wider Arabic social contexts, therefore enabling us to carefully examine any changes in Arabic political discourse, post Arab Spring.

Apart from introducing key concepts and approaches to discourse, this chapter introduces the reader to the concept of discourse, culture and identity. This will be in particularly useful when we consider the way speakers identify themselves in relation to in-groups and out-groups, in a changing social and cultural context.

2

Discourse, Framing and Representational Strategies

In the previous chapter we have reviewed some of the approaches to discourse analysis, including CDA and its key approaches. This chapter will introduce the reader to key approaches and frameworks on representational strategies in discourse, by introducing and examining the notion of framing and positioning in discourse.

Representational Strategies in Discourse

Discourse is not produced at random or from a vacuum, as it is often the product of a strategy employed by producers to convey their own message. The strategy reflects the way of thinking and the producer's frame of reference, and it is not a randomly produced product, but in most cases, if not all, it is carefully orchestrated and delivered in a way that supports the producer's own agenda, or at least the way producers wish others to perceive it.

In this section we aim to demonstrate that discourse is a product of the producer's ideas, beliefs and attitudes. It is used to reflect and represent the producer's views of the world. Machin and Mayr (2012: 77) assert that the discourse we employ when representing different actors and actions is not neutral and there are always clues in the discourse of the culture and identity of the person or action represented. In their own words, 'there exists no neutral way to represent a person. And all choices serve to draw attention to certain aspects of identity that will be associated with certain kinds of discourses' (Machin and Mayr 2012: 77). Take, for instance, the following example: 'Muslim man arrested for fraudulently claiming benefits' (2012: 77). Machin and Mayr highlighted the word 'Muslim' and argued that there are other ways of 'characterising the man' without referring to his Muslim background; the writer could have referred to him as 'A British man' or an 'Asian man', which could have reflected in a broader way his belonging, away from his religious affiliation. By referring to his religious identity the speaker sought to express his or her ideological opinion which tends, in this case, to be anti-Muslim. Secondly, by characterising the man as a Muslim, the writer aims to refer to a particular group or a faith, and this could have a knock-on effect on the way this particular group or faith is perceived.

According to Machin and Mayr (2012: 78), the above example 'locates the story in a news frame emphasising his "otherness"'. Although the man's actions could have been conducted by any ordinary British person, it could be argued here that the attribution of Muslim is designated to aggravate the act and heighten tension, especially after the 'bombing of the London transport system' (2010: 78) in 2005. Following this unfortunate event, 'Muslims often became represented through news frames that emphasised their threat to British society and resistance to cultural values' (Machin and Mayr 2012: 78). What is striking about the above example is the focus on his religious identity rather than his nationality. He could have been referred to as a British man since he was born in Britain (Machin and Mayr 2012). The representation of the man in this context could be interpreted as an attempt to 'ideologically square' the public against the man, and by not labelling him as a British man, the reporter dissociated himself or herself from the man and his act. This type of framing, which is conveyed through language, serves as a reminder of how ideology shapes and is shaped by discourse.

The communicator often has a wide range of lexical choices, which are used to represent different purposes. To borrow Machin and Mayr's words:

> the choices they make will never be neutral but will be based on the way they wish to signpost what kind of person they are representing, or how they wish to represent them as social actors engaged in action. These choices allow us to place people in the social world and to highlight certain aspects

of identity we wish to draw attention to or omit. (Machin and Mayr 2012: 103)

In a nutshell, the choice of discourse reflects the way we see the world, represent actions and others, and make clear statements about events and actors. Such representations can be either explicit or implicit through lexical and grammatical choices.

In his analysis of representation of ethnic minorities in the press, Van Dijk (2000) concluded that ethnic minorities are often presented in the active form if they have committed anything bad. However, the passive form is used when things are done against them. He has provided the following examples to illustrate his points: 'Muslims win a transfer out of too "white" jail' (*Daily Mail*, 21 March 2008); 'Terrorism convicts granted move from "white" jail' (*Daily Telegraph*, 21 March 2008).

According to Machin and Mayr (2012: 105), both examples convey a negative connotation 'because prisoners should not be given privileges'. The two examples could also be interpreted to show that the author sought to convey the meaning that these convicts should not be granted these privileges. But, again, the agents of both sentences could have been masked, or, at least, presented in broader terms such as 'some prisoners'.

Machin and Mayr (2012) described three aspects of meaning when analysing agency:

1. Participants (which includes both the 'doers' of the process as well as the 'done-tos' who are at the receiving end of action; participants may be people, things or abstract concepts)
2. Processes (represented by verbs and verbal groups)
3. Circumstances (there are adverbial groups or prepositional phrases, detailing where, when and how something has occurred). These aspects will be explained below (Simpson and Mayr 2010: 66 in Machin and Mayr 2012: 105).

In this section, we will draw on Machin and Mayr's (2012) approach to analysing CDA. This approach offers some very practical steps on how to analyse discourse, providing some valuable tools and mechanisms on conducting CDA. In their analysis of CDA they have provided a variety of aspects of representational strategies in discourse, some of which are outlined below. This representation is seen through different aspects of textual analysis as well as through the lenses of framing. Before we embark on these strategies in more detail, a review of the literature on framing would be very useful, as it would allow us to define, discuss and debate a variety of perspectives on this concept.

Framing

Any discussion of representational strategies in discourse necessitates a closer look at the framing strategies employed in discourse, as these are key to understanding the production and consumption of discourse and its processes. According to Kinder and Sanders (1990: 74) framing is a cognitive process which operates as 'internal mind structures' and 'devices impeded in discourse'. While framing constitutes part of news discourse, it is also part of the socio-cognitive structure of society (Entman, 2004). By socio-cognitive we mean the internal mind structure, which frames and shapes the production of discourse. This internal mind structure holds the key to the producer's set of beliefs that govern the nature and type of discourse produced.

Likewise, Lakoff (2004) believes that 'frames are among the cognitive structures we think with'. In other words, frames function as a filter through which people interpret messages and guide their thoughts. It is a cognitive process and a strategy used in discourse (Lakoff 2004; Kinder and Sanders 1990: 74).

Gitlin defines frames as 'persistent patterns of cognition, interpretation, and presentation, of selection, emphasis and exclusion by which symbol-handlers routinely organize discourse' (1980: 7). Put simply, framing is a pattern through which discourse is formulated and interpreted. It is the frame of reference, which governs speakers' thoughts and interpretation of events and actions. The manner by which we choose to describe an individual does not only reflect the cognitive internal structure, but the way we perceive that individual; this perception will find its way into our actions which are often mirrored in the language or discourse we generate.

In this respect, Goffman (1974) emphasises aspects of interpretation and explanation of discourse and attaches them to the individual's perception of actions and events surrounding them. Likewise, Reese defines framing as a set of 'principles that are socially shared and persistent over time, that work symbolically to meaningfully structure the social world' (2001: 11). One would second Reese's statement that framing constitutes part of a set of beliefs and principles that govern the production and consumption of discourse, and it is through these principles that events and actions are framed in the way they are. Framing can take a positive or negative connotation depending on the producer's own principles and stance towards issues surrounding them. Framing can, therefore, be expressed in semantic forms through selective appropriation, where speakers or discourse producers can use lexis to frame individuals, groups and actions. Such production of lexis, as mentioned above, emanates from a set of beliefs, ideologies, policies of individuals and organisations. In the context of media, for instance, the production of news texts is often in line with the editorial policy of news organisations and reflect 'certain social practices, ideologies and orders of discourse' (Al-Hejin 2012: 302).

Positioning

According to Moghaddam and Harré (2010: 2), positioning is about 'how people use words (and discourse of all types) to locate themselves and others'. Words become no longer those semantic tools that reflect certain meanings, but charged with meanings that position actors, socially, culturally and politically. It is through words that persons and groups, for instance, could be described 'as "trusted" or "distrusted", "with us" or "against us", "to be saved" or "to be wiped out"' (Moghaddam and Harré 2010: 2).

Positioning has also been described as 'the process through which discourse constrains identities' De Fina (2011: 271). This definition, which has been coined by social theorists, has been reviewed by Davies and Harré, who considered it 'as the discursive production of a diversity of selves' (Davies and Harré 1990: 47) in De Fina 2011: 172). De Fina's reviewed definition underscores the point that identities are 'plural' as they are connected to social, cultural and discursive practices which reflect people's actions to 'social situations and discursive practices in which people are involved, but also that they are relational since people continuously position themselves, are positioned by others, and position others' (De Fina 2011: 272). While identities remain attached to individuals, they are often formed by individual practices in interpersonal settings. These are a set of norms and practices displayed by individuals, which identify them in relations to other groups or social contacts. These identities or set of practices often contribute to positioning individuals vis-à-vis others in different contexts, through their practice, be it an action or a reflection of the language used in particular contexts and settings. These types of identities displayed by people could be said to be a response to individuals in certain contexts and practices, and these identities are more often than not designed to show the speaker's roots, norms, set of beliefs, cultural and political orientations.

Dealing with identity and discourse would be incomplete without referring to culture as it is inextricably linked to discourse and identity. Keating and Duranti (2011: 331) considered culture to be 'made up of practices and knowledge passed down from one generation to the next, the learned and shared behaviour patterns characteristic of a group'. These practices do not only form the day-to-day routine of their practitioners, but they are shaped in the discourse which itself often mediates aspects of these practices. It 'mediate(s) between the past and present, potential and actual, invisible and visible, immediately given and imagined' (Keating and Duranti 2011: 331). Keating and Duranti have argued that discourse would be meaningless if it was divorced from the context in which it is generated/constituted, including the social and cultural contexts (2011: 337). They believe that 'discourse and culture mutually constitute one another' (2011: 353). Discourse, as discussed in Chapter 1, shapes and is shaped by many internal and external factors, including culture. The two are inextricably linked and culture influences the use of discourse, while the latter clearly shapes culture. 'Discourse is what makes human cultures possible and unique' (Keating and Duranti 2011: 331). It is through discourse that culture is described and represented, as discourse is a reflection of the producer's political, social and cultural beliefs; Fairclough's framework, described in Chapter 1, provides the main tools and mechanisms for deciphering such a relationship between discourse and society. The contextualisation of discourse in its wider social contexts offers a key to a good understanding of the cultural elements that constitute discourse.

Discourse Representation

Discourse representation

> is a major site in which social positioning is constructed in discursive practice. Ranging from nominalizations to direct quotations, these representations are the discursive means by which one text is positioned within another text and through that positioning the authors of the texts are also positioned both in relationship to broader sociocultural practice. (Scollon 1998: 218)

This level of positioning can be seen at the level of clauses and sentences. Individuals, groups and actions are often represented differently depending on the level of vocabulary and lexis selected to describe these people. According to Fairclough, the vocabulary provides 'sets of preconstructed categories, and representation always involves deciding how to "place" what is being represented within these set of categories' (1995b: 109). To illustrate this statement further, Fairclough (1995b) refers to the act of killing and how it is represented within these set of categories. A violent death of people at the hand of others could be represented differently. Some might refer to it as 'killing', others may chose to label it 'murder', 'massacre', etc.

The choice of lexis, as mentioned above, represents peoples' preferences, which reflect their own beliefs, values and attitudes. Such a representation can also be seen in the use of grammar. According to Fairclough, 'the grammar of English differentiates the following process types: Action, Event, State, Mental Process, Verbal Process' (1995b: 110). In his differentiation between an action and event, Fairclough (1995b) emphasises that an action involves both the participant-types. That is, the doer of the action and the recipient of the action (such as police kill the thief). In an event, however, the actor is often absent, and the sentence often has an intransitive structure, where the doer of the action is absent (e.g. 'Fifteen killed').

The use of grammar and the choice of grammatical concepts to represent an event may not always be innocent and their usage may have something to do with the producer's own ideas and personal beliefs. As referred to above, there are always 'alternative ways of wording any (aspect of a) social practice, that alternative wordings may correspond to different categorisations often realise different discourses' (Fairclough 1995b: 114).

The use of vocabulary is just one aspect of representation. Fairclough (1992) also uses discourse representation to refer to the traditional term 'speech reportage', simply because different people report speeches from different angles, using different structures and lexis to express their viewpoints. Although it is challenging to establish how ideologies are represented in discourse, some elements of textual analysis and their interpretation in relation to their context of production could help in deciphering such a relationship between discourse and the producer's own beliefs. Elements of textual analysis could include, but are not limited to, presupposition, negation, metadiscourse, etc.

As previously mentioned, there is a dialectical relationship between discourse and society. There is also the dialectical relationship between discourse and subjectivity. According to Fairclough, subjects are 'constituted in discourse, but they also engage in practice which contests and restructures the discursive structures (orders of discourse) which position them' (1992: 123). This includes restructuring, which reflects the subjects' ideological perspectives, and which are often put forward implicitly through what Leech refers to as a 'semantic engineering' (Leech 1981: 48–52).

To elaborate further on Leech's concept, the notion of semantic engineering is crucial to the way discourse is constituted and introduced. It does not only reflect the meaning but serves as a vital sign of the ideological perspective underpinning the production of discourse. Textual analysis is crucial to understanding and interpreting such signs of discourse, which are often carefully engineered. They can serve as a springboard for the interpretation and explanation of these semantic elements. However, methodologically this would require a careful consideration of the link between the macro and micro elements of discourse, some of which will be discussed in Chapters 4 and 5.

Semantic Labelling

According to Lopez, semantic labelling using cultural elements draws upon the knowledge and beliefs of that culture creating 'social scenarios' based on the cognitive frames of that culture (2002: 312). These cognitive frames are often deeply rooted in the beliefs of the producer. Van Dijk argues that semantic labelling of groups, geographical location and events is not merely based on their evaluative description, but it reflects the sociopolitical position of the group producing the label (1995a: 259). Consequently, these cultural labels help readers to identify, interpret and form an opinion on issues and events; hence it is an important process in the production of news discourse as this requires careful selection of the appropriate label for intended readers. This choice of lexis is often designed to position the other or categorise them by their own culture, identity or a social group. The following section will discuss aspects of positioning in details.

Individualisation versus Collectivisation

In news reports and in media in general, participants and actors, depending on the context, are often nominated as individuals or a collective group. By individually nominating participants the reporter tends to express his or her empathy with the individual, especially if the individual is portrayed as the victim (Machin and Mayr 2012). Again, as alluded to above, this could have some emotional impact on the receiver and could contribute to arousing feelings of empathy towards the individual, especially if he or she is the victim. On the other hand, the nomination of groups, especially in cases where they are perceived as perpetrators, could arouse feelings of hatred towards this group. Take for instance the following examples (Machin and Mayr 2012: 80):

1. Two soldiers, Privates John Smith and Jim Jones, were killed today by a car bomb.
2. Militants were killed today by a car bomb.

In the first example, the two soldiers have been named. By specifying their names, the writer has humanised them and this could be designed to attract the reader's empathy. The second example, however, refers to a group of individuals who are not identified, but are given a label that has a negative connotation. The question here is whether the wording in this example is innocent or whether it reflects the author's ideological stance. The author could have, for instance, used other wordings to convey similar meaning, such as 'a group of fighters', or 'a group of people', which do not carry any negative connotation.

The issue of representation is vital to understanding the type and nature of discourse. In this book we will be looking at how different actors represent others and are represented in discourses. This will enable us, for instance, to examine how the two actors (i.e. the Arab public and leaders) perceive each other through their discourses. One way of looking at this is by examining the binary of 'us' and 'them' in their discourses.

Pronoun versus Noun: The 'Us vs Them' Division

Pronouns like 'us', 'we' and 'them' are often used 'to align us alongside or against particular ideas' (Machin and Mayr 2012: 84). Text producers often adopt different approaches in communicating and representing others, as well as representing their own ideas. They can appear very inclusive and make their own ideas as 'ours' (Oktar 2001).

The use of 'we' and 'ours' can be very inclusive and is often designed to engage readers or recipients of discourse, and, in some cases, it is considered as an invitation to share one's point of view and beliefs. This is frequently used by politicians in times of conflict to rally their people behind them. It is occasionally presented in the form of Us vs Them. This dichotomy has been seen by most scholars as the effective way of arousing supporters' emotion, in order to gain their support. However, Fairclough (2000: 152) has commented on how the pronoun 'we' can be very confusing and, at times, very vague, as it is often used by politicians to convey their own statements.

In this book we will examine the use of 'we', 'us' and 'them' in the discourses of the Arab public and Arab leaders. We, in particular, seek to identify how protesters are addressed in leaders' speeches, and how protesters themselves address leaders and whether they use the dichotomy Us vs Them to represent themselves. If such a type of discourse exists, then what connotation does it have in terms of governance and social change?

Grammatical Positioning of Actions

Richardson (2007: 207) argues that the structuring of sentences could be used to ideologically represent actions in different ways. This is often accomplished through backgrounding certain actions and foregrounding others (Machin and Mayr 2012: 114).

Van Dijk (1991) has also examined how actions could be magnified or 'played down' (Machin and Mayr 2012: 114), depending on their position in the sentence. The grammatical structuring of sentences could emphasise actions by placing them at the beginning of the sentence, or it could play down its importance by placing it later in the sentence (Machin and Mayr 2012: 114). Van Dijk states that '[E]vents may be strategically played down by the syntactic structure of the sentences, for example, by referring to the event in a lower [later, less prominent] embedded clause, or conversely by putting it in the first position when the events need extra prominence' (1991: 216). Machin and Mayr (2012: 115) have given this example to illustrate Van Dijk's quotation:

1. The university management made severe staff cuts.
2. After extensive reductions in government funding, the university management made severe staff cuts.

In the first example, the action is emphasised by referring to the doer of the action, while in the second example the action is placed at the end of the sentence, emphasising the action less.

Grammatical positioning would be very useful in our attempt to study the leaders' political speeches during the Arab Spring, and how grammatical positioning is used to represent actions and groups, in particular the protesters.

Nominalisation

The way of providing actions/news could hide or omit the doer of the action at times, depending on the purpose and function of the report. The use of passive and the absence of the active could be used to conceal the agent of the action, or provide less focus on the doer of the action: 'The civilians were killed during a bombing raid [by the American bombers]' (Machin and Mayr 2012: 137). In this sentence the agent of the action was left out, and the reader left wondering who carried out the action. By changing the sentence into the active form, the focus will be on the doer of the action, and in the example above the American action will be emphasised, as follows: 'The American bombers killed the civilians in the raid' (Machin and Mayr 2012: 137).

It is clear from the above example that civilians have been killed by the American bombers. The doer of the action is conspicuously emphasised through the active form. The use of the passive and active forms to convey meanings depends on the strategy of the speaker or writer, as well as their intention and ideological orientation that could affect their choice of lexis.

Effects of Nominalisation

Machin and Mayr (2012) have highlighted the following effects of nominalisation (2012: 140–4):

1. 'People are removed and therefore the responsibility for the action has been removed.'
2. 'Nominalisation can clearly hide both the agent and the affected since our vision has been channelled and narrowed.'
3. 'Nominalisation can remove any sense of time.'
4. 'Since actions become a thing, it can be counted, described, classified and qualified through the resource of the normal group, but this means that the causality is now of a secondary concern.'
5. 'Nominalisation can function as new participants in new constructions.'
6. 'Nominalisations can themselves become stable entities that will enter common usage.'
7. 'The process is still in the sentence, so the text accumulates a sense of action but avoids agents, time and specificity through simplification.'
8. 'The text is becoming more dense or compressed. Details of events are reduced.'

Metonymy

Although metonymy is a rhetorical device that is used to substitute another expression, phrase or concept, it is often used for ideological reasons, one of which would be to conceal the main actors (Machin and Mayr 2012).

The use of expressions such as 'the White House', 'Downing Street' and 'The Kremlin' is to conceal the politicians who reside at these places, and who have full responsibility for the actions taken and the policies made. Instead of referring to the 'British government' or the 'Russian government' the writer resorts to the headquarter of these governments to avoid directly referring to the people who are occupying these places, and their policies. Moreover, the use of expressions such as 'the opposition leader' is often designed to conceal the name of this leader, especially in contexts where there are more than one opposition party. In this case, the identity of the person remains anonymous and this could serve the purpose of the writer.

Personification/Objectification
'Personification means that human qualities or abilities are assigned to abstractions or inanimate objects' (Machin and Mayr 2012: 171). 'Democracy will not stand by while this happens' (ibid.). According to Machin and Mayr, democracy in the latter example has been personified to conceal the main actors. Democracy is often used by politicians and parties to refer implicitly to themselves or their parties. The concept is used for different reasons and in different contexts. It is used in conflicts to drum up support and rally the public behind politicians and their policies. It is also used in contexts where politicians try to appear as the champions of democracy, in particular when referring to non-democratic opposition or enemies.

One could clearly read into this that by using a concept such as democracy, speakers aim to legitimise themselves as defenders of the free world and hence the call for democracy as a process that protects those freedoms and rights.

Personification is a key concept in Arabic discourse and it is often used to 'sharpen up and upgrade the linguistic competence of writing and speaking. It provides users the appropriate and effective stylistic mechanisms required for eloquently forceful discourse. Thus, Arabic rhetoric makes language meet the communicative needs of the language user' (Gholmani, Montashery and Khorrami (2016: 58). It is often associated with eloquence, creativity and high language communicative skills. According to Abdul-Raof (2006) there are three constituents of rhetorical speeches. These are:

> (i) word order (ilm al-ma'ani) that is concerned with semantic syntax,
> (ii) figures of speech (ilm al-bayan) that is concerned with allegorical and non-allegorical significations, linguistic allusion, and linguistic signalling, and (iii) embellishments (ilm al-badi) that shows the language user how to bestow decorative lexical and semantic features upon his or her speech activity. (Gholmani, Montashery and Khorrami (2016: 58)

In Arabic discourse in general and in a political discourse in particular, rhetorical features are used to demonstrate high communicative register by displaying features of the above constituents. For instance, the use of simile where a person is associated with something that is original and has rare qualities that are designed to express the uniqueness of that person by associating them with the original features. The use of personification and rhetorical features in Arabic are designed for persuasion purposes, as well as a reflection of high standard status, as eloquence in Arabic is highly valued.

According to Abdul-Raof (2006), constituents of figures of speech in Arabic rhetoric are: simile, allegory and metonymy. Allegory is divided into cognitive and linguistic, the latter consists of metaphor and hypallage. These constituents represent key Arabic rhetorical features, which are often used to ensure better and effective communication in a highly recognised style of delivery, which is a key feature of political discourse. It is also a feature of competency in MSA, where leaders demonstrate a good command of the language as it is associated with privilege, charisma and authority. These speeches are very formal and address the public sphere in general regardless of the level of education or the political background. Arab regimes use political speeches to communicate key strategic issues as well as issues pertaining to individual Arab countries.

Hedging

Authors often use hedging 'to create a strategic ambiguity within their claims' (Wood and Kroger 2000 in Machin and Mayr 2012: 192). By using hedging, speakers and writers tend to give themselves a room to manoeuvre, which helps them to avoid being specific and to be broader in their claims. While speakers and writers aim to deliver their discourse in a clear manner, they tend to 'avoid directness or commitment to something' (Machin and Mayr 2012: 192). This is a good strategy which does not only allow the writer/speaker to maintain their distance, but also protects them from any 'unwelcomed responses' as a result of their discourse. 'Hedging can be used to distance ourselves from what we say and to attempt to dilute the force of our statements and therefore reduce chances of any unwelcome responses' (Machin and Mayr 2012: 192). For example: 'Some people say that multiculturalism is outmoded, but, in fact, it is still orthodox thinking' (Machin and Mayr 2012: 192).

The *Daily Mail* newspaper uses hedging here to avoid directness. One could argue, Who are these people? And why their identity is kept hidden? The *Daily Mail* is not alone in this context, as most of media's reporting tends to use hedges to avoid being specific, or to use anonymous sources under the pretext of protecting informants or their source of information. This strategy allows the media to keep its distance, leaving the reader to second-guess these sources.

While hedging grants speakers/writers some flexibility in distancing themselves from the story or practice, it has some serious implications on understanding the message, which remains broad and more often vague. In the media context, it could also be interpreted as part of the lack of responsibility and professionalism as the message is delivered in a way that allows multi-interpretation of the discourse, which could lead to undesirable interpretations, undermining therefore the essence of the meaning of the text.

Overlexicalisation
Another useful element for the analysis of discourse is overlexicalisation. This is where lexical items are heavily repeated in a text, either through the same lexical item or through its synonymy. Although this is a familiar aspect in Arabic discourse, its use and contextualisation could be very useful in determining the type and nature of discourse employed.

In her discussion of media representation of others, Merskin (2004: 158) wrote:

> mass media in the United States have generated and sustained stereotypes of a monolithic evil Arab; these stereotypes constructed all Muslims as Arabs and all Arabs as terrorists. Using representations and language in news, movies, cartoons, and magazine stories, the media and the popular culture have participated in the construction of an evil Arab stereotype that encompasses a wide variety of people, ideas and beliefs.

Merskin's words are a vivid example of how media promotes and enhances stereotypes, where communities are vilified, degraded and made to look as the enemy. This media narrative, while it does not constitute a true representation of the other, could fuel feelings of anger and hate towards the other. The June 2017 attack in London, when Darren Osborne drove a van into a crowd of Muslim worshippers near the Finsbury Park Mosque, is a tangible example to be cited here. Osborne killed one person and injured at least nine others. Reports suggest that Osborne's action was influenced by media reports and documentaries on Muslims. While some may argue that the media is just doing its job of investigating and reporting stories of Muslim practices in the UK, others claim that the media stereotype and negative reporting on Muslims contributed to this attack. In some reports, the media is unable or unwilling to distinguish between Islam and extreme individuals who have different motives, similar to Osborne's. This lack of ability or unwillingness to separate the two has often contributed to creating an image where all members of the in-group are tarred with the same brush and labelled as one. Jackson (1996: 65) identified this type of representation in American movies where 'barbarism and cruelty are the most traits associated with Arabs'. This deeply rooted stereotype, which has been constructed in media and films, could have some serious repercussions on human relations, both nationally and internationally, and could exacerbate tension between communities. The media should therefore exercise caution, balance its reports in a manner that does not compromise freedom of expression, and at the same time contribute to building bridges rather than creating tension and friction between different communities.

While media representation of events can be motivated by a host of reasons, this idea of making the other 'the common enemy' is often used by some politicians to drum up support, and this is known to be 'a method of social control, of reinforcing values of the dominant system, and of garnering participation in the maintenance of those beliefs' (Merskin 2004: 159). Post 9/11 could be a good example to list here, when the Bush Junior administration labelled Al-Qaeda and Taliban as the common enemy, urging other nations to oppose them and, where possible, fight them. This was made clear in his well-known speech 'you are either with us or against us'. To use the 9/11 tragedy to control not only American citizens but governments and officials of sovereign nations could be seen as unwise and may have a lasting effect. When nations rallied behind Bush to wage war on Iraq, long-term devastation was the result, with millions of Iraqis displaced, others killed and livelihoods ruined in the pursuit of 'the common enemy', Saddam Hussein. This move, which had unintended consequences, was widely supported by the media, which represented Saddam Hussein and Iraqi officials as the enemy who may have contributed to the 9/11 atrocities. The media was been mobilised to support 'the cause', without questioning the motives of the Bush administration, and whether Iraq possessed weapons of mass destruction, which turned out to be untrue following investigations of the possession of WMD by Saddam. This lack of accountability on the part of the media has shown that politician do not only manipulate the public, but use the media as a vehicle to support and promote their own agenda, at a time where they should be scrutinised for their actions.

Bush's 2003 address to the American people positioned Saddam as an evil person who threatened the security of the United States and its allies in the region. By framing Saddam as evil and a menace to the values of the United States, Bush sought to rally Americans to support his announced war on Iraq. According to Lasswell:

> for mobilisation of national hatred the enemy must be represented as a menacing, murderous aggressor, a satanic violator of the moral and conventional standards, an obstacle to the cherished aims and ideals of the nation as a whole and of each constituent part. Through the elaboration of war aims, the obstructive role of the enemy becomes particularly evident. (Lasswell 1995: 18–19)

Lasswell gives the example of Ronald Reagan in the 1980s when he considered the Soviet Union as the common enemy and the 'focus of evil in the modern world'. Twenty years later, the same label was adopted by Bush when he called North Korea, Iran and Iraq an 'axis of evil'. If Reagan created the Soviet Union as his common enemy, Bush identified three nations as a common enemy, but pursued Iraq as the arch-enemy number one, which led to the overthrow of Saddam Hussein and his regime in 2003.

In both cases, the two American presidents constructed an image of a common enemy who should be defeated because of its threat to the national security. The fact that the enemy is represented as the other who resents American values and way of life, is a tangible example of not only controlling the public and media but mobilising the public behind the president; a strategy, as mentioned above, used by different leaders for different purposes, including securing their positions or drumming up support.

In her analysis of the concept of making a common enemy, Merskin (2004: 159) commented that this concept is 'important in organizing evolutionary-based survival strategies that rely on perceptual and behavioural patterns that are fundamental part of human nature'. Indeed, history has taught us that when leaders are weak or are on the verge of being thrown over by their fellow politicians or citizens they resort to creating a common enemy that would not only divert attention from their wrongdoing, but would rally everyone under the umbrella of protecting national interest. The Falklands War in the 1980s is a good example to cite here. At a time when Thatcher was in trouble with her party, especially those who opposed her policies, the Falklands War cemented her position and rocketed her popularity as a leader who defended British interest, making her a stronger leader after being weak and on the verge of being deposed. The media played a significant role here in portraying her as the Iron Lady who stood up for the British interest.

Spillmann and Spillmann (1997: 50–1) point out 'the development of the collective unconscious that comes to support viewing others as enemies'. They describe enemy image construction as 'a syndrome of deeply rooted perceptual evaluations that take on the following characteristics: negative anticipation, putting blame on the enemy, identification with evil, Zero-Sum thinking, and refusal to show empathy'.

Worth (2002) asserted that:

> America's discovery of an enemy who is not merely an enemy, but 'evil,' has impeccable historical credentials. In a long history of responding to real and perceived threats, it seems clear that this large, heterogeneous country defines itself in part through its nemeses. Such bellicosity can serve as a convenient tool for unification where differences among 'us' can be minimized, erased, or overlooked with a powerful 'them' or 'other'. (Worth 2002: 1 in Merskin 2004)

Merskin (2004) explains that this strategy of overlooking opposition is clearly demonstrated in Bush's speech about those who support or harbour Al-Qaeda and its affiliates, saying 'they will hand over terrorists or they will share in their fate'. This reinforces Bush's doctrine, discussed above, 'you are either with us or against us'. This refusal to show empathy to those impartial nations who do not wish to take sides has created some tension between those nations and the United States. The fact that Bush characterised the enemy as evil and that any supporters of this evil would 'share in their fate' shows his strategy of isolating the enemy, and this became clearer when he compared Al-Qaeda to Nazism (Merskin 2004):

> We have seen this kind before. They are the heirs of all the murderous ideologies of the 20th century. By sacrificing human life to serve their radical visions, by abandoning every value except the will to power, they follow the path of fascism, Nazism, and totalitarianism.

By comparing Al-Qaeda and its associates to Nazism, Bush sought to magnify his attack and depict the enemy as equal to Nazism. This intertextual link, one could argue, is designed to remind his audience of the atrocities committed by the Nazis in order to magnify the threat of Al-Qaeda and its violent act which left 3,000 civilians dead. By assimilating Al-Qaeda with the Nazis, Bush sought to mobilise the national and international public to support the war on Afghanistan in 2001.

Bush's discourse could be considered as the means by which he 'constructs his strategies of action' (Moaddel 1992: 359). This strategy of action becomes visible when the Bush administration, after a period of discussion, debate and justification, decided to launch its military campaign in Afghanistan. This justification of action was represented in different discourse strategies, either through the attribution strategy of Us vs Them, or the use of selective appropriation, discussed earlier in this chapter. The adopted strategies reflect some stereotypes in the way particular groups and nations are being described and characterised. In her definition of stereotypes, Merskin asserts that 'stereotypes are collections of traits or characteristics that present members of a group as being all the same. This signifying mental practice provides convenient shorthand in the identification of a particular group of people' (Merskin 2004: 160). Some of these stereotypes emanate from a set of beliefs and ideologies that producers of discourse may have towards certain groups, actions or cultures. So these ideologies 'can be observed in people's attempts to formulate their strategies of action and in the activities and artifacts of its producers' (Moaddel 1992: 359).

The construction and reconstruction of reality by the media and other means of communications often reflect the ideological orientations of these media organisations. Take, for instance, the Egyptian media pre and post the Arab Spring. Before the overthrow of Mubarak, the Egyptian media in almost unequivocal terms were supporting the regime and very critical of the demonstrations, questioning the rationale behind it. However, the same media turned against Mubarak as soon as he decided to step down, taking therefore the side of the revolutionaries. It sounds very hypocritical but the Egyptian media played a role during the uprising by constructing inaccurate and often false narrative of demonstrations, labelling some of them as externally influenced and mobilised, and that the majority of the Egyptian people are in support of their president and government. They often resort to nationalistic songs and patriotic emblems to emotionally engage and deter revolutionaries from carrying out their action. News and current affairs programmes are full of praise for Mubarak and his government, showcasing their achievements and loyalty to the country. However, the same media turned against Mubarak as soon as the announcement of his resignation was made public. The media then switched sides and considered the revolutionaries' demands legitimate. While one would recognise the hybrid political situation in Egypt and the complexity of the matter, equally one would question the integrity and impartiality of the Egyptian media when dealing with domestic issues pertaining to governments and regimes.

In this regard, Tienari et al. (2003: 379) asserts that 'discourses can be activated, performed, and connected in a process in which the actors strive for specific goals'. When Bush compared Al-Qaeda to the Nazis, he sought to reactivate the horror and the trauma of the past to magnify his description and intake on the present. Bush's goal here was to drum up support, both nationally and internationally for his planned action to wage war on Afghanistan and later in Iraq, but his action could also be said to have been designed to marginalise Al-Qaeda and the Taliban and deprive them of any support. Bush here used 9/11 events discourse to intertextually connect to the past, by comparing Al-Qaeda to the Nazis. He constructed a new reality, where a new 'enemy' surfaced, described as a 'evil, murderous and bloodthirsty one'. Bush's discursive strategy of drawing on a specific event that occurred in the past is used to demonise the enemy, cement and 'legitimise' the speaker's 'position and achieve particular ends' (Tienari et al. 2003: 379). Bush's example and intertextual link to the Nazis' past reinforces the approach of Tienari et al. (2003) that discourses are an 'inherent part of the sociocultural practices that are embedded in social and societal contexts'.

This is often more evident in the way subjects position themselves vis-à-vis certain events, and based on this positioning they construct their narrative and produce their own discourse, which is often stimulated by past practices contextualised in living social and political contexts. Drawing on Bernstein's notion of positioning and its relation to the distribution of power, Daniels (2007: 98) concluded:

> given that, in Bernstein's terms, positioning is a systematic relation to the distribution of power and principles of control, it is argued that this approach to our understanding the notion of social positioning as the underlying, invisible component which 'figures' practices of communication and gives rise to the shaping of identity.

Leontiev (1978: 10) linked people's activities to their social position. The magnitude of their action is measured by their social position and the sway they may have on others using their power to influence, reconstruct narratives and change the world surrounding them, be it local, national or international.

'In periods of crisis [. . .] language changes rapidly and becomes part of the political process' (Olsen and Harvey 1988: 451). We have witnessed this in times of conflict, when the language of diplomacy becomes language of threat, menace and military, and this is often channelled through local and national media to mobilise the public and gain support for any planned action. Take, for instance, the Iraq war and the language which preceded it. In the UK, knowing that the public was against the war as demonstrated in the march organised by the anti-war coalition, Blair constructed a new narrative and adopted a new discourse designed to magnify Saddam's threat, which was regarded as imminent and constituting a danger to British citizens and British interests in the region. The language used, which reflected Blair's political process of deposing Saddam Hussain, reflected and constructed a new discourse, which was used in parts to mobilise the public and to degrade the opponent. It could also be argued here that this new narrative was imposed by the political process and Blair's agenda of mounting a military campaign against Saddam. As mentioned earlier, in order to drum up support, Blair resorted to making Saddam the enemy, who was a threat to the national and international security. In order to cement his argument, Blair resorted to the discourse of the other, where Saddam was depicted as 'evil', who was a threat to the 'international community and his own people'. Blair's political discourse was amplified to support his own political decision of waging war on Iraq by vilifying Saddam and constructing him as the enemy number one. This new constructive image serves as the main rationale for Blair's action, which others have rejected, arguing that it was taken well in advance and was designed to stand by Bush's decision of waging war on Iraq.

Discourse of Revolutions

Dealing with revolutions often involves dealing with the causes and consequences of these revolutions. The analysis would most likely focus on the pre-revolution period by examining the causes and drives that have triggered certain revolutions; these could be economic, social, cultural or political. These causes are often formed as a bloc of grievances that certain people, citizens or groups have against regimes and governments. However, it should also be acknowledged that these groups, people and actors are not homogeneous groups and may not have the same grievances as will be discussed in the case of the Arab Spring.

When Arab revolutions swept Tunisia, Egypt and Libya, most of the analysts traced this back to what they consider to be 'the level of corruption and aggression that has characterised these societies for many years'. The economic situation and deprivation in other countries has served as a catalyst for these revolutions and uprisings. The lack of opportunities, the spread of unemployment, corruption and the hegemony of elites over power and politics have all contributed to the abrupt eruption of these uprisings and revolutions. These grievances, which for so long have been muted and in some cases made invisible and forced underground, surfaced immediately and rapidly as soon as they were triggered by catalysts. No one could imagine that one incident in a very remote Tunisian village would change the political landscape of the Arab world. Mohammed Bouazizi, who was an ordinary man who suffered unbearable injustice and marginalisation, took drastic action and set himself ablaze in a very dramatic and emotional scene that left millions of Tunisians unhappy with the situation, and which fuelled feelings of unrest across the country, culminating in the overthrow of Ben Ali's regime. But the Tunisian

Jasmine Revolution was just the beginning of a series of revolutions to sweep the Arab world, some of which have been successful in overthrowing and replacing regimes; others, unfortunately, have led to civil war, such as the case of Libya, Yemen and Syria.

While the causes and consequences of revolutions are the debate of different scholars and political analysts, most agree that these revolutions have not only impacted the political landscape in some of these countries, but they have also contributed to the creation of a new political discourse and register, which reflect both the internal changes to the political landscape, and social and cultural changes affecting these societies. This emancipation of discourse could be witnessed in the public sphere, the media and political discourse. It embodies aspects of criticism and appraisal for political leaders through multiple usage of discourse attributions, where Arab government and regimes have become the opposition and were at the receiving end of a very critical discourse.

In his analysis of the Orange Revolution in Ukraine, Wilson refers to some of the causes of the revolutions, which go beyond the economic grievances and the need to establish a government to improve economic conditions. Their demands seem to have broader universal political goals, and as he puts it:

> there was a revolution of expectations . . . there was a real desire for regime change, not just a new president. The mood in the *Maidan* did not just indicate support for Yushchenko or Tymoshenko personally; it was the articulate anger of a people finding their voice . . . students wanted a change in political culture, the poor wanted a change in political culture, and small medium-sized businesses wanted a change in political culture . . . the key sentiment was 'kick the bastards out', and that is what revolutions are all about . . . it was a protest against a rotten system of government . . . and the hope that something better would take its place. (Wilson 2005: 199, 202)

As the above quotation suggests, the Orange Revolution was triggered because of a multiplicity of reasons, which go beyond the bread-and-butter issues. Following Wilson's assertion, this was motivated by cultural and political factors, unlike Arab revolutions, which were triggered because of the economic grievances and level of corruption and poverty, as well as unemployment that became rampant in most of those countries that witnessed these revolutions.

To trace the Arab revolutions to cultural dimensions would be, in my view, an inaccurate representation of the situation in these countries. The fact that these revolutions erupted unexpectedly and without prior notice shows how spontaneous they were, and could explain the absence of leaders who may claim responsibility.

While the Orange Revolution had visible leadership and organisers and their demands were laid out clearly, in the case of the Arab Spring the political leadership emerged after the dust settled on these revolutions and when the democratic process had been initiated to fill in the power vacuum that emerged after the resignation, the flight or killing of someone. In all cases, Islamic parties emerged as the strongest political force, the most organised and well- structured movements, as demonstrated in the political processes of post Arab revolutions: mainly parliamentary and presidential elections, as well as local elections in other Arab countries.

While '"democratisation" and "democratic consolidation" are the basic categories in which the majority of scholars traditionally describe progressively directed social changes globally and in the post-communist region in particular' (Zherebkin 2009: 207), evidence for the reason for Arab revolutions tends to focus on the economic and social issues, rather than explicit political reasons, as manifested in the Orange Revolution. This has been manifested in the type of slogans raised in protests. The constructed discourse in this regard could be said to be a discourse of economic deprivation and suffering.

In his article, 'Ideologies and Social Revolutions: Reflections on the French Case', Sewell considers the French Revolution as a 'social revolution', as the intention was to aim for a 'restructure of the society from top to bottom and across the board' (Sewell 1985: 76). He went on to assert that

> the French, Russian, and Chinese revolutions were 'social' not only because they included revolts from below and resulted in major changes in the class structure, but because they attempted to transform the entirety of people's social lives – their work, their religious beliefs and practice, their families, their legal time. (Sewell 1985: 77)

While Sewell's description of the motives and drives of the French Revolution apply to the French context, the social reform and reconstruction of the society from top to bottom were certainly not the explicit characteristics of Arab revolutions. As alluded to earlier, this is because Arab revolutions lacked political organisation and were economically driven, meaning that these revolutions were intended to achieve better living conditions, which are directly linked to economic reform. The drastic reconstructing of society was not the main drive of these revolutions, judging by the slogans used.

Similar to the Arab revolutions, Moaddel points out that the Iranian Revolution

> proceeded so quickly that it took foreign observers and even the revolutionaries themselves by surprise . . . The rapidity with which the revolutionary movement proceeded, the unanimity of the public demand for the overthrow of the Shah through mass demonstrations that crippled one of the strongest repressive regimes in the Third World, the decline of secular politics, and the increasing importance of religious ideology in the revolutionary movement. (Moaddel 1992: 353)

The outcome of the Iranian Revolution bears some similarities to Arab revolutions in terms of their rapidity, and unexpected results, such as the overthrow of regimes, as is the case with the Shah, and leaders of other Arab regimes (i.e. Mubarak, Ben Ali, Gaddafi, etc). Although they do not have the same structure and political organisation, these revolutions do have a lack of freedom and economic deprivation as a common factor. While the Iranian Revolution was driven by the Islamic movement led by Ayato Allah Khomeini, Arab revolutions were driven by the shared interests of a mosaic of stakeholders who had different political ideologies. To borrow Moaddel's words, the Iranian revolution

> provides little support for the argument that ideology reflects class consciousness and interests. The connection between capitalist development of the 1960s and 1970s and the growth of revolutionary Islam was too complex to support a simplistic correspondence between revolutionary ideology and the ascending mode of production. (Moaddel 1992: 358)

The Iranian Revolution was very explicit in its discursive strategies and was tangible in the Iranian revolutionary leadership in formulating 'their strategies of actions and in the activities and artifacts of its production' (Wuthnow

1989: 81 in Moaddel 1992: 359). These strategies of actions are mirrored in the discourse produced by the revolutionary movement. In the case of Iran, the Islamic discourse was prevalent and was designed to mobilise the Iranian supporters and offer an alternative discourse to the existing one: a move which was designed to position the Iranian Revolution as an Islamic revolution, aimed at conservative elements who support Khomeini and his movement.

Following Wuthnow's definition of ideology, it could be said that Arab revolutions were the product of the protesters' beliefs and ideologies, despite the fact that this was not clear at the beginning. The spontaneity of protests and gatherings and the lack of visible leadership would not support Wuthnow's definition, but, equally, it could be argued that the fact that these movements and protests are taking place, they reflect, though not explicitly, the passive nature of these ideologies, as analysts came to conclude that certain groups and organisations were behind this move. This action, which is often a culmination of a set of beliefs, is frequently shaped in the type of discourse produced. As Moaddel points out, 'ideology is best conceptualised as a discourse consisting of a set of general principles, concepts, symbols, and rituals used by actors to address problems in a particular historical episode' (Moaddel 1992: 359). In order to understand these discourses and their intent, a contextualisation of their production and, where possible, their consumption would allow a clearer interpretation and explanation, providing us therefore with an insight into the type of language and discourse produced.

This brings us to Fairclough's assertion of the dialectical relationship between discourse and society, and how discourse shapes and is shaped by an individual's social, cultural and political stance. In the case of Iran, for instance, Moadell (1992: 360) asserts that:

> various groups and social classes in nineteenth and twentieth century Iran has been noted by most historians and area specialists. The bazaaris often used religious rituals and symbols in their mobilisation efforts to change or resist unpopular policies initiated by the state. In its turn, the state resorted to religion to justify its action.

It is apparent from this quotation from Moadell that religion has been used as the pillar around which actions are decided, or for ideological reasons religion has been used to justify actions and decisions. This has paved the way for the 'rise of Islam as the dominant discourse of the opposition' (Moadell 1992: 360) in a context where secular discourse witnessed a decline. However, this new movement, which put Islam front and centre, emerged after decades of glorifying 'the Iranian kingship and ancient history while overlooking the Islamic period' (Moadell 1992: 360). This has helped the opposition to reconstruct their religious national identity, as demonstrated in their 'revolutionary Islamic discourse' (Moadell 1992: 360). However, the rise of the Islamic discourse in Iran was not a new phenomenon, but could be seen to be a progression of the emergence of Islamic movements and more importantly the rise of 'Islamic modernism, which become dominant in the late nineteenth and early twentieth centuries' (Moadell 1992: 361), supported by scholars and intellectuals such as Sayyid Jamal Uddin 'al-Afghani', Sayyid Ahmad Khan, Muhammad 'Abduh, etc. This new wave of Islamic intellectuals has paved the way for some very organised Islamic movements, calling for the *Al-ṣaḥwa al-Islāmiyya* (Islamic revival) adopting a new Islamic discourse that considered Islamic law as one of its tenets. The emergence of this new discourse came as the backdrop to the decline of liberalism as manifested in regimes such as the Shah's. In addition to the Islamic discourse, which has been used to justify their action, a discourse of reprimand has also emerged to discredit liberals by pointing to their deeds and political behaviourism, which was in support of Western democracies, and domestically does not comply with the Islamic law, as these intellectuals argued. This was sufficient for these intellectuals to consider regimes as 'traitors', 'corrupt' and 'Western puppets'. Such a naming and labelling strategy is supported by religious texts to cement their arguments and discredit their regimes.

These revolutions have not only brought about social and political change, but have led to the inception of new language and discourse, which has been manifested in the new usage of vocabulary. 'Vocabulary is a far more volatile object, changing rapidly in the face of technological, social, political, and cultural developments [. . .] since vocabularies are not stable or clearly fixed objects' (Olsen and Harvey 1988: 452), drastic events such as revolutions often lead to the coinage of new vocabulary, as we have witnessed in the Arab Spring, where collocation adjectives with weekdays becomes a practice across different Arab countries during the Arab Spring event. Examples of this include:

جمعة الغضب *jumuʿat alghaḍab*/Friday of outrage; جمعة الصمود *jumuʿat al-ṣumūd* /Friday of steadfastness; جمعة التحدي *jumuʿat attaḥad* / Friday of challenge; جمعة الحماية الدولية *jumuʿat al ḥimāya al dduwaliyya* / Friday of international protection. جمعة النصر لشامنا ويمننا *jumuʿat al naṣer lishāminā wa yamaninā* / Friday of victory Levant and Yemen ; جمعة نصر من الله *jumuʿat naṣer min Allah* / Friday of divine victory.

This new vocabulary has become part and parcel of Arab revolutions and culture. Since Friday is considered a holy day in the Arab and Muslim world, such a coinage is a culture-bound vocabulary. The revolutionaries here have expressed their feelings through religious connotations. Linking emotional well-being to Friday as a holy day is very revealing indeed. It gives the whole act a religious blessing, although it could be said that revolutionaries chose Friday as the day of action because it is a day of rest, and that revolutionaries have used it to maximise their impact and attract more sympathisers as they leave Friday prayers. Whatever the motives for considering Friday as a major day for action, it could be said that the new discourse often collocated with Friday, which reflects the protesters' willingness and desire to sacrifice their weekend (Friday) for magnifying their action and mobilisation. These practices are often designed to rally support around the cause of 'freedom and liberty' and 'employment and corruption'. However, what can be noticed from different revolutions is how the opposition or protesters utilise any clampdown on protesters to rally support and advance their cause. The example of the Egyptian regime allegedly allowing thugs riding horses and camels to take revenge on protesters, in fact strengthened the protesters' resolve and culminated in massive protests in Tahrir Square, which eventually led to the demise of the Mubarak regime. The Egyptian example is not the only one where the opposition used the regime's brutal action to mobilise the public. In January 1978, in Iran, Khomeini's supporters staged a protest against the Shah, but the police repressed the protesters, which brought different religious and secular groups to protest against the Shah (Moadell 1992: 366). This is a clear example that 'coercive power played a crucial role in shaping events as rival contenders manipulated ideology to fit their goals' (Moadell 1992: 370).

This manipulation could be explicit and implicit, depending on the type of discourse used and the target group. According to Moadell (1992: 370), the Iranian Revolution created a discourse which 'dictated political change through revolutionary action and glorified martyrdom and self-sacrifice. It emphasised unity within the Islamic community and warned of the presence of counter-revolution.' The Iranian Revolution has produced a discourse that 'encodes and reproduces the ideological structures at play' (Thorne et al. (1999: 123): a structure where liberal discourse has been replaced with a conservative one, as reflected in the revolutionary slogans and speeches.

Our understanding of Iranian revolutionary history is accessed through the use of language and discourse. To use Achugar's words:

> we access the past through language. The memories we have of the past are mediated by language. Discourses about the past distinguish the events or 'what occurred' (the historical 'facts', even if they are provisional and open to revision) and the narrative of 'what has been said to occur' (interpretations of those facts). (Achugar 2007: 523)

By examining the discursive practices of the Iranian Revolution, one cannot help but notice similarities in terms of the motives and strategies employed against regimes. The popular discontent over the economy and living conditions were used as main strategies to mobilise the public to take action against regimes. Having said that, the Iranian Revolution has another explicit motif, which is the replacement of the Shah's regime with an Islamic regime. This was manifested in different discourses of the Iranian opposition, both in exile and in Iran. The slogan that 'Islam is the solution' was one of the most popular slogans used during the Iranian Revolution. Contrary to the Arab Spring, this last motif was almost absent or could be called discreet, with the main focus being on economic and social grievances. Indeed, the changes that occur at the social, cultural and political levels are mediated by the language and discourse. As pointed out earlier, discourse shapes and is shaped by society.

Revolution and Leadership

In his analysis of the Arab Spring from the prism of the Iranian Revolution of 1979, Nabavi (2012) alluded to the fact that the successful Iranian Revolution was attributed to the visible leadership of the Khomeini, who was directing the revolution from exile, and therefore setting up clear aims and objectives as well as expectations, which gave the revolution focus and direction as well as a sense of purpose:

> the reason why the Islamists won the day in Iran was twofold. The first and foremost reason was the person of Ayatollah Ruhollah Khomeini, and the role that he played in shaping the unfolding of events, both during and after the revolution. He gave a sense of direction to the protesters from exile, particularly when he moved to Neauphle-le-Château in Paris, refusing any form of compromise with the Iranian regime in the course of the revolution. (Nabavi 2012)

Compared to the Arab Spring, the revolution was considered 'leaderless, amorphous, and fluid as during the Spring time of the Peoples in 1848. A polyphony and sometimes cacophony of voices arose and quickly swelled. But these voices could not draw on real political authority, not to speak of organizational discipline' (Weyland 2012: 924). The involvement of a large segment of society and the spontaneity of the whole thing took Arab regimes by surprise, despite the repressive measures employed by some of them (Rosiny 2012: 2). What makes the Arab Spring revolutions successful is the ability of the protesters to identify themselves as nationals, avoiding their political affiliation (i.e. socialist, liberal or Islamist), which has minimised conflict and friction between different groups. This has strengthened their appeal and unified people against the system (Rosiny 2012: 5). This leaderless movement has culminated in a variety of voices and perspectives, which tend to represent different political orientations, but are unified in their struggle for change at all levels, a change which ensures better living standards, fairness, equality and democracy. The overwhelming majority, however, is discontent with the poor living standards.

In the context of the Egyptian Revolution, Khamis (2011: 1169) asserts that 'two of the most striking aspects of the Egyptian uprising were its loose structure and its lack of identifiable leaders, as it was largely a grass-roots movement that had a bottom-up, rather than a top-down, structure'. He also commented on the protesters' discipline and organisation as well as their integrity: 'the protests were organised and led largely by a loose network of young people, most of whom demonstrated significant capacity for organisation, discipline, restraint, and integrity, resulting in a unique, peaceful, and youthful revolution' (Khamis 2011: 1169). In his analysis of the Egyptian Revolution and its organisation, Khamis concluded that the Arab Spring lacked 'the prerequisites of democratization, as defined in the Western context, such as vibrant and well-organized political parties with a strong and popular base of support, structural reform, an active and dynamic political life, and an energetic civil society' (Khamis 2011: 1169).

Khamis' conclusion has strengthen the claim that Arab revolutions were leaderless and were not governed or supported by any political party or movement in that respect, although reports later on suggested that the Muslim Brotherhood was discreetly mobilising people and encouraging their supporters to take to the street. Others have commented that the organisation and discipline of the protesters mirrored the Muslim Brotherhood's disciplined action and organisational social structure, a claim dismissed by Muslim Brotherhood leadership, insisting that the protests were random and reflected the protesters' discontent with the status quo.

Arab Spring: Transnational Arab Media versus Social Media

The success of some Arab revolutions took everyone by surprise, and this has opened debate as to the reasons for this. While most of the reports have credited social media for the massive popular protests that have swept the region, others have argued against this, asserting that social media impact has been exaggerated, and that it has little influence on the protests because the internet penetration in most of the Arab countries was very slim and only a small percentage of the population had access to social media. Others have argued that Egyptian activists, for instance, made great attempts in the past to use social media to mobilise the Egyptian population, but to no avail, as has been pointed out by Aday et al. (2012):

> Egyptian activists had been trying to ignite a revolution using blogs and social media for a decade, with little sustained success. The hundreds of thousands of people who made the Egyptian revolution by coming into the streets on January 25, 2011, did not learn about it through Twitter or Facebook. They saw it on Al-Jazeera, or out their windows. Internet

penetration in Yemen, which has made one of the most sustained and resilient protest movements, is roughly 2 percent, while the Gulf countries, with the highest regional rates of Internet penetration, have experienced little protest. (Aday et al. 2012: 4)

Aday et al. asserted that the Arab Spring occurred because of 'broader social conditions such as economic and political stagnation, political activism via social movements, and many small decisions by key actors such as political regimes' (2012: 17). They supported their argument with the claim that social media being hailed as the catalyst for the Egyptian Revolution flies in the face of the fact that little access was given to social media, especially after 'the Egyptian government shut down the Internet and short message service (SMS) (Aday et al. 2012: 7). Apart from the role that transnational media have played in promoting and mobilising the Arab public, Abou El Fadl (2013: 309) commented that Friday congregational prayers have played a significant role in fuelling revolutions in countries such as Egypt, Yemen, Syria and Tunisia. He went on to argue that Friday sermons have contributed to this, as often imams would deliver sermons pertaining to freedom and liberty. Prepared spiritually and their cause being justified religiously, some of these demonstrators would take to the street protesting the status quo. While Abou El Fadl is right that Friday congregational prayers contributed to mobilising and bringing large crowds out, these demonstrations were not limited to Fridays but took place every day of the week prior to the overthrow of the regimes. As asserted earlier, Fridays have been used as key demonstration days where millions of Arabs would take to the street to protest. What makes Friday protests interesting is that each Friday has been given a name based on the priorities of the protesters, such as Friday of Outrage, Friday of Human Rights, Friday of Justice, Friday of Victory, Friday of Resistance, etc. By naming these Fridays, the organisers sought to remind protesters and regimes of their multiple grievances and quest for justice and democracy.

Al-Jenaibi (2014: 248) reported that when he asked his subjects about the timeliness of social media and old media, 'most respondents saw the two about equal'. His subjects have rated the new and old media 'comparatively in terms of reliability' (Al-Jenaibi 2014: 249). In terms of the priority and preference for news, Al-Jenaibi found that his subject would resort to old media as the first port of call for checking news, but would use social media to verify news stories (2014: 249). Al-Janaibi's interviewees consider social media to be complementing traditional media and that 'traditional media still had an appeal at a time when the population faced cultural illiteracy' (2014: 253). However, despite the advantages of social media and the freedom it comes with it, some of Al-Janaibi's interviewees felt that the freedom available with social media needed to be subject to some rules. People needed to find the laws governing these freedoms, without defeating democracy, modifying the laws of expression in ways that were civilized and responsible. (2014: 253).

After studying surveys and interviews with media professionals, Al-Janaibi concluded that social media has a significant influence on 'the social and political change, and its specific impact on the aims and daily production of Arab media' (2014: 254).

Social Media and the Arab Spring

'The use of the internet by marginalised groups has been identified with counter public theory' (Faris 2010 in Al-Jenaibi 2014: 243). Faris (2010) defined counter public as 'parallel discursive arenas where numbers of subordinated social groups invent and circulate "counter discourses" to formulate oppositional interpretations of their identities, interests, and needs' (Faris 2010: 2). This counter narrative, which has been organised via social media, emerged as regimes controlled state-owned and private media which has been mobilised to support the regimes against the protesters, who were often considered 'unpatriotic', 'extremists' and 'foreign agents'. Against this barrage of propaganda, protesters resorted to social media, in some parts to promote their cause and mobilise the public to support them. While social media has been the catalyst for this, conviction and word of mouth, coupled with family networks, have contributed immensely to the success of these revolutions. The argument that social media alone has been behind the revolutions is far-fetched and this is simply because not every citizen in the Arab world has access to the internet, due to illiteracy, low income and lack of availability of internet broadband, especially in the period leading to the downfall of Mubarak, when the internet was cut.

Al-Jenaibi (2014: 250) conducted an interview with media experts in the UAE and found that people share the point of view that social media contributes to informing users and developing their social, cultural, religious, economic and political knowledge. Apart from expanding people's knowledge, Al-Jenaibi asserted that social media is often associated with social and political change, although others, as alluded to earlier, may contest this and consider it a preconception of social media post 2011. They consider 'the interactive forum of social media as a powerfully expressive medium for change' (Al-Jenaibi 2014: 251) And this link to the social and political change become entrenched in users' minds after the collapse of some Arab regimes. As experts and researchers were working tirelessly to identify the driving factor for this abrupt political change, others have made up their minds and reached their own conclusions that social media is the driving force, especially in a culture where traditional media 'was bound by "domination" and a "monopoly" grip' (Al-Jenaibi 2014: 251).

This dichotomy between social media and traditional media has been touched upon by Al-Jenaibi's interviewees who indicated that social media is much better and practical in 'disseminating and receiving news' (252). To use one journalist's words in this regard, 'using mainstream media doesn't provide easy access for the public compared to social media . . . I like social media because it is easy and immediate'. Another of Al-Jenaibi's interviewees highlighted the main pros of social media compared to traditional media, asserting that the dissemination of information by social media is speedy and often reaches a wider audience.

Judging by the comments of Al-Jenaibi's interviewees, social media remains popular compared to traditional media. Social media is practical, up-to-date and delivers news and information in a timely fashion. While speed and dissemination of news and information remain the main attributes of social media, some would question the authenticity of the news and material disseminated across social media. What about the fake news that has marred social media?

Al-Jenaibi's interviews and surveys, however, suggest that 'social media has not largely replaced traditional media, and in fact one is often used as a cross-check against the other in a complementary manner' (2014: 254). Al-Jenaibi asserts that there is 'a correlation between visiting an old media/corporate website and the verification of a news story heard through social media tools' (2014: 256). Al-Jenaibi's findings seem to support those views, which express a lack of trust in social media and its dissemination of news and information. This lack of endorsement raises many questions as to whether social media is considered the first or second source of news. Al-Jenaibi's findings suggest that it is considered second as its news and information are verified through traditional media.

The diversity of these protests varied from country to country, although it could be said that economic grievances remain the main cause for this. 'The reactions of the regimes have also ranged from cautious concessions to violent repression' (Rosiny 2012: 1). However, these protests came at the backdrop of years of social and economic protests, where protesters were 'protesting the hardships and despotism for years' (Rosiny 2012: 2). What is interesting about this movement is its transnational nature and its domino effect, which saw many other Arab countries engulfed in waves of protests.

According to Rosiny, these rapid protests and the 'movement's spontaneity and largely leaderless nature initially surprised the regimes and undermined suppression strategies they had formerly employed, such as arresting political leaders and villainizing protesters as foreign agents' (2012: 2). While the new movement caught everyone by surprise both in its rapid development and its organisation, which continue to attract many dissatisfied people, some Arab governments resorted to the old style of accusing protesters as 'agents of foreign powers' (Egypt, Bahrain, Saudi Arabia), as 'saboteurs' (Syria), and as 'rats and cockroaches' (Gaddafi in Libya) (Rosiny 2012: 3). Despite this strategy of blaming and labelling, protests grew even larger defying all sorts of accusations. However, as regimes failed to persuade their citizens to resume normality, and with the continuation of protests, some have resorted to repression to establish normal life, but this failed spectacularly as it led to civil war in some countries, mainly Syria, Yemen and Libya, some of which are still raging today.

The success of these transnational Arab movements can be traced to three main causes:

1. The advent of technology and the use of social media to communicate amongst the minority who have access to these facilities, and who were very vocal in calling for wider protests.

2. The economic hardships and living challenges encountered by citizens, which has fuelled the protests across the Arab world and motivated many politically illiterate people to join protests, with no demands except for a call to improve their living conditions.
3. The role of transnational Arab channels in mobilising the Arab public across the Arab world. The fact that some of these channels could reach a wider audience has contributed to sharing and broadcasting protests and demonstrations across the Middle East. These transnational channels have dropped their normal schedules for weeks to focus on these movements, with a particular focus on mass movements in Arab capitals. The narrative and discourse of some of these channels, coupled with revolutionary music and emotional scenes, such as those of people living in abject poverty, have fuelled some of these protests. Apart from the broadcasts of these channels, they have provided online platforms for discussion and debate, allowing protesters to share messages of encouragement, comments, and motivating stories designed to mobilise people to join protests. The discourse employed by some of these channels is also worth noting. The discourse of deprivation, poverty, hardship, repression, stifling of liberties, etc. has been prevalent in the coverage of most of the channels.

However, some have contested calling the uprisings in Tunisia and Egypt Twitter or Facebook revolutions. For instance, Comninos (2011) examined ICT access in these countries and argued that statistics suggest that the internet penetration in these countries is very low, for instance, only 7 per cent of Egyptian inhabitants are Facebook users, which is a tiny proportion, and this casts doubt on the argument that Facebook was responsible for the revolutions. Comninos asserts that 'from the ICT access and usage figures [. . .] it is clear that there is no necessary correlation between ICT access and unrest. Social networking users comprise a minority of the population' (2011: 5).

Judging by the statistics for ICT users, which are very slim, I think Comninos's argument does have some truth in it, as the vast majority of citizens in Egypt and Tunisia do not have access to social media. The question remains, did the tiny minority which has access to the internet lead to the demise of three of the longest ruling regimes in the region? One should take this with a pinch of salt as the evidence does not substantiate this claim, especially if you consider the masses of people involved in the protest, which defies the statistical evidence of ICT users in these countries.

The advent of ICT has changed the communication landscape across the Arab world. Social media 'offers new appealing possibilities to people to express themselves in a variety of ways and freely participate in major events because they are more decentralised and less hierarchical and are based on democratic structures' (Bardici 2012: 16).

Since the eruption of the Arab Spring, there has been a wider discussion as to the role of social media in social and political change. According to Bardici, social media allowed Egyptian protesters to 'plan, organise, and execute leaderless movement actions. Mobilisation is interrelated with cyberactivism in that it can help foster civic engagement' (2012: 19). The same point has been reinforced by Khamis and Vaughn (2011) who asserted that social media fosters freedom of expression and allows networking, which is vital to civic engagement. While some may have their doubts about social media and the ability of its users to stage successful revolution, Bardici (2012) and Iskander (2011) are of the view that social media has contributed immensely to the Egyptian Revolution, pointing to the fact that social media has enabled the protesters to 'magnify and expedite the process of revolution' (Bardici 2012: 19). While there is agreement that social media can facilitate and promote political activism, the question remains on what scale, and what impact does it have on the wider population, some of whom do not have access to the internet.

Khamis (2011) associated the success of social media to the social and political movements that endorse and use social media as a means of communication to transform and mobilise societies. He asserts that 'new Arab media should be preceded by active social and political movements if they are to have an impact on transforming and liberalizing the societies to which they belong' (2011: 1166). Khamis acknowledged the significant role social media played in the Egyptian Revolution and summarised it as: 'enabling cyberactivism, a major trigger for street activism; encouraging civic engagement, by aiding the mobilisation and organization of protests and other forms of political expression; and promoting a new form of citizen journalism, which provided a platform for ordinary citizens to express themselves' (2011: 1163).

He goes on to say that social media was integral in mobilising the Egyptian public.

The trigger for the Egyptian Revolution has been 'the corruption, the dictatorship, economic distress, and humiliation that they had been experiencing, several protests movements were already active in the Egyptian political arena' (Khamis 2011: 1164). These reasons, which had been boiling beneath the surface exploded on the January 25 revolution. Khamis believes that the success of the Egyptian Revolution could be attributed to three main groups that managed 'to combine street activism with cyberactivism' (2011: 1164). These are: the National Coalition for Change, the April 6 movement, and the 'We are all Khalid Said'. Khamis (2011) argued that these groups had been very active since 2005 and used social media to organise a myriad of activities. However, the question is why were they unsuccessful in mobilising the public to take to the streets in 2005? While some may argue that the public was not ready then, or that communication was not so effective, then this may raise the question of social media and its ability to mobilise the Egyptian people. The fact of the matter is that the revolution was triggered by the Tunisian Revolution, which was been widely covered by transnational Arab media, and this reached the Egyptian people through Al-Jazeera Mubashir (Al-Jazeera direct) and other media apparatus, including social media, of course.

As has been mentioned in previous sections, the role of social media in sparking the Arab Spring has been overestimated and underestimated by some. Irrespective of which perspective you support or hold, one could argue that there are host of reasons and drives that have sparked the Arab Spring. To limit it only to social media might be seen as an overestimation, as other factors do not support this, including internet penetration, the economy and the widespread illiteracy. However, this does not rule out all together the main contribution that social media has played in this regard. This has been reinforced by many scholars, including Atton (2004) who argued that the internet has helped and facilitated social mobilisation as online messages are 'read and disseminated more easily than printed pamphlets, flyers or bulletins. This modern form of spreading information in recent social movements has proven to be an efficient way of targeting a bigger audience and delivering information in a faster and cheaper way among civilians with the same interests' (2004: 3). In the context of Libya, Papaioannou and Olivos asserted that social media has encouraged 'new cultural values based on human rights and political freedom, in particular participation in free elections, are disseminated via Facebook, highlighting Libya's transition from an authoritarian regime towards democracy' (2013: 108). They went on to reiterate social media's role in 'articulating collective goals, building solidarity and organizing actions' (2013: 111). Similarly, and in the context of Tunisia, protesters used social media as a tool to communicate and mobilise people (Ryan 2011). Social media has also been used to transfer and report protests on the ground (Khamis and Vaughn 2013: 72). This has been seen as a good mechanism for engaging and encouraging activism. 'The international community has recognised the importance and impact of the use of social media in articulating social change. Nevertheless, the Internet still has limitations regarding access, censorship and affordance' (Khamis and Vaugh 2013: 111).

Conclusion

This chapter has reviewed some of the concepts and approaches related to framing and representational strategies in discourses. We have examined how different actors position and represent themselves and others based on their own social, cultural and political beliefs. The chapter has also introduced us to the discourse of revolutions as well as the role of media in instigating and promoting these revolutions. In the Arab Spring context, a discussion of the role of traditional and social media has been established, offering different perspectives on this. This chapter is vital to our subsequent chapters as it introduces readers to key concepts and terminologies to be adopted in the course of our analysis.

3

Framing, Representation and Conflict in Arabic Discourse

This chapter will consolidate the previous two chapters by examining the notion of Us vs Them. It will look at how the Arab people present and position themselves vis-à-vis their leaders during the Arab Spring. The discursive construal of the Us vs Them binary will be identified and its representation through language will be demonstrated. This chapter will offer a textual analysis of a set of speeches and slogans of the Arab public during the Arab uprising of 2011. The focus will be mainly on the Arab people's use of particular names and labels to describe and identify their regimes. The data covers the beginning of the uprising until the downfall of the regimes in those countries that have witnessed revolutions. Some of the data is taken from media organisation websites, activists' websites and social media, etc. By examining the above-mentioned strategy, it is hoped that more light will be shed on the development and changes in discourse, and further insight into the type and genre of the relationship governing the Arab public and Arab regimes in these countries will be offered. In my analysis, I will draw on the approaches/ frameworks of Fowler et al. (1979) and Van Dijk (1991), which are relevant to this research, as they offer the relevant tools and mechanisms for examining the attitudes and ideologies of speakers through their language use.

The main approaches to discourse, framing and representation have been succinctly reviewed in the previous chapter. In this chapter, however, we will examine the discourse of Arab revolutions with particular reference to the notion of Us vs Them naming and labelling. By doing so, we will be able to gain an insight into the type of discourse used by the Arab public pertaining to their leaders. In order to access this type of discourse, the frameworks of Fowler et al. and Van Dijk will be adopted for the analysis of data, which will focus on the language representation and how discourse has been used to represent Arab regimes.

Theoretical Background

Ideological Structures of Discourse

As discussed in Chapter 2, CDA deals with the production and reproduction of power, dominance and asymmetry in discourse. As power and asymmetry are defined 'in terms of the relations between social groups or organisations, such discourse generally will be ideologically based' (Van Dijk 2015: 72–3 in Wodak and Meyer 2015).

Van Dijk argues that ideas, beliefs, power and abuse, and racism, amongst others, find their way to discourse and are exemplified in what he calls 'ideological discourse structure'. Van Dijk cited the following as aspects of ideological discourse structures:

Polarisation. Polarising between groups through the concepts of *US* and *THEM*, where the in-group is presented positively but the out-group is presented negatively. This representation allows the positive and negative representation to control the structure of discourse based on the ideological belief of speakers, whose discourses are legitimised because of their institutional power.

Pronouns. Pronouns can be used to express collectivism and inclusivity as a group or organisation such as we/us/ and exclusivity and otherness such as they/them, the other – who are painted to be different, the outsiders who constitute a menace to the group organisation and society. This ideological structural discourse is intended to polarise communities, create enmity and establish a hostile environment that push communities and groups further apart.

Identification. Members of groups and organisations identify themselves in relation to their group, emphasising a sense of belonging reflecting their own ideological beliefs. This is often highlighted in affiliating oneself with a group or an organisation. Van Dijk's examples of 'as a feminist . . .'; 'as pacifist . . .' illustrate this very clearly.

Emphasis of positive self-descriptions and negative other-descriptions. In his analysis of positive-self description and negative other-descriptions, Van Dijk asserted that the in-groups tend to focus on their positive attributions while ignoring all together their negative characterisations. However, they would emphasise the negative description of the other and disregard their positive attribution, with a sole intention of associating them with bad things and removing their positive attributes and this is often designed to tarnish the reputation of these groups, if not, belittle them. 'This rhetorical combination of hyperbolic emphasis and mitigation of good or bad things of in-groups and out-groups is called the **Ideological Square**' (Van Dijk 2015: 72).

Activities. Groups identify and describe themselves based on their own activities and the things they do. The 'we do' thing is clearly highlighted and the things that should be done are underlined to show that the group is the key defender of the group, community or country (Van Dijk 2015: 72). The main contribution and the plans of the other are ignored and often considered illegitimate and a threat to the in-group. This has often led to the marginalisation of the in-group.

Norms and values. Ideologies are reflected in the expression and display of norms, beliefs and values, which are magnified and often glorified to show the positive value of the in-group, while degrading the outgroup for not adhering to such norms and values such as freedom, equality, liberty, justice, etc. A good example to consider here is Bush's speech after the 9/11 attack where these ideologies have been displayed clearly and used as values to rally the country against the other, who have been vilified and considered the enemy of the country. Bush's ideological demonstration has also been exemplified in his plans of spreading freedom and democracy to the Middle East and his willingness to defeat the enemy, who stands against these values.

Interests. Ideological discourse embodies references to power and interests. People's social, cultural and political interests are often articulated in the type of discourses we generate: 'ideological discourse typically features many references to our interests, such as basic resources (food, shelter, and health) as well as symbolic resources such as knowledge, status, or access to public discourse' (Van Dijk 2015: 72).

These ideologies often find their way into the language and discourse of the speaker or producer. They are presented in different forms depending on the attributes. For instance, to highlight 'Our good things and Their bad things, we may use headlines, foregrounding, topical word or paragraph order, active sentences, repetitions, hyperboles, metaphors and many more. Conversely, to mitigate Our bad things, we may use euphemisms, passive sentences, backgrounding, small letter type, implicit information and so on' (Van Dijk 2015: 74).

In his discussion of racism in discourse, Van Dijk examined the UK Independence Party's discourse in the 2014 European elections and concluded that UKIP has used several strategies to express its ideological stance, opposing immigration. For instance, he mentioned the use of numbers (26 million) to magnify the issue and attract support, the use of command such as 'take control', possessive pronouns such us 'our country', as well as the use of modality by introducing images to maximise the effect of fear and mobilise the public to support the party's ideological belief. Such strategies are designed to push UKIP's ideologies to be supported and acted upon by the public through voting for them and advocating their message. UKIP's argument is structured around the negativity of immigration and the significant impact it has on UK citizens, painting therefore a picture that EU migrants are responsible for the increase in unemployment in the country. 'This attitude is based on a more fundamental racist *ideology* polarizing in-groups and outgroups, and enhancing the superiority or priority of (ethnic) in-groups' (Van Dijk 2015: 74).

The concept of Us vs Them has been present in the UKIP's discourse and it has taken different forms and strategies. Connecting people's hardships and lack of opportunity to the other (immigrants) is explicit in their literature and discourses. The vilification of the in-group and holding them responsible for the economic situation in the country is designed to attract support from those who have been affected by the economic crisis in the UK. While the blame should be solely on the government and elected officials for the state of the economy, innocent migrants have been held responsible for the situation, by painting them as the main competitors who have arrived to steal jobs and opportunities from their UK counterparts, a claim Van Dijk said is baseless and lacks reasoning.

In dealing with the discourse of US vs Them, Van Dijk referred to the Social Component in discourse. This component reflects the power, dominance, control and abuse, which often reflect the institutional asymmetrical structure of discourse. This allows the formulation of the binary power groups and dominated groups. To borrow Van Dijk's words, 'part of this societal account of discursive domination and resistance has been formulated in terms of *social cognition*, that is, as the specific knowledge, attitudes and ideologies shared by the members of these societal organizations' (Van Dijk 2015: 70). These social practices frequently shape and are shaped by discourses, mediated, according to Van Dijk, by cognition which reflects the shared knowledge, beliefs and ideologies of groups and communities.

According to Oktar (2001: 319–20) the strategy for constructing ideological communication consists of four moves:

1. Express/emphasise information that is 'positive' about us.
2. Express/emphasise information that is 'negative' about them.
3. Suppress/de-emphasise information that is 'positive' about them.
4. Suppress/de-emphasise information that is 'negative' about us.

The above-mentioned moves constitute Van Dijk's 'Ideological Square' which represents the positive self and the negative other.

In his analysis of how Turkish media, mainly Cumhuriyet and Akit, represent and reconstruct ideologies of different parties that have different conflicting views on the Turkish political landscape, by adopting a transitive analysis of the discourse of 'secularists' and 'anti-secularists', Oktar found that the media representing these groups has made heavy use of the binary of Us vs Them, where the positive self has been emphasised and expressed and the positive other has been de-emphasised and suppressed, while the negative other has been highlighted and emphasised. Examples of this include: *we are democrats, we are tolerant, we are powerful; they are bigots, they are reactionary, they are fakers*, etc.

These examples of representation of the self and the other are produced by the political parties, but are re-produced and reconstructed by the Turkish newspapers that are supporting different groups. This reconstruction of political ideologies is designed to support the political ideologies of the actors that share the same ideologies through the representation of their positive practices. Oktar concluded that

> the analysis of syntactic structures of the op-ed articles appearing in Cumhuriyet and Akit reveals an ideology that portrays the ingroup as embelished with positive attributes while the outgroup is consistently associated with negative attributes, such as non-democratic, intolerant, oppressive, etc. Therefore, there is structural evidence of positive self-representation and negative other-representation in the secular and anti-secular discourses of Cumhuriyet and Akit, respectively. (Oktar 2001: 343)

In his final conclusion of the analysis of ideological representation in both newspapers, he asserted that:

> ideology is an important determining factor in the organization of discourse in terms of social representation of us versus them; that is, what we are, what we typically do, what our aims and values are in relation to them, and what they are, what they typically do, what their aims and values are in relation to us. (Oktar 2001: 344)

The emphasis is that the in-group are different and often 'represent our negative mirror' (Oktar 2001: 344).

In the United States context, Oddo (2011) examined Franklin D. Roosevelt and George W. Bush's 'call-to-arms' speeches. He carefully examined the strategies used for the legitimisation of their acts, examining therefore the binary of Us vs Them in four speeches, two for each president. Oddo concluded that both 'FDR and Bush drew upon similar thematic formations and rhetorical strategies in their attempts to lead the public into war' (2011: 308). He also found out that both presidents have utilised the semantic binary Us vs Them to polarise the nation and garner support for legitimising their wars. Different strategies have been utilised including the misrepresentation of 'both past and future events to legitimate immediate violence in the here-and-now' (2011: 308). In his analysis of the speeches and subsequent conclusion, Oddo charged both presidents with manipulation as both 'achieved their rhetorical (and material) objectives 'by omitting very important information, by lying, or by distorting facts' (Van Dijk 2006: 364 in Oddo 2011: 308).

Oddo remarked on what he calls 'expanding and delimiting US' in the presidents' speeches. The notion of victimhood was expanded to convey the message that an attack on soldiers or civilians is an attack on the whole nation and civilised world. He also noted that the two presidents expanded their rhetoric to include other enemies while addressing those who attacked the United States. In the case of Roosevelt he expanded the hostile rhetoric to Japan before their attack on Pearl Harbor. Similarly, Bush expanded his hostile rhetoric to Saddam, despite the lack of evidence linking him to the 9/11 attack (Oddo 2011: 304–5). This strategy is often designed to prepare the public for future conflicts with designated states. This could be considered the first step in a series of announcements and speeches where the named enemy becomes the focal actor of the call-to-arms rhetoric. In the case of Saddam, for instance, we noticed that Iraq became front and centre in Bush's speeches post 9/11. These speeches often carry out descriptions and representations of Saddam as 'evil', 'dictator' and the real threat to his own people and United States' friends and allies in the region, affecting therefore America's interests in the region.

> *Iraq has attempted to purchase high-strength aluminium tubes and other equipment needed for gas centrifuges, which are used to enrich uranium for nuclear weapons. If the Iraqi regime is able to produce, buy, or steal an amount of highly enriched uranium a little larger than a single softball, it could have a nuclear weapon in less than a year. And if we allow that to happen, a terrible line would be crossed. Saddam Hussein would be in a position to blackmail anyone who opposes his aggression. He would be in a position to dominate the Middle East. He would be in a position to threaten America. And Saddam Hussein would be in a position to pass nuclear technology to terrorists.* (Bush 2002)

In his comment on the above extract from a speech delivered by Bush in 2002, Oddo made the following remarks:

> Bush's representation of the future is highly modalized. It begins with a conditional (*if*) and a modal auxiliary (*could*): *If* Iraq is able to produce or obtain a small amount of enriched uranium, it *could* have a nuclear

weapon in less than a year. Bush then continues to slip from this propositional future to still more worrisome hypothetical future (*would*) possibilities: Saddam Hussein *would* be in a position to blackmail those who oppose him, dominate the Middle East, threaten America and pass nuclear technology to terrorists. Of course, by unpacking all of the explicit and implicit 'ifs' in Bush's utterances, it is easy to see the remoteness of the dark future he construes. Yet Bush presents this distant and highly contingent future as likely enough that we must take immediate military action to stop it. After all, Bush suggests that this future will come about *if we allow* it to happen. (Oddo 2011: 303)

Bush's representation of the dark future of the Middle East and the consequences of Saddam's ownership of WMD has proven to be a misrepresentation of the reality in Iraq in 2002. When the dust settled on the war, which created the very dark future that Bush spoke about, in the sense that it opened the door for sectarian conflicts, created ISIS – which had never dreamed of making Iraq the headquarters for its fanatical ideas – it became evident that the pretexts for war were inaccurate and misleading. The use of the conditional (ifs) and buts are good indicators that in the absence of tangible facts, hypothetical scenarios are created to mobilise public opinion to support one's claim. Bush's strategy of polarisation, spreading of fear and 'manipulation', in Oddo's words, has been used in some Arab regimes' speeches during the Arab Spring. Their strategy, as will be discussed later, has been based on limiting the scale of these uprising and associating them with a small group of Islamists. This strategy of limiting and constraining the event by associating it with small groups could be interpreted as a tactic to spread fear amongst citizens that the contemplated future would be worse if Islamists take power. While it was clear that the uprisings, as discussed in Chapter 4, were triggered by economic grievances and widespread unemployment among the youth, some Arab officials continue to lay the blame on foreign forces as well as on 'rogue Islamist' groups. This strategy is twofold. First, by using the strategy of foreign forces/powers, officials have sought to mobilise the public to support them and warn that any uprising would support the foreign powers and subsequently impact the national interest, if not the system of governance. The second strategy is designed to sow fear in the West that the uprisings are the making of Islamists who will be very hostile if they lay their hands on power. One would characterise these strategies as internal and external strategies, one designed for citizens and the other for Western powers. However, judging by the level of uprisings and involvement of different groups and parties, it could be said that both strategies failed spectacularly as they ignored the key grievances of protesters, which were genuinely reflective of the situation on the ground.

Leudar et al. (2004) carried out a study on membership categorisation in the context of 'doing violence in political discourse', where they examined the use of Us vs Them in Bush, Blair and Bin Laden's speeches post 9/11. They found that the use of Us vs Them reflects the divisive nature of their discourses. As in Oddo's work, Leudar, Marsland and Nekvapil found that Bush and Blair use 'Us' to refer to the 'civilized world', 'freedom-loving nations', 'democratic nations', while 'Them' refers to the 'terrorists', the 'evil' and 'uncivilized'. They see themselves as part of their nations and the wider free world that loves and defends freedom and democracy. While religion was not an explicit criteria for categorisation of membership for Bush and Blair, although they implicitly alluded to it, Bin Laden's categorisation was based on religious reasoning. His use of 'we Muslims', 'Our Muslim brothers' and 'Islam' speaks to his reasoning and categorisation, while he represented the other as 'crusaders', 'infidels', 'aggressors'.

What is remarkable about this study is that the three speakers have used language to categorise themselves as part of a certain group, rejecting the other as the outsider who is hostile and seeks harm to their in-group. They therefore called upon all their associates to support their cause and defend their 'oppressed sons, brothers and sisters'. This is done through the binary of Us vs Them, while different opinions within the group have been rejected outright and these people have been considered as traitors or a menace to the group. For instance, in Bin Laden's speech there was a reference to 'Ulama (religious scholars) who, according to him, do nothing to defend the Islamic faith and its followers, discrediting their authority as true representative of Muslims.

In their examination of mood effects on intergroup discrimination, Forgas and Fiedler (1996: 28) noted that, judging by research in the field (Tajfel 1970; Tajfel and Forgas 1981), the distinction between us and them can often 'bring about biased perceptions and judgments, and even prejudiced behaviors'. They have drawn on Berkowitz (1993) who asserted that feelings of negativity could serve as a catalyst for 'aggressive action tendencies toward outsiders' (in Forgas and Fiedler 1996: 28). Forgas and Fiedler referred to other studies that have associated affective states with 'anxiety, fear and anger, and even good or bad moods tend to interfere with people's ability to process group-related formation adequately' (Forgas and Fiedler 1996: 28–9).

The categorisation of individuals into distinct groups may fuel feelings of discrimination against these groups. Following Tajfel's minimal group paradigm, which assigns participants to groups, Forgas and Fiedler remarked that the affiliation with in-group and out-group was 'sufficient to bring about a marked tendency to discriminate in favor of the in-group' (1996: 29).

According to Gilmore and Somerville (1994: 1341), such a stereotype can arise from practices and experiences acquired from 'fairy tales and comics, in the schoolyard and on the playing field, from television and cinema, and from the media'. The role of media in reinforcing such a stereotype is well documented in numerous studies, and such a stereotype can lead to the formation of groups and movements that may call for social change. The following section will deal with social change and movement.

Social Change and Movement

Marshall (1994: 489) defines social movement as 'an organized effort by a significant number of people to change (or resist change in) some major aspects of society'. I am adopting Marshall's definition when examining Arab revolutions and subsequent political and social change in countries such as Egypt, Libya and Tunisia. We will examine whether social movements in these countries have contributed to these changes and the likelihood that these changes have been shaped in their discourses, via the use of Us vs Them binary. As alluded to on numerous occasions in this book, movements for social change in the Arab world during the Arab Spring have been anonymous – it was not clear who is behind them, or who was leading. But what was clear is that groups of individuals, incentivised by the same cause of economic grievances, have taken to the street to protest against these conditions, in the hope of changing the situation for the better.

The Us vs Them binary helps articulate the ideological belief of discourse producers, who often 'share evaluative beliefs, viz, opinions. Organized into social attitudes' (Van Dijk 1995b: 18). Van Dijk has given the example of feminism to illustrate this point. He goes on to say that 'feminists may share attitudes about abortion, affirmative action or corporate "glass ceilings" blocking promotion, or other forms of discrimination by men. Ideologies, then, are the overall abstract mental system that organize such socially shared attitudes' (1995b: 18). These attitudes are internally shared, agreed and often acted upon within the group or movement. In the case of the Arab Spring, the attitudes displayed by social movements have created an internal structure, beliefs and ideas that are anti-regime, anti-poverty, anti-unemployment and anti-injustice. These beliefs are shared within the movement and acted upon, culminating in the uprisings which have seen the overthrow of some Arab leaders, while substantial reforms have taken place in others. These newly formed attitudes and beliefs were expressed through the dichotomy of Us vs Them, where Arab regimes and governments were categorised as the other, 'Them', who oppose the group's attitudes, beliefs and hopes for economic prosperity, freedom, democracy and justice. This newly emerged discourse, which I would call the Arab anti-establishment discourse, has broken certain taboos of loyalty and allegiance to their leaders. This has been manifested in the discourse of reprimand, which breaks with the tradition of politeness, at the heart of which is respect and loyalty for leaders. While this is something to be expected in Western countries, in the Arab world it is making history, as the norms and customs that govern social and cultural practices have been challenged by these new social movements, culminating in a new discourse and practice; a discourse of reprimand, challenge and accountability was revealed and enhanced by the new social movements. These newly surfaced practices could be categorised as ideological practices of a movement that is in favour of new social and political practices, forming therefore new ideological beliefs supported and endorsed by new groups. In this respect, Van Dijk (1995b: 18) pointed out, 'ideologies of groups and group relations are constructed by a group-based selection of relevant social values'. As mentioned above, the new Arab social movement has constructed new practices such as liberty, democracy, freedom of expression, justice and economic prosperity.

Why has interest in the new ideological beliefs emerged recently in the Arab world? According to Van Dijk (1995b):

> any property of discourse that expresses, establishes, confirms or emphasizes a self-interested group opinion, perspective or position, especially in a broader socio-political context of social struggle, is a candidate for special attention in such an 'ideological' analysis. Such discourse structures usually have the social function of legitimacy dominance or justifying concrete actions of power abuse by the elites.

Such a power is maintained through the constant upgrading of the interest of the powerful, while any information that contradicts powerful groups is 'downgraded, and information about outgroups be given more prominence by assigning it to a more prominent category' (Van Dijk 1995b: 29).

In the early stages of Arab revolutions, stated-owned media downgraded the protesters' demands and considered them to be illegitimate, and pushed by tags and agents of foreign powers. As protests and demands increased, the state-owned media became very aggressive in its tone, discourse and attitude towards protesters. A discourse of 'traitors', 'outsiders', 'foreign agents', 'radical Islamists' were used to discredit and tarnish some of the protesters. The state-owned media ignored outright some of the protesters' demands and regarded their actions as supported, triggered and driven by foreign powers and groups. However, the protesters considered their protests, which were staged to protest against poor living standards, injustice and inequality, to be legitimate. These burning injustices served as the key trigger for millions to take to the streets and demand political and social change. Although ideologies are often associated with dominant groups, 'oppositional or dominated groups also share ideologies' (Van Dijk 1995b: 21). As discussed earlier, protesters have different ideologies to those expressed by Arab officials and governments. The fact that they oppose official policies vehemently and propose their own vision, which stems from their own beliefs and shared ideologies, shows their persistence in changing the status quo. Although one might argue that the protesters' ideologies were not explicit and were invisibly underlined by beliefs or distinct ideologies of individual parties, the discourse employed did suggest that some of the protesters support the political and social change in line with some political parties' policies. But this was very challenging to prove at the time, as the heterogeneity of the protesters dominated the uprising, making it very difficult to pinpoint the whole movement to a party/group.

While some of the protesters' demands were legitimate and reflected their desire for change, some of these demands spring from protesters' ideological beliefs, which shape their practices and discourses. Some of these ideologies, although they are not always aware of them, remain tacitly embedded in the protesters' practices. To borrow Van Dijk's words, 'underlying ideologically based attitudes about others may not always be conscious, and so the subtle details of dialogical interaction are not always fully controlled and controllable' (1995b: 31–2). Ideologies 'influence social interaction and coordination, group cohesion, and the organized or institutionalized activities of social members aimed towards reaching common goals' (Van Dijk 1995: 32).

Indeed, ideologies create a sense of division and polarisation among social groups, which often threatens aspects of harmonisation and the cohesion of communities. The adoption of US vs Them reflects such a division and the incohesion of groups and communities. In politics, such a divide is a normal practice and parties try their best to express their beliefs and stances vis-à-vis a range of political, social and cultural issues. Discourse, therefore, is considered to be 'an inherent part of socio-cultural practices that are embedded in social and societal contexts . . . particular discourses are enacted and, to a large extent, constituted in a specific process and context' (Tienari et al. 2003: 379).

In the context of the Arab Spring, protesters' discourses were confined to specific themes and demands, while Arab governments reconstructed and re-enacted a new discourse register, based on national security argument. The security-based discourse was designed to protect regimes and government against the growing protests, but this strategy failed to achieve its objectives as protesters rejected this claim and persistently continue to call for the overthrow of the regimes and their governments. Against the backdrop of resilience and persistence, some Arab regimes have shifted their strategies and acknowledged protesters' demands as legitimate and promised to address them. In a series of speeches, regimes have called on protesters to end their protests and to come to negotiations with the government, but this has not lessened protesters' grievances and their suspicion of the regimes' abrupt change of strategy. This exemplifies the lack of trust and the gravity of the situation in most of Arab capitals. However, different Arab leaders have adopted different discourses to defuse the situation. These discourses fluctuate between commands and pleas, harsh tones and gentle address, religious and secular discourse, formal and informal use of the language and, at times, a vernacular has been used to appeal to a wider section of the society. Such appeals fall on deaf ears as millions of protesters took to the streets calling for a change of regime in Egypt, Libya, Tunisia, Syria and Yemen. Protesters' demands marked a new shift in their discourse towards their leaders, adopting a very critical approach which has broken social and cultural taboos.

Arab Public Discourse: Positive-Self and Negative-Other

This section examines the discourse of the Arab public through the use of slogans during the Arab Spring. It will in particular highlight the main strategies and discourses utilised, reflecting therefore the social and political changes that have swept the Arab world during this time. It will demonstrate the social changes that have affected the Arab public, as reflected in their discourse; it will also provide an insight into the attitudes and behaviour displayed by the public towards their regimes and governments. Put simply, it will help us to understand how Arab leaders are represented in the Arab public discourse.

The Discourse of Shahīd and Nafdīk

The death of Mohammed Bouazizi, who died fighting injustice in his small town of Sidi Bouzid in Tunisia, was held by many Arab protesters to be shahid (martyrdom). The support for Bouazizi has been given a religious connotation to amplify the solidarity and magnify the cause. The use of the phrase '*Kulunā Bouazizī*' (we are all Bouazizi) resonated across Tunisia and the Arab world in a symbol of support and solidarity against injustices. This discourse of '*Kulunā*' (we are all) then become a copycat across the Arab world and there is not a single demonstration, where the phrase has not been used.

The phrase '*nafdīk*' is used in Arabic to show honour and loyalty to the deceased by avenging or sacrificing life for him or her. This discourse of retribution and vengeance against Arab regimes is new to the culture, society and politics, as it replaces well-known and documented phrases of loyalty to regimes such as '*bi rūḥi bi dami nafdīk yā ra'īs*' (we sacrifice our blood and soul for you (president)) and *'naḥmīk'* (we protect you). This transition of discourse from loyal citizens to mobilised opposition reflects a new change in the social and cultural fabric of Arab society. This new discourse has exacerbated what is often portrayed in the Arabic media as a healthy relationship between the governor and the governed, and has shown that the traditional discourse of fear and silence has given way to a discourse of reprimand and accountability for some Arab regimes. The switch of the use of *'nafdīk'*, which was traditionally associated with supporting Arab regimes, to supporting citizens against their regimes is a new phenomenon and unprecedented in the Arab world. This shift in the reallocation of terminology reflects the new binary of Us vs Them: citizens against their regimes, where praise changes to reprimand, and loyalty to opposition.

In the Egyptian context, the death of some protesters has mobilised protesters who used different online fora to communicate their rejection of Mubarak's long reign. But the biggest and largest platform has been the street and Tahrir Square, where millions of Egyptians converged to say loud and clear, and in no equivocal terms, 'No' to repression and the targeting of protesters. This has pushed protesters to call for the departure of the Egyptian regime, borrowing the Tunisian slogan of *'irḥal'*, which has become one of the most popular slogans in the Arab Spring.

The Discourse of 'irḥal' *(Leave)*

Demonstrators were very measured in their slogans at the beginning, where slogans reflect the economic upheaval and indecent living circumstances. However, as protests grew in size and scope, protesters and their strategy became very bold. Their demands for better living standards gave way to political demands, including the call for regimes to 'step down' and 'leave'. The use of the verb *'irḥal'* (leave) became a popular slogan across the region. The verb is used in its imperative form, expressing order and command from protesters to regimes. This is, again, a shift in the social hierarchy, as orders and commands are associated in Arabic culture with power, authority and high rank. However, by using the verb *'irḥal'* in its *amer* (imperative) form protesters have shifted authority from regimes to protesters, displaying their power. This transition in discourse is very revealing; in many ways it serves as an indicator that there is a shift in the asymmetrical structure of Arab societies, where the powerful become powerless and the powerless become powerful, with full authority and control. While this appears normal in some Western societies, in the Arab world this is a coup against the political, cultural and social norms that have governed Arab societies for so many years.

As protests gathered momentum, the protesters started to express their various demands, some of which were political and social, including the call for the resignation of Arab leaders. This is unprecedented in Arab public discourse, which is characterised historically with slogans of loyalty and respect. However, the Arab slogans have marked a departure from this tradition, adopting a new discourse of defiance, reprimand and challenge. The following examples of protesters' slogans are evidence of this shift.

The use of the imperative, coupled with insult, as in the following example: '*Irḥal yā chayṭān*' (leave oh devil) is a clear indication of the change in Arabic public discourse and a tangible sign of the mobilisation and empowerment of the Arab public. The shift from receiving orders to giving them is clearly manifested in the direct use of the imperative where wide range of commands, including calls for resignation, have been performed. This is a new shift, not only in the discourse itself, but in the political culture of some Arabic countries. The shift in the political culture no longer supports the hierarchy, where power and authority are dominant, and where respect and loyalty are the norm. The culture of respect that prevailed for decades has been reversed with the arrival of the Arab Spring, which has empowered the powerless and stilled confidence in those fluctuating minds. Such a change in the political culture finds its way into the Arab public discourse, which became very revolutionary, both in its tone and semantics, reflecting a visible change in the culture and structure of society. As discourse reflects social and political change, it could be said that the slogans of '*irḥal*', 'slogans of reprimand' and 'slogans of insult' are tangible examples of this change. The question that imposes itself here is: Why this sudden change?

Whatever the reasons behind this shift, it could be said that the slogans and the protesters' voices reflected a genuine awareness of their rights and obligations. Their expectations, which had been suppressed for many years, emerged along with an attitude of defiance and challenge. This new change has empowered and strengthened the demands of protesters, injecting confidence and feelings of positivism in their actions and behaviour, as will be discussed in the next section.

While Arab regimes have been trying hard to deal with this new phenomenon, they themselves have used different discourses to describe protesters, such as the discourse of *mukharibūn* (vandals), *khawana* (traitors); *madsūsīn* (agents). These labels were intended to drive a wedge between protesters and the wider public. They have been portrayed as foreign agents who intend to cause harm to their motherland. What is more interesting is the gradual discourse employed by regimes. To start with, protesters were ignored and marginalised, but in the face of solid resistance and international condemnation, this strategy gave way to a discourse of dialogue and peaceful negotiations. Arab leaders have called for *ḥiwār* (dialogue) and *muṣālaḥa* (reconciliation) but this attempt has been rejected outright by protesters who themselves have adopted a new slogan of *muḍāharāt silmiyya* (peaceful demonstrations), as will be discussed in the following section.

The Discourse of 'silmiyya' (Peaceful)

Realising the importance of peaceful demonstrations, the discourse of *silmiyya* became a slogan reiterated by every single protester to prevent demonstrations sliding into violence, which could give regimes a pretext to crackdown on these demonstrations.

The discourse of *silmiyya* was designed to stage peaceful and civilised demonstrations, allowing protesters to exercise their rights. It has also been used to warn Arab officials that their intention is to protest peacefully and any clampdown on their demonstrations would be unjustified. However, in some cases, demonstrations have been infiltrated by protesters who used violence, despite the opposition of the majority of protesters. These actions have been used as pretexts by governments to clampdown on protesters. The emphasis on peaceful demonstrations is exemplified in many slogans such as '*silmiyya silmiyya*' (peaceful peaceful).

It could be said here that the significance of civilised protest is understood, with the protesters expressing their discontent in an orderly manner. These protesters have used the discourse of *silmiyya* to send out the message that their demonstrations are peaceful and civilised, while protesting their lawful rights. The discourse of *silmiyya* has become a shared slogan across the Arab world and has been used to mobilise protesters to ensure peaceful demonstrations.

The shift in discourse here is exemplified by the full awareness of the protesters' rights and obligations, as well as their rationalisation of the event, contrary to other protests, where anger was avenged on others, or, at times, the police, with acts of violence. The use of *silmiyya* discourse could be considered a shift in the strategy of protesters, but also displays their maturity and their awareness of the requirement for protests, as well as their responsibility for their own actions. Their maturity is not only visible in the way they conduct themselves, but in the type and nature of demands raised in the protests.

The Negative Other in Arabic Public Discourse

Whilst demonstrators have adopted a discourse of *silmiyya* to protest their rights, their opposition to their leaders has been exemplified in the discourse of reprimand and accountability, where feelings of dissatisfaction about various aspects of social and political life have been explicitly expressed. This includes their reprimand of Arab regimes for curtailing freedom of expression, restricting political activism, and for the lack of opportunities for young people.

We have seen at the beginning of this chapter how Arab regimes have rejected from the outset demonstrations and considered them the work of mobs and criminals, which could be interpreted as a strategy designed to tarnish the protesters' reputation and credibility. Despite this, protesters continue to call for the overthrow of some regimes, using different labels and lexis. In the context of Egypt, Mubarak was labelled as '*Ṭāghūt*' (dictator), '*ẓālim*' (oppressor), '*qātil*' (murderer/assassin).

As Lahlali (2014: 10) pointed out 'the slogans are very definite and, in some cases, very personal, particularly those referring to Mubarak. This made the conflict very personal between Mubarak and the Egyptian people'. The following examples demonstrate this.

Example 1

"ويسقط مبارك العميل"

Down with Mubarak, the puppet/agent

"وصامدون حتى يرحل الطاغية"

Persevering until the downfall of the tyrant

"ويسقط الفرعون والزبانية"

Down with pharaoh and tyrants

"يسقط الطاغوت"

Down with the tyrant

"ودم الشهداء لن يضيع"

The blood of the martyrs will not go in vain

"لن تخدعنا الحلول الجزئية"

We will not be deceived by partial solution

It seems from the above example that protesters have used the binary Us vs Them in their slogans. 'US' here represents the nation, protesters, democrats, etc. and 'THEM' refers to Arab regimes, which are negatively represented, with clear reprimand. This has marked a significant shift in the discourse of Arab citizens. To call a regime 'murderer', 'dictator', 'tyrant', etc. is unprecedented in the modern history of the Arab world and marks a shift in the political discourse. This new discourse has caught everyone by surprise and neither the culture nor the politics allows for such a new development, which could only be described as a discourse of rebellion, reflecting the highly charged emotions of discontent. This new discourse does not only depict the protesters' criticism and reprimand of their rulers and superiors, but the gravity and scale of the situation. Their highly charged slogans, which compare Mubarak, for instance, to *pharaoh*, are a clear departure from the slogans of 'long live president', heralding a new discourse of criticism and reprimand. Their tenacity of seeing change through, and their persistence in having their demands met is very telling about the new public sphere in these Arab countries; a public that is determined to change the current status quo. Their demands are explicit, as epitomised in the following examples.

Example 2

"مطالبنا: إسقاط الرئيس، حل مجلسي الشعب والشورى المزورين، إنهاء حالة الطوارئ فورا، تشكيل حكومة وحدة وطنية انتقالية، برلمان منتخب يقوم بعمل التعديلات الدستورية لإجراء انتخابات رئاسية"

> *Our demands are: bring the president down; dissolve both fake chambers of parliament; immediate lifting of the emergency law; form an interim national unity government; an elective representative parliament, which will amend the constitution and hold presidential elections.*

What is fascinating about the above extract is not the well thought out series of demands and their sequence, but the manner in which these demands have been made. The absence of politeness and respect in this example, where superiors are usually addressed with dignity and respect, reflects the new changes in the public sphere discourse. The use of imperative in Arabic is often associated with order and command, and it is designed to mask the agent, avoiding direct reference to the doer of the action, which implicates the call for a third party to take action. This is completely new to the Arabic culture, where demonstrators have taken on regimes and started calling for action.

In Arabic politics and culture, the elderly, rulers and leaders are symbols of power and authority, meaning therefore that respect, loyalty and obedience are required for these people, as their authority is unquestionable. However, the Arab Spring has revealed the opposite of this long-established norm. We have witnessed leaders being degraded, sworn at, and held responsible for their actions. While one would argue that this is a feature of revolutions and demonstrations, where protesters avenge their anger in those responsible, the context and culture are extremely significant here. This could be justified and accepted in countries that have a long tradition of freedom of expression and where symbols of power are held accountable, despite their rank and hierarchy; in the Arabic context, however, culture and society dictate that leaders are above criticism and reprimand. Citizens know it, politicians understand it, and the system upholds it. The fact that demonstrators have broken this tradition by creating a new discourse and forming new rules and norms that challenge the existing ones demonstrates the drastic change in the culture and politics of the Arab world. This shift in discourse is underpinned by the shift in the social and political thinking, which erupted unexpectedly and created a new culture of accountability. This transition is evident in example 2, introduced earlier.

The above examples have marked a shift in the production of discourse and have given way to a new discourse, which emphasises the power and authority of the voiceless ordinary citizens. The change has given them both confidence and a sense of ownership of their own country. Example 2 illustrates quite vividly the direct clash between protesters and their leaders. The protesters were very direct in their call for the removal of Arab regimes. This directness is new to Arabic political discourse, especially because, as discussed earlier, it broke the cultural norms and political practices in Arab societies.

By default, Arab regimes have historically created a unitary political landscape where certain red lines have been reinforced transnationally. These have been broken as protests rage across different Arabic capitals. Protesters have used the copycat approach, where slogans have been adopted across different Arabic countries, and where protesters have learned from each other how to avoid certain restrictions imposed by the regimes. Solidarity protest groups became visible across borders, which made it very difficult for them to be controlled. This has created a homogeneous regional protest, where demands and aspirations have been shared and echoed using identical slogans.

Positive Self and Negative Other in Arabic Political Discourse

Representation of Them (Protesters) in Political Speeches

As discussed earlier, one of the missing elements in the blame and remorse strategies used by Arab leaders is the direct nominalisation and representation of actors. According to Machin and Mayr (2012: 77) 'in any language there exists no neutral way to represent a person. And all choices will serve to draw attention to certain aspects of identity that will be associated with certain kinds of discourses'. In the political leaders' speeches, the identity of those responsible for the uprising remained concealed and have been represented in generic terms as 'mobs', 'criminals' and 'foreign agents' but no single group or party has been blamed for the uprising, although there are references to 'extremists' and 'people in the pay of foreigners', but no names or actors have been singled out. The demonstrators have been represented as the people who wish to do harm to their own country; people who envy the progress and stability of their country; people driven by their own ideological ideas and stance on things, but these people remain unidentified. While the identity of these people remains a mystery, their representation falls within the category of otherness, which suggests that they are not Arab citizens – although they are – but they have been represented as the other, and as holding a great grudge against their own country, leaders and people.

Representation of Foreign Actors in Arabic Political Speeches

While Arab leaders have focused on their internal events and acknowledged that they were led by local citizens, there is a reference to external actors who are allegedly behind the uprisings. Arab leaders have avoided naming any actors or describing them as such, but there is a clear reference to hidden powers who are instigating and fuelling protests. In Ben Ali's speeches there is a reference to external forces who are behind the inciting of violence and fuelling protests, and the fact that some of the 'gangs' are in the pay of foreigners. But, Ben Ali refrained from naming or providing any further explanation or description of these foreign hands which are meddling in Tunisian internal affairs. One could conclude from the example below that Ben Ali was referring to Islamic groups by describing them as extremists who are in the pay of foreigners, but it has been left to readers to come to their own conclusions about this.

Example 3

أحداث وراءها أياد لم تتورع عن توريط أبنائنا من التلاميذ والشباب العاطل فيها. أياد تحث على الشغب والخروج إلى الشارع بنشر شعارات اليأس الكاذبة وافتعال الأخبار الزائفة، استغلت بدون أخلاق حدثا أسفنا له جميعا وحالة يأس نتفهمها كانت حدثت بسيدي بوزيد منذ أسبوعين.

مناوئون مأجورون ضمائرهم على كف أطراف التطرف والإرهاب

Incidents [were] committed at the instigation of parties who have not hesitated to engage our children among the students and unemployed youth. These parties, who incite violence and going out into the street, spreading hollow slogans of despair and fabricating, from scratch, misleading and erroneous information, have dishonestly exploited an incident that we all regret and a state of understandable despondency occurring in Sidi Bouzid for two weeks.

Hostile elements in the pay of foreigners, who have sold their souls to extremism and terrorism.

(Ben Ali's speech, 10 January 2011)

The above example refers to parties that oppose Tunisia and hold a grudge against its people. Ben Ali has not named any groups or parties, but his message remains vague as to who instigated these uprisings. Again, this strategy drives a wedge between protesters in an attempt to defuse the growing protests, but this comes to no fruition. It could be because the protesters did not believe Ben Ali's story. As protests grew, we noticed that reference to gangs, criminals and extremists disappeared, only to be replaced with a discourse of appeal and commitment to taking action to eradicate poverty, unemployment and injustice, and to establishing freedom of expression, freedom of the media, and democracy.

The only explicit foreign actor mentioned in Ben Ali's last speech before his resignation was Gaddafi, who was praised for the support he provided for Tunisia and its people. Gaddafi's offer of allowing Tunisians to cross over to Libya and join the Libyan workforce was praised by Ben Ali as a brotherly gesture and a great support for Tunisia and Tunisian people at a time of great need. But, this was again one of the many ways to absorb protesters' anger and frustration. The irony is that even Gaddafi found himself battling waves of protests against his rule, which subsequently culminated in his overthrow and death.

While the three leaders have referred implicitly or explicitly to the role foreign actors had in instigating and inciting uprisings, there was a degree of difference as to who was behind this. Gaddafi was the most explicit of them all, directly pointing the finger at the United States, Britain, France and others. He even went on to justify their involvement, suggesting that they are after 'the wealth of [my] country', whereas Ben Ali and Mubarak remained vague and provided no names. This could be explained by the fact that both used diplomatic language, whereas Gaddafi's was confrontational. But Gaddafi's discourse did not stop here, it went further and attacked some of these countries for planning to destroy his prosperous country and reduce it to chaos.

It could be said from the above examples and discussions that Ben Ali's and Mubarak's speeches were very generic in their terms and diplomatic in their tones when it comes to foreign actors, while Gaddafi was very specific and direct, using the naming and shaming strategy, with some very negative descriptions and representation. However, Al-Gaddafi's critical and confrontational discourse was not limited to foreign actors only, but was extended to protesters who rose against him, as demonstrated in the following extract.

Example 4

نحن أجدر بليبيا من تلك الجرذان وأولئك المأجورين، من هم هؤلاء المأجورين المدفوع لهم الثمن من المخابرات الأجنبية ؟!، حفنة من شذاذ الآفاق المأجورين من هؤلاء القطط والفئران التي تقفز من شارع إلى شارع ؛ ومن زنقة إلى زنقة ، في الظلام.
الآن مجموعة قليلة من الشبان المعطاة لهم الحبوب، يغيرون على مراكز الشرطة هنا وهناك مثل لفئران
لكن هناك مجموعة قليلة مريضة مندسة في المدن، تعطي الحبوب ؛ وأحيانا حتى النقود

We are more worthy of Libya than those rats and hirelings. Who are those hirelings, paid for by foreign intelligence services?!
A handful of alien hirelings – these cats and mice that jump from street to street, alley to alley, in the dark.
Now, a small group of young men, who were given pills, are raiding police stations here and there like rats.
However there is a small group of sick people which has infiltrated cities and are circulating drugs and money.

In the Libyan context, THEM were presented as traitors, cockroaches, in the pay of foreign agents; they are labelled as 'cats', 'rats', 'cockroaches' who work in the dark. Al-Gaddafi considered this a small group of young people who have been influenced by drugs and have been pushed to commit criminal acts. He has reiterated the same discourse, where the blame falls on a minority of youth who are allegedly supported by foreigners. He called upon Libyan citizens to get rid of these foreign agents who have no recollection of their history or sacrifices of their ancestors. Gaddafi repeated the phrase 'minority few' several times to convey the message that the uprising is not a representation of the Libyan people, but a minority of foreign agents. To reinforce his message and intensify his criticism of the 'minority in the pay of foreign agents', he heaped criticism on some of the foreign powers by referring to their aggressive actions against Libya and Libyan people. He also touched upon what he calls sacrifices and victories against 'the tyrannical might of America, Britain, and the nuclear states'. His discourse here is designed to portray himself as the strongest leader who fought the West and faced their aggression.

Example 5

أخاطبكم من هذا المكان الصامد؛ هذا البيت في طرابلس، الذي أغارت عليه «170» طائرة ؛ تقودها الدول النووية الكبرى أمريكا وبريطانيا والحلف الأطلسي. «40» طائرة بوينج، تزود هذه الحملة بالوقود، تخطت كل القصور؛ وكل المنازل؛ وكل بيوتكم، كل بيوتكم تركتها ، تبحث عن منزل «معمر القذافي»، لماذا؟

I am addressing you from this steadfast place. This house in Tripoli, which was raided by 170 planes led by the greatest nuclear states, America, Britain and NATO. Forty Boeing planes were assisting in refuelling the campaign. They bypassed all palaces and all houses – all your houses, they left your houses behind – looking for the house of Muammar Qaddafi. Why?

نحن قاومنا جبروت أمريكا؛ جبروت بريطانيا، الدول النووية؛ قاومنا جبروت حلف الأطلسي ، لم نستسلم ؛ وكنا نحن صامدون هنا . الآن مجموعة قليلة من الشبان المعطاة لهم الحبوب، يغيرون على مراكز الشرطة هنا وهناك مثل الفئران

We resisted the tyrannical might of America, Britain and the nuclear states. We resisted the tyrannical might of NATO. We did not surrender. We remained steadfast right here.

Now, a small group of young men, who were given pills, are raiding police stations here and there like rats.

ولما أغارت علينا أمريكا قاتلناها؛ وفرنسا في الجنوب قاتلناها؛ وسقط الاستعمار

When the United States attacked us we fought; we fought France in the south; and then colonialism/imperialism fell.

«90» في المائة منه للشركات الأمريكية وأنتم عندكم «10» في المائة ؛ والآن (90) في المائة لكم و(10) في المائة للشركة الأمريكية فقط

90 per cent of the oil was for American companies and you only received 10 per cent, but now 90 per cent is for you Libyans and 10 per cent for American companies.

(Gaddafi's speech, 22 February 2011)

While there is little reference to foreign actors in Mubarak and Ali's speeches, Gaddafi's speeches were full of reference to Western powers as in نحن قاومنا جبروت أمريكا ؛ جبروت بريطانيا، الدول النووية ؛ قاومنا جبروت الحلف الأطلسي (*naḥnu qāwamnā jabarūta Amrīcā, Britanyā, al-Duwal annawawiyya, qāwamnā jabarūta al-ḥilfī al-aṭlasī* / We resisted the tyrannical might of America, Britain and the nuclear states. We resisted the tyrannical might of NATO). In an attempt to persuade protesters, Gaddafi referred to the Libyan glorious history when Libyan fighters defeated Italy, Britain, the United States and others. He referred to the fight against what he called 'the hegemony of America'. He used the opportunity to remind Libyans of their own history, when Libyans took on different nations and 'defeated them'. ولما أغارت علينا أمريكا قاتلناها ؛ وفرنسا في الجنوب قاتلناها ؛ وسقط الاستعمار (*wa lamā aghārat 'alaynā Amrīcā qātalnāhā wa faransā qatalnāhā wa saqaṭa al istiʿmār* / when the United States attacked us we fought; we fought France in the south; and colonialism/imperialism fell). Gaddafi's discourse was very explicit in blaming foreign powers for the uprising, warning Libyans that 'foreigners' intention' is to control oil and Libyan wealth, as they did 'before the first Libyan revolution', when '90 per cent of Libya's oil was taken by the United States'.

Similar to Mubarak and Ben Ali, Gaddafi spoke at length about his service and sacrifices for the country. He referred to his glorious days when he led the revolution and liberated the country from what he considered to be foreign invasion. This, of course, was designed to remind Libyan youths of their history and, similar to Ben Ali and Mubarak, to galvanise support and rally people against what he considered the minority few whose main intention was to destroy Libya. The other in Gaddafi's discourse has been represented as the 'enemy' from within, who are encouraged by foreigners to create chaos and destruction.

The common feature of the three leaders' speeches is their citation of glorious moments in their history and their association with these struggles and victories. This discourse of promoting the self and its positive attributes was used in final speeches of these leaders when the tide turned against them. In Gaddafi's last speech, it was a review of the Libyan history and the struggle against the West, in an attempt to refresh Libyans' minds and educate the new generation who have 'limited knowledge of their history', according to Gaddafi. Despite his tough rhetoric, Gaddafi's speeches showed a shift in terms of the action required. His flexibility in acknowledging the discontent of some tribes, their grievances and demands, his proposal of forming 'committees' and municipalities to address local concerns could be seen as a shift in his discourse when addressing the majority of Libyans. His discourse of empowerment of citizens to take control of their own destiny could be regarded as a tactic designed to calm down protests and reduce any anger against the system of governance and distribution of wealth. Like other Arab leaders, Gaddafi offered concessions and acknowledged certain concerns raised by citizens. However, his discourse was characterised by the harsh tone of 'revolutionary leader' whose sole aim was to defend Libya from foreign powers and their agents in the country.

These foreign powers have been presented as 'thieves', 'invaders', 'meddlers' and 'enemies of Libya'. They are the 'bad guys who meddle in the country and sought to destroy it by instigating and inciting innocent youth to take to the street'. This discourse of blaming the other has been adopted by other Arab leaders, and while it may have some truth in it, it could be said that Gaddafi, like others, sought to shift the blame from himself and his government to foreign actors. This blame was more evident in his reference to 'brotherly' Arab countries, who used their media to incite uprisings and promote 'chaos and disorder'. Here, again, he was very explicit by referring to Qatar, the host of Al-Jazeera channel.

Arabic Political Discourse and Semiotic Representation

The Semiotics of the Arab Spring

The above-mentioned examples present cases where the image and the text stand side by side communicating the same message. Both the image and text are in harmony.

Another example is an image without a caption, allowing readers to offer their own interpretation. This could led to different interpretations, emanating from different perspectives and ideologies. While the multiplicity of perspectives is a healthy phenomenon, the wide-ranging interpretations may not do justice to the content of these images.

The third aspect is when the text is explicit but the image offers different interpretations, depending on the context and the way the image is presented.

While images have been used to promote protesters' activities towards toppling Arab regimes, post Arab Spring has shown different images: images of destruction, fighting, killings and revenge. The images vary from those demanding freedom and prosperity to scenes of destruction and continued conflict amongst different factions and parties – which have rendered some of the countries a war zone, rather than places of liberation, where democracy was expected to prosper. This power struggle has taken some of these countries years back as basic living conditions are lacking in countries that have so much potential. So the discourse of freedom, prosperity and independence has been replaced with a discourse of violence, conflict and revenge. This type of discourse has emerged as factions and groups try to fill the power vacuum emanating from the lack of trust between different tribes, as in the case of Libya. What we have witnessed is a tribal discourse, rather than a national one; a discourse putting the interest of regions and tribes before the national interest. In the case of Yemen, religion has filled the power vacuum as Sunni and Houthi factions battled it out in an attempt to hold power in Yemen.

Representation of Arab Leaders in Images
Machin and Mayr assert that the 'representation of objects and settings could be used to communicate more general ideas and discourses . . . images may seek to depict specific people and how these people can be used to connote general concepts, types of people, 'stereotypes' and abstract ideas' (2012: 96). They go on to say that texts and images may have different affordances. In the context of the Arab Spring, we will be looking at images displayed by protesters and images covered in the media. These images will be selected randomly, irrespective of the type, genre and ideological orientation of the media, as this research is not examining a specific media outlet or newspaper.

A protester holds a photo showing the late Egyptian President Hosni Mubarak's face crossed out in red evoking the colour of blood (Figure 3.1). The photo shows Mubarak looking composed and serious. Another protester holds a smaller crossed-out photo of Mubarak, with 'Dictator Mubarak, get out of Egypt' written on it in Turkish. The crossing out on the photos is over Mubarak's face, which shows that he is no longer required to carry out his duties. The usually agreeable nature of Mubarak's picture and his smiles in streets and squares are in stark contrast to the image held by protesters, who are shouting slogans and appear to be very discontent.

The writing and the distorted image of Mubarak reflects the protesters' attitudes and feelings towards him; feelings of rejection and a desire for change. Crossing Mubarak's face out in red serves as an indication that he is no longer wanted and that he should resign his position. It could also be

Figure 3.1 Hosni Murabak's face crossed out

seen as an ultimate warning to Mubarak. This would have been extraordinary a few years back, but the Arab Spring protests show a shift in attitudes on the part of Arab public both inside and outside their counties.

The representation of Arab leaders in images is very rich indeed. It embodies a sense of rejection of Arab leaders, both in text and image. The crossing out of faces and the slogans are clear signs of this rejection. But this is an unprecedented shift in the way protesters present their leaders' images; it is in stark contrast to the traditional way of hailing leaders as heroes, champions, reformists and guardians of their nations. Their photos and images have decorated walls and streets and they were hailed as fathers of nations, deserving nothing but respect and loyalty. This shift in both the discourse and culture shows deep grievances and a departure from the traditional values of respecting authority to challenging leaders. Again, as discussed in other sections, this shift has broken years of fear of authority and power and adopted a new culture of questioning, challenging and speaking the truth. The other striking issue here is the explicit messages conveyed through these images, held by people who are not trying to hide their identy, showing courage and challenging their own leaders. The Arab Spring has paved the way for a new era of defiance coupled with a sense of humour (Abu Hatab 2016).

While Mubarak's picture has been defaced (Figure 3.1) and reflects the protesters' desire for his departure, Figure 3.2 shows a picture of Gaddafi, torn into two pieces, with his face crossed out; an act as violent and aggressive as if his face was riddled with bullets.

Figure 3.2 shows a face crossed out in red and torn into pieces, conveying a message of revenge. The fact that Gaddafi's image has been defaced reflects the protesters' anger and frustration, and what makes this torn image so compelling is that it has been decorated with slogans in English and Arabic: 'enough is enough', '42 years of Gaddafi's oppression' and '*istibdād*' (tyranny). Gaddafi's face has been turned into a mosaic of slogans in Arabic and English covering all of his face. Although there is no caption to describe the image, it could be interpreted as 'you are no longer required', 'your time is over', but it also conveys feelings of detestation and rejection. This is in contrast to the tradition of long live sir. Such a shift in discourse and semiotic representation of leaders is due to the empowerment of protesters, their

Figure 3.2 Gaddafi's face crossed out and torn into two pieces

freedom from the security apparatus in Libya and other Arab countries, and their desire to communicate their messages to internal and external audiences.

Given the history of Libya and Gaddafi, the image of him crossed out and torn into two pieces is a shift in the way he has been perceived, as most Libyans would associate him with power, authority and control, but the irony here is that the most powerful man in Libya could not protect his own image from being defaced. The image is also a reflection of the situation on the ground and post-revolution Libya, where civil war has been raging for some nine years, with different factions fighting each other over the control of Libya. Gaddafi's image is just an example of the whole Libyan map, which is torn and riddled with bullets and destruction.

In contrast to Gaddafi's crossed-out and torn face, Ben Ali's image remains intact, but has been decorated with a caption of 'wanted' (Figure 3.3).

The most striking thing about Figure 3.3 is not only the slogan of 'degage' (leave), but that of 'wanted'. Although the image depicts a calm and composed Ben Ali, the caption tells a different story of a wanted fugitive. The fact that he is 'wanted' suggests that he is in hiding, but Ben Ali not only hid, but also fled his country. For the protester who holds the image, Ben Ali

Figure 3.3 'Dégage' (leave) and 'wanted'

will remain a fugitive as he left the country for good. What is striking about the caption and slogans is that they are written in French and English, giving them an international appeal.

The slogan above the image of Ben Ali describes him as 'a dictator (dictateur)' who has left, but the search for him is ongoing, as exemplified by the word 'wanted'. For the protesters who hold the slogan 'Ben Ali Degage', Ben Ali is a 'dictateur' (dictator), this is a historical moment as it allows them to express themselves in different languages and convey their absolute rejection of Ben Ali, without any fear of intimidation or imprisonment. It should be mentioned here that Ben Ali left for Saudi Arabia in 2011, where he died and was buried. The young protesters, who appear to be very excited and jubilant, are holding up banners and the Tunisian flag as a symbol of patriotism, and they are also reminding Tunisians and the rest of the world of their rejection of the status quo. Protesting openly against an Arab regime and using demeaning terminologies such as 'dictator' and 'degage' consitutes a new shift in the discourse of the Arab public towards their leaders, a symbol of empowerment and confidence in their own voice and action.

What is most striking is the shift in the way which Ben Ali's pictures have been displayed; from the charismatic leader whose image greets every passer-by on the streets of Tunisia, to a leader whose picture has been surrounded and decorated with reprimanding slogans. It is as if to say, the only thing you deserve now is rejection and humiliation. Again, the context of displaying images of a late leader is very revealing and offers a variety of interpretations as to the importance of Ben Ali post Jasmine Revolution.

The Use of the National Flag as a Symbol of Identity
Contrary to the images displayed in the previous section, which show total rejection of some Arab leaders, the national flag has been consistently present in all demonstrations across the Arab world in an attempt to show unity and patriotism. National identity has been communicated through the discourse of '*waṭan*' (nation), showing unity under the national flag. The display of the national flag is a clear expression of the protesters' national identity and patriotism, which have been questioned by some Arab leaders. The use of the flag was the rallying factor that brought protesters together, irrespective of their political, religious and social background (Figure 3.4).

By using the national flag, protesters sought to make the distinction between the regime and the state. By embracing the flag they demonstrated

Figure 3.4 Protesters holding national flags

their loyalty to their homeland, but rejected their leaders. This consolidates their message that they wish no harm to their motherland, but they reject their leaders outright and call for their resignation. In the three cases above, national flags were present at every protest, irrespective of its size. Another observation is that party or organisation flags were absent and this demonstrates the protesters' desire to unite under the national flag, despite their different ideologies. At a time of conflict, the national flag was the rallying factor, under which all protesters united to show their nationalism and patriotism.

Discussion

Homogeneity and Heterogeneity of Arabic Political Discourse

It becomes apparent from the above analysis that when considering Arabic political discourse the political culture and practice of individual leaders and states are paramount to understanding these discourses and their connotations, since different Arabic countries tend to practise or adopt different political approaches and systems. The Libyan political system, for instance, is quite different from the Egyptian and Tunisian, as there is no parliament, no parties and no elected leaders. According to Gaddafi, it is a socialist system based on the idea that people can govern themselves by themselves. This diversity has been visible in the discourse of Gaddafi, who, unlike Ben Ali and Mubarak who resigned their positions, insisted that he is not an elected president and therefore he has no position to resign from. His discourses were also different in many ways. While Ben Ali and Mubarak adopted a reconciliatory and diplomatic tone, Gaddafi went on the attack, criticising and casting doubts on the protesters' intentions, and associating them with foreign agents. This diversity of practice and discourse shapes and is shaped by the social and political structures and systems of the individual Arab state. Having said that, it should be pointed out here that the traditional structure of Arabic political speeches has been maintained by the three leaders.

In terms of its tone and style, Gaddafi's discourse was more direct, confrontational and replete with expressions of fear, threat and menace for protesters who took to the street. His speeches could be characterised as revolutionary speeches, where the military tone and style were ever present.

This could be due to the character of Gaddafi, who called himself 'the revolutionary man from the tent'.

As for the Arab public discourse, it was homogeneous in its content, slogans and style. The same slogans have been used across different Arabic countries, the same grievances have been expressed loudly by protesters. These include demands for freedom of expression, better living standards and the resignation of leaders and officials. In contrast, leaders' speeches have shown some differences due to the political culture of different Arabic countries, which suggests that the Arab public sphere is transnational, while the speeches and strategies of political leaders are domestic. The homogeneity of the Arab public sphere could be attributed to the shared desire for political, economic and social change, which has been promoted by transnational and social media across these countries. One example that could be listed here is the copycat of slogans used during the Arab Spring. The labelling of Friday protests has shown some similarities across different Arab countries, which suggests that protesters communicate and interact transnationally with each other.

Multilingualism in Arabic Public Discourse

Observers of the Arab Spring will notice that protesters have expressed their concerns and raised their demands in a variety of ways, including by the use of cartoons and slogans. As this is an Arabic protest, spanning most of the Arabic countries, one would think that demands would be conveyed in the Arabic language only. However, Arabic was not the only medium through which protesters' concerns have been expressed. Other languages such as French and English have been used to express these demands. While the motives behind the use of different languages are unclear, a few explanations for this phenomena spring to mind. One could argue that the use of foreign languages allows protesters to communicate their demands and concerns to a wider audience. Another interpretation could be that slogans have been written in foreign languages to attract the attention of the international community and mobilise support for their demands and actions. Others would argue that this is a sign that protests have been led by the educated middle-class youth. The use of multilingual slogans could also be interpreted

REPRESENTATION AND CONFLICT IN ARABIC DISCOURSE | 109

as a sign of tolerance, literacy and a high level of education, suggesting that protesters are fully aware of their own demands. The only difference, however, is that French was dominant in Tunisia while English was heavily used in Egypt.

Whichever interpretation one may consider, the fact of the matter is that these protesters were desperate for their voice to be heard internally and externally, and the use of different languages could achieve this purpose, as Figure 3.5 demonstrates.

The above examples suggest that the use of foreign-language slogans are often related to actions against regimes such as 'Degage' (leave), 'get out' (leave) *irḥal* (leave). And these are designed to attract the attention of, and appeal to, the international community to take action. Again, this marks a new shift in the discourse of slogans, where traditionally monolingual slogans have been used for domestic consumption. The desire to be global and interact with a global audience is very visible in this shift in the use of discourse.

Figure 3.5 Multilingual slogans

Conclusion

In this chapter we have examined the shift in the discourse of the Arabic public and Arab leaders' speeches. This shift came about as a result of social and political changes that have engulfed most Arabic countries. The widespread protests and the persistence of protesters in their demands has led to a new discourse that reflects this change. This persistence, when magnified, could lead to concessions, moderation and acceptance of the other. It could also change the dynamics of the society, actors and stakeholders, where the powerless become the most powerful and the powerful become the mundane. This shift in the structure and conception of society finds its way in how we interact with others. Examples of the analysis in this chapter have taught us that discourse reflects power and solidarity, as well as weakness. Significantly, they have shown the power of protesters through their assertive, confident and challenging discourse, while revealing the vulnerability of Arab leaders as they face this magnitude of unprecedented protests. Discourse, therefore, can change any time when the forces of change are persistent and politically or socially mobilised against the powerful other (i.e. rulers, leaders, regimes, etc.). As persistence and awareness increased, so did the concessions and negotiations of Arab leaders.

4

Doing Arabic Discourse: Micro-Analysis of Arabic Political Discourse

In this chapter we shall offer a practical analysis of extracts from both Arabic political speeches and public discourse in the context of the Arab Spring. This guide will take us through the application of key discourse analysis concepts and tools that are deemed relevant to understanding different dynamics of Arabic discourse. It will also offer a clear insight into the notion of framing and positioning in the context of Arabic discourse. It will introduce new concepts and terminologies such as personification, individualisation, collectivisation, foregrounding, backgrounding, metaphors and personal pronouns, amongst others.

Micro-Analysis of Arabic Political Discourse

Framing/Positioning and Grammar in Arabic Political Discourse

The discussion of political speeches of several Arab leaders in previous chapters has demonstrated the fluidity of these speeches and the changes they embody in content, style, register and tone. There were shifts in the position and style of political speeches as protests gathered momentum. These shifts are not only related to the language and tone of discourse, but reflected in the attitudes of political leaders, who have adopted different approaches and strategies, coupled with a discourse of self-criticism and critical reflection in dealing with the situation. The new approach has given way to a discourse of inclusivity and mutual understanding, where opposition and protesters' demands have been acknowledged and listened to, as the following example demonstrates.

Example 1

والأخطاء موجودة في أي نظام ودولة، ولكن المهم الاعتراف بها ومحاسبة مرتكبيها، وأنا كرئيس جمهورية لا أجد حرجاً في الاستماع الى شباب بلادي

Mistakes can be made in any political system and in any state. But, the most important thing is to recognise them and correct them as soon as possible and bring to account those who have committed them. As a president I find no shame in listening to my country's youth.

(Mubarak's speech, 11 February 2011)

The above excerpt demonstrates that Mubarak's discourse has departed from the asymmetrical, which reflects the hierarchy of society and the power of the leader, to a reflective and compromising discursive approach, where mistakes have been admitted and shortcomings have been recognised, with a clear statement on how to overcome them. The idea of holding officials accountable (محاسبة مرتكبيها *muḥāsabat murtakibīhā*/to hold to account its perpetrators) for their shortcomings is a new phenomenon and demonstrates a complete departure from the traditional official discourse, suggesting therefore evident transition in discourse, as the following example makes clear.

Example 2

(. . .) أكرر اللجنة المستقلة، التي ستحقق في الأحداث والتجاوزات والوفيات المأسوف عليها تحديد مسؤوليات كل الأطراف، كل الأطراف بدون استثناء، بكل إنصاف ونزاهة وموضوعية.

(. . .) I repeat: an independent committee, which will investigate the incidents, abuses and regrettable deaths, to delineate the responsibilities of all sides, all sides without exception, with equity, integrity, and impartiality.

ونحب نؤكد أن العديد من الأمور لم تجر كيما حبيتها تكون، وخصوصا في مجالي الديمقراطية والحريات، وغلطوني أحيانا بحجب الحقائق وسيحاسبون.

I would like to affirm that many things didn't work the way I wished, especially in democracy and freedoms. They have sometimes misled me, by hiding truths, and they will be held accountable for that.

(Ben Ali's speech, 13 January 2011)

The above two examples show a clear shift in terms of discourse and accountability. It is uncommon in the Arabic culture for leaders to reprimand members of their own circle in public. However, Ben Ali went on record and announced the formation of a committee to investigate corruption at the highest level of the hierarchy, which is alien to the system of governance in most Arabic societies. Again, this is another tangible example of the transition in the leaders' discursive practices. Ben Ali's negative discourse employed in relation to members of his government represent this shift in discourse, where praise and commendation have been replaced with reprimand and admonishment. It also suggests that Ben Ali positioned himself closer to protesters by reprimanding members of his own government. While Ben Ali's speeches show his criticism of members of his government, it also shows a level of weakness, dysfunctionality and lack of trust, as clearly indicated in the use of *ghalaṭūnī* (misled me). In normal circumstances, this type of discourse remains private and within the confines of the government, but in this case Ben Ali broke with tradition and went public; first, to show his integrity and second, to divert the blame from himself and lay it on members of his government. In his speech he sought also to demonstrate a shift from the position of a vulnerable president, who has been misled by members of his own government, to a strong president who is decisive and willing to take action as demonstrated in *wa sayuḥāsabūn* (and will be held accountable). This dichotomy shows Ben Ali's state of confusion as he decided to abandon his government and position himself on the side of the Tunisian people, but it was too little too late, as expressed by demonstrators.

Grammatical Positioning and Persuasion in Speeches

Overlexicalisation, Repetition and Emphasis in Arabic Discourse
While leaders' speeches focus on addressing the situation and ending protests which pose a threat to their existence, the microstructure of these speeches is very revealing indeed. The most striking feature in these speeches is the

use of *tawkīd* (emphasis) at the beginning and across paragraphs. Most of the speeches start their paragraphs with إن (*inna*) (indeed, verily) to emphasise the content of the paragraph and subsequent content. The use of إن in Arabic serves many functions, including emphasis, and shows the importance of the message and content to be introduced. إن (*inna*) and لقد (*laqad*) were foregrounded in most of the speeches and would usually start paragraphs to emphasise the leaders' speeches and actions. Mubarak's speech to the nation in January 2011, for instance, consists of seventeen paragraphs, fifteen of which start with إن or لقد. This is very revealing indeed as it makes quite explicit the significance of persuasion in this speech and other speeches. It shows that Mubarak was concerned about the situation, hence his heavy use of emphasis. However, Mubarak was not alone in adopting the strategy of *tawkīd* (emphasis), Ben Ali used the same strategy where *Inna* and other emphatic particles have been utilised to reinforce his speeches. Again, *Inna* appears to be the most dominant emphatic particle in his speeches.

Repetition is another type of emphasis used by political leaders, especially in their last speeches of the uprising. Before we delve into the analysis of some of these examples, a definition of repetition will be very useful in this regard. Repetition is defined as 'multiple instances of an idea or word, and the greater the number of repetitions the more we notice it' (Reynolds 1995: 185). Lahlali argued that repetition can be 'deliberately used to reinforce different political strategies' (2012: 1). He goes on to assert that repetition could be used for persuasive and emotional purposes, which would impact the audience (Lahlali 2012). Although repetition in Arabic is often considered to be part and parcel of the Arabic language structure (Johnstone 1991), in the Arab Spring political leaders' speeches, repetition has been used as an element of emphasis and persuasion. Similarly, Rieschild (2006: 21) is of the view that a 'word or a phrase with intensity as part of its denotation makes emphasis more explicit'. He asserted that rhetoric can have a great 'influence on the formation of public attitudes, opinions and will (identity construction, manufacturing of consent and solidarity)' Reisigl (2008: 258). Repetition can be considered a part of overlexicalisation, which Teo (2000: 20) defines as 'results when a surfeit of repetitious, quasi-synonymous terms is woven into the fabric of news discourse, giving rise to a sense of overcompleteness' (in Machin and Mayr 2012: 37). Machin and Mayr, however, see overlexicalisation as 'a sense of over-persuasion and is normally evidence that something is problematic or of ideological contention' (2012: 37). They attribute some of the overlexicalisation to the persuasion process and 'ideological contention'.

It could also be said that repetition has been used to impact recipients by performing sentimental and emotional acts (Mazraani 1993: 265–7). Multiple examples from the Arab Spring illustrate this. The overuse of repetition in Ben Ali's last speech could be interpreted as a means of drumming up support by arousing the emotions of the Tunisian people. The constant repetition of his regret for the casualties, his determination to turn things around, and his repetition of his services and sacrifices to the country, were all intended to have an emotional impact on Tunisians.

Example 3

نكلمكم اليوم، ونكلمكم لكل في تونس وخارج تونس، نكلمكم بلغة كل التونسيين والتونسيات، نكلمكم لأن الوضع يفرض تغيير عميق... تغيير عميق وشامل.

I am addressing you today, all citizens in Tunisia and abroad. I am speaking to you in the language of all Tunisians. I am speaking to you now because the situation dictates a change, yes, a deep and comprehensive change.

تونس بلادنا الكل، بلاد كل التوانسة، تونس نحبوها وكل شعبها يحبها ويلزم نصونها

Tunisia is the country of all of us, the country of all Tunisians. We love Tunisia. All the people love it, we have to safeguard it.

وأنا فهمتكم، فهمت الجميع: البطال، والمحتاج والسياسي واللي طالب مزيد من الحريات، فهمتكم، فهمتكم الكل.

I have understood you all, the jobless, the needy, the political and all those who are calling for more freedom. I understood you, I understood you all.

نكلمكم لأن الوضع يفرض تغيير عميق.. تغيير عميق وشامل

I address you because the situation dictates deep changes, deep and comprehensive changes.

ولذا أجدد لكم، وبكل وضوح، راني باش نعمل على دعم الديمقراطية وتفعيل التعددية. نعم على دعم الديمقراطية وتفعيل التعددية.

Once again, I wish to say clearly I will work to promote democracy, to promote democracy and pluralism.

ونحب نكرر هنا، وخلافا لما أدعاه البعض، أني تعهدت يوم السابع من نوفمبر بأن لا رئاسة مدى الحياة، لا رئاسة مدى الحياة

I would like to say again, and contrary to what some claim, I pledged on November 7, that there would be no lifetime presidency, no lifetime presidency!
وأسفي كبير كبير جدا، وعميق جدا، وعميق جدا، فكفى عنفا كفى عنفا
My sadness is deep. My sadness is deep and profound, very deep and very profound. Enough violence! Enough violence!

(Extracts from Ben Ali's speech, 13 January 2011)

As the above examples demonstrate, there is an emotional plea manifested in Ben Ali's overlexicalisation of certain verbs and nouns. The repetition of *fahimtukum* (I understood you), *nukalimukum* (I/we address you) is designed to establish a close rapport and line of communication between the president and Tunisian people. It could also be said that Ben Ali has shown some leadership skills here by listening to citizens' demands and grievances, and promising to address their concerns. By resorting to repetition he sought to reinforce his message with the hope of persuading and dissuading those protesters from carrying out their actions. However, his repetition could be considered an indication of his weakness, especially because it highlights his plea, which could be understood as seeking sympathy and empathy from the public. In the Arabic culture, repetition can be seen as a sign of desperation and can be used to impact recipients emotionally. What is striking about Ben Ali's repetition and overlexicalisation is his focus on patriotism to impact Tunisians. His repetition of Tunisia as a country that belongs to all and that is loved by all is intended to rally support under the Tunisian flag; however, his repeated and pleading discourse fell on deaf ears. It appears that Ben Ali played on the sense of belonging and identity to rally Tunisians to support him after other attempts had failed. The Arabic saying الوطن يعلو ولا يعلى عليه *Al-waṭan ya'lū wa lā yu'lā 'alayhi* (the homeland is above all) remains one of the strongest tools for rallying citizens. This entails that the interest of the homeland should come first and that any differences and conflicts should be resolved to safeguard the nation. This traditional Arabic saying has been used to put the homeland first and any personal or party interest should come last. One could argue here that Ben Ali's repetition of homeland has been designed to remind Tunisians that the interest of Tunisia should come first, ironically from a president who, others may argue, did just the opposite during his rule of

Tunisia. It is apparent from the above discussion that Ben Ali has resorted to the homeland to persuade Tunisians of his proposed changes; however, his message of the homeland, loyalty and patriotism did not come across as protests showed no sign of abating.

In his use of repetition, Ben Ali relied on two strategies: being generic and specific in his discourse. It was general when referring to all Tunisians without exception, utilising the inclusive *kul* (all), followed by specific mentions of individuals and groups for persuasive purposes. The use of *'ām* (general) and *khāṣ* (specific) in speeches is often designed to rally support by appealing to the overwhelming majority of the population. However, this strategy of appealing to all was unsuccessful as protests grew unabated. In the case of Ben Ali's speeches, although repetition was very explicit as reflected in his continuous repetitions of full phrases and sentences, this did not yield any results and protests continued until Ben Ali fled for exile.

In the context of Libya, overlexicalisation was one of the overwhelming features of Gaddafi's speeches. While other Arab leaders have used overlexicalisation moderately, Gaddafi used it extensively, repeating words, phrases and synonyms. This could be attributed to his lengthy, unscripted speeches. The overlexicalisation could also be attributed to his frustration and anger towards protesters, and is a clear indication of his anger and disappointment of what was happening in Libya. This disappointment found its way into his own discourse, which was intended to persuade Libyans to take control of their own country and expel what he called 'drug takers', 'al-Qaeda affiliates' and 'foreign agents'.

What is striking about Gaddafi's speeches is the overlexicalisation of 'Libya' and '*thawrā*' (revolution) in an attempt to distance himself from the scene and focus on what he called the nation and revolution. His speeches, contrary to those of other Arab leaders, embody a revolutionary tone, explicitly linked to the past and history of Libya, with a clear reference to freedom and independence from foreign powers, as has been reiterated on numerous occasions. This has been seen as a scaremongering tactic designed to deter protesters from pursuing their action of change.

What makes Gaddafi's overlexicalisation different from that of other leaders is his direct and confrontational style, where specific names of people and groups, as well as names of foreign powers, are repeated constantly.

His direct approach and focus on certain groups made his speech appear very repetitive.

As for Mubarak, overlexicalisation is present in his reference to victories over Israel, the liberation of Sinai and the building up of the army during the presidencies of Sadat and Nasser, which were key moments of greatness for him. His act of liberation and raising the Egyptian flag over Sinai was the high point of his career, as he put it.

Agency in Arabic Political Discourse

Ahearn (2012) defines agency as 'the socio-culturally mediated capacity to act'. Through the use of explicit or hidden pronouns, which more often than not reflect the ideological reasons behind it, agency is often used as a manipulative strategy to serve one's action (Fairclough and Fairclough 2013). The decision to make agents explicit or implicit often emanates from ideas and beliefs, making discourse very charged and lacking in innocence. Speakers, as Machiavelli pointed out, 'should have anything blameable administered by others, favors by themselves' (1985: 75). To borrow Jarraya's words, in political discourse the use of agency 'is a strategy employed to achieve a specific objective, the deliberate manipulation of the addressee through the use of deictic pronouns' (Jarraya 2013: 10).

When examining leaders' political discourse, two main issues present themselves: explicit and implicit agents in their speeches. Agency here is linked to the Us vs Them and binary. When 'their' action is negative, the agent is explicit and when 'our' action is negative the agent is concealed and remains anonymous, as the following examples demonstrate.

Example 4

أحداث عنيفة دامية أحيانا أدت إلى وفاة مدنيين وإصابة عدد من رجال الأمن، قامت بها عصابات ملثمة أقدمت على الاعتداء ليلا على مؤسسات عمومية وحتى على مواطنين في منازلهم في عمل إرهابي لا يمكن السكوت عنه

Violent incidents, sometimes bloody, which have killed civilians and caused injuries to several officers of the security forces, have been perpetrated by hooded gangs who have attacked public institutions during the night and even assaulted citizens at home, in a terrorist act that cannot be tolerated.

إن هذه الأحداث أعمال قلة من المناوئين الذين يغيظهم نجاح تونس

These incidents are the work of a small group of hostile elements who are offended by the success of Tunisia.

لقد ركب هؤلاء المغالطون موضوع البطالة بتوظيف حالة يأس فردية مثلها يتكرر في جميع المجتمعات و في عديد الأوضاع

These ill-intentioned elements have used the issue of unemployment, exploiting an isolated act of desperation, as happens in all societies and in many situations.

نحن أجدر بليبيا من تلك الجرذان وأولئك المأجورين، من هم هؤلاء المأجورين المدفوع لهم الثمن من المخابرات الأجنبية

We are more worthy of Libya than those rats and hirelings. Who are those hirelings, paid for by foreign intelligence services?!

وإذ نعرب عن بالغ أسفنا للوفيات والأضرار التي نجمت عن هذه الأحداث

We express our regret for the deaths and damage generated by these incidents.

وقد أخذت العدالة مجراها للتحقيق في ظروف وملابسات هذه الأحداث وتحديد المسؤوليات فيها

Justice has taken its course and clarified the conditions and the ins and outs of these incidents, to determine those responsible.

In the above examples, the active form has been used to refer to the negative action of the protesters by explicitly referring to their bad deeds. The active form has been used to name and shame those who are responsible for the uprising. In these examples, Arab leaders have been very explicit in specifying the agent when there is a negative representation of them. The use of 'minority few', 'gangs', 'sick people', 'rats and cockroaches', as agents of action, who are associated with 'instigating', 'stirring', 'exploiting situations', 'responsibility for chaos and disorder'. The agent here is explicit and visible, and this could be designed to hold the doers of the action responsible, but could also be intended to tarnish their reputation and undermine their action, by emphasising its negativity. One cannot help but notice the strategy of blame and shame through the use of the active form, where the agent is explicit when describing negative actions. However, the agent is often concealed and the passive is used in relation to the negative representation of 'Us'. By concealing the agent, it is hoped that the in-group negative depiction and attributes will remain anonymous.

There is explicit reference to casualties in the examples above, where leaders have expressed their sincere regret for these fatalities and the damage caused, but made no reference to who has inflicted these fatalities.

وإذ نعرب عن بالغ أسفنا للوفيات والأضرار التي نجمت عن هذه الأحداث

We express our regret for the deaths and damage generated by these incidents.

The agent in the above example has been concealed, and this is probably because some blamed the police and security agencies for their heavy crackdown on protesters, which left casualties. One could argue that this was a deliberate way of concealing and hiding the 'brutality' of the police and state, for which leaders are responsible. The suppression of the agent is often regarded as an ideological action by the speaker/writer to conceal the identity of the doer of the action in contexts where speakers share, endorse and advocate the action, irrespective of its consequences and repercussions.

In the above examples, Arab leaders referred to casualties but made no mention of who caused them and why. It could be argued that leaders tend to distance themselves from what happened, allowing a space for interpretation as to who was responsible. By emphasising the negativity of the protesters, leaders and government officials hope that recipients and consumers of this discourse will hold some of the protesters accountable for their actions, but, as subsequent events have made clear, this did not materialise. This shows a lack of persuasiveness on the part of leaders. The Arab public continued to sympathise with protesters, as manifested by the growth of these protests.

It could be concluded here that the suppression of the agent in the above examples is designed to suppress the truth and protect those who have caused such actions, in an attempt to distance leaders from any future accountability for the action of their security agencies. This is clearly visible in the last example, where 'justice took its course to investigate the incidents and identify responsibilities'. The question here is who is going to investigate what? Both agents are absent from this example: the investigator and the investigated. While agents are absent in the last examples, in the first five examples agents were explicit and represented negatively in a very demeaning manner. This brings us to the conclusion that 'Our' agents are present when positive actions are attributed to them, but are absent when they are associated with negative actions; on the other hand, their agents are present when they are associated with negative actions, but absent when they are associated with positive actions.

The Use of Deictic Pronouns in Political Speeches

Many studies have examined the function of deictic pronouns in the context of political discourse. Fairclough and Fairclough (2013) and Wilson (1990) associated the use of deictic pronouns with ideology and manipulation. In his analysis of Ben Ali's political speeches, Jarraya (2013) came to the same conclusion that Ben Ali used the deictic pronouns for ideological and manipulative reasons. By resorting to this strategy, he sought to gain the empathy and support of the people.

The Use of the Deictic First Singular Pronoun

Traditionally, in Arabic political speeches, the first plural pronoun is used as a mark of respect and as a sign of the power and authority of the speaker. For this reason, it is rare when the singular pronoun 'I' is used in formal speeches. Although it is uncommonly used in Arabic formal speeches, it could be used to claim self-assertion and direct responsibility for one's actions. The use of '*anā*' in formal Arabic speeches is often associated with '*anāniya*' (selfishness), which could, at times, be considered a sign of self-confidence and authority. The use of '*anā*' (I) is avoided in most cases as it is considered a sign of arrogance and egotism, which are socially and culturally discouraged.

'We' and 'I' in Arabic Political Speeches

Ben Ali and Mubarak resorted to *naḥnu* (we) to show inclusivity and demonstrate that they are ordinary citizens like anyone else. This inclusive strategy is designed to divide protesters into two camps: those who may feel strongly about economic and social inequalities, and those who are politically motivated and call for the overthrow of regimes. By using 'we', leaders have adopted an inclusive tone and approach, hoping to marginalise other groups who have political motivation and have been stirring demonstrations. The use of 'we' is very strategic in the sense that it shows their collectivistic action and inclusion, tacitly arguing therefore that any shortcoming is the responsibility of all. They only used 'I' when they sought to appeal to their citizens and talk about their achievements and services for their respective countries, but this was not prevalent in all of their speeches. In Gaddafi's speeches, however, the use of 'I' featured frequently, compared to Ben Ali's and Mubarak's. This reflects Gaddafi's leadership style and his fervent belief in power, authority and strong command.

Foregrounding and Backgrounding in Speeches

While *inna* (indeed) has been designed to emphasise action and persuade citizens of their leaders' speeches and actions, one cannot help but notice that in addition to repetition and emphasis, political leaders resorted to foregrounding key aspects of their speeches, some of which are related to the positive-self, services and achievements, while protesters' bad actions have been foregrounded but their good actions have been backgrounded. Take for instance the following examples:

Example 5

والجميع يعلم كم هي كبيرة عنايتنا بحاملي الشهادات العليا

Everyone knows how much effort we put into employment.

أحداث عنيفة دامية أحيانا أدت إلى وفاة مدنيين وإصابة عدد من رجال الأمن قامت بها عصابات ملثمة

Violent incidents, sometimes bloody, which have killed civilians and caused injuries to several officers of the security forces, have been perpetrated by hooded gangs.

أحداث وراءها أياد لم تتورع عن توريط أبنائنا من التلاميذ والشباب العاطل فيها

Incidents [were] committed at the instigation of parties who have not hesitated to engage our children among the students and unemployed youth.

(Extracts from Ben Ali's speech, 10 January 2011)

As the above examples show, protesters' negative actions have been foregrounded to attract the reader's attention to what the speaker calls 'hidden agents', 'mobs'. This foregrounding, which reflects the level of negativity of the other, is designed to rally citizens against these groups, with the hope of stopping the uprising and defaming these groups. However, the discourse was not explicit as to who these groups and ringleaders are. This broad description and lack of clarity dissuaded most citizens from supporting and rallying behind the leaders' call for unity against these groups. The scale of economic grievances and social injustices were not on the side of the leaders. The uprising was triggered first and foremost by the injustice against Mohamed Bouazzizi, a fruit vendor, whose self-mutilation triggered the Tunisian people to take to the streets to protest against inequality, injustice and low living standards. This had a domino effect on other Arab countries such as Egypt, Libya, Syria and Yemen.

Foregrounding and Remorse

As protests gathered momentum, the police intervened to stop them. However, the heavy-handedness of the police interference as they sought to stop demonstrations exacerbated the situation and inflamed protests further, with more protesters taking to the streets. In their speeches, the leaders of Egypt and Tunisia expressed their sorrow and issued apologies for the casualties. In expressing their remorse, leaders foregrounded their apologies and expressions of sympathy in their speeches to show their solidarity with protesters and their families. By foregrounding these emotions and feelings, these officials have sought to win the protesters over and distance themselves from the police's attack on demonstrators. What is striking about this is the repetition of expressions of remorse in their speeches and the promise to hold those responsible accountable for their actions.

Example 6

لم أقبل يوما / وما نقبلش / باش تسيل قطرة دم واحدة من دماء التونسيين
I won't accept that another drop of blood of a Tunisian be spilled.

أسفي كبير كبير جدا، وعميق جدا، وعميق جدا، فكفى عنفا كفى عنفا
My sadness is deep. My sadness is deep and profound, very deep and very profound. Enough violence! Enough violence!

يزي من اللجوء للكرطوش الحي، الكرطوش موش مقبول، ما عندوش مبرر
Stop using live ammunition. Live ammunition is not acceptable, and is not justifiable!

(Extracts from Ben Ali's speech, 13 January 2011)

In his expressions of remorse for the casualties, Ben Ali has used both Modern Standard Arabic and Tunisian colloquial Arabic to express his feelings.

The repetition of expressions of remorse is also very revealing and is designed to show sympathy with the audience. These expressions have been foregrounded to appeal to the wider Tunisian society. Ben Ali's call to cease the use of live ammunition is also intended to distance himself from the action of his police force, for whom he is directly responsible. In terms of Arabic political discourse, this is unprecedented as it is expected that the leader should have full control of what is happening in the country and under his command. Firstly, recognising mistakes and offering apologies to the nation live on air is not a characteristic of Arabic political discourse, nor is it a common practice of Arab leaders. These actions are often carried out discreetly and with a very low profile. This is indeed a transition in the approach, discourse and political culture in the Arab world. Of course, these are special circumstances requiring direct action, and demonstrating the leaders' sense of humility and recognition of the scale of event. While some have argued that this is a genuine shift in discourse and political culture, others continue to argue that it is a tactic used by leaders to absorb the anger and discontent of the protesters. Whatever the intention behind this change in discourse, there is strong evidence that these new discourses, both in substance and structure, invite citizens for dialogue and discussion to resolve some of the issues that have triggered these uprisings. However, the question remains: does this shift in discourse entail a change in the social and political landscape of these countries?

Previous research has linked change of discourse to a change in society in general, but during the Arab Spring, the drastic and unprecedented change of discourse in leaders' speeches did not reflect the change in the political landscape as the asymmetrical structure remained the same and the system of governance witnessed no change. In the absence of visible and tangible change at the societal level, it could be argued that the shift in political discourse is temporary, as it does not mirror the social structure, which remains unchanged. What we witnessed in the Arab Spring was a change of discourse, which reflects the changing mood and attitude of the country against the governing elite. In terms of presenting and addressing some of these changes, we witnessed that these leaders' speeches embody a new strategy of foregrounding and backgrounding, which can be summarised as follows. Leaders' positive attributes and actions are foregrounded; their empathy and sympathy with the public are foregrounded, but their bad actions are backgrounded (i.e. casualties, heavy clampdown on protesters, individual freedoms, etc.). However, the protesters' positive attributes are backgrounded while their negative attitudes are foregrounded.

Table 4.1 mirrors the findings of other studies, but what is remarkable is the scale of positive foregrounding used in these speeches, which means two things: firstly, it shows the leaders' desperate situation and their urgent appeal and emphasis on the positive-self. Secondly, it reveals the magnitude of the event and the authority that the opposition has displayed. The leaders' discourse has foregrounded the demonstrators' negative attributes and these significantly outweigh the positive attributes, which could be interpreted as an attempt to tarnish the reputation of protesters. These changes occur at individual and collective levels, as will be discussed in the following section.

Individualisation versus Collectivisation

As discussed in Chapter 2, 'people can be depicted as individuals or as a group' (Machin and Mayr 2012: 100). However, in the political speeches of Arab leaders, individualisation is replaced with a group of people called 'mobs' and 'criminals', while collectivisation represents the whole society. This is designed to shed the blame on those who have contributed to or led the uprising, accusing them of being criminals and gangs, in an attempt to discredit their action and isolate them from the wider society. Take for instance, the following example from the Tunisian and Egyptian contexts.

Foregrounding	Backgrounding
Our positive attributes: services, sacrifices, achievements, attitudes, personal attributes Our human aspects (emotion, sentiments, sympathy and empathy, etc.) **The other:** Their negative attributes: their bad actions, their link to others, their threat to the national security, their novice approach to political matters, their extreme views on issues pertinent to the country	Our negative attributes: our unpopular actions, failed actions and lack of responsibilities **The other:** Their positive attributes: their achievements, their contributions, their call for justice, freedom and democracy

Table 4.1 Foregrounding and backgrounding in Arab leaders' discourses

Example 7

أولادنا اليوم في الدار، وموش في المدرسة، وهذا حرام وعيب لأن أصبحنا خائفين عليهم من عنف مجموعات سطو ونهب واعتداء على الأشخاص

Our children are confined at home today, they are not in school. This is totally immoral and shameful, because we have become afraid for their safety, from the acts of violence, looting and attacks perpetrated by small groups of bandits. This is a crime, this is a criminal act, not a protest, and this is sinful.

(Ben Ali's speech, 13 January 2011)

إن أحداث الأيام القليلة الماضية تفرض علينا جميعا شعبا و قيادة الاختيار ما بين الفوضى والاستقرار

The events of the last few days require us all as a people and as a leadership to choose between chaos and stability.

ستخرج مصر من الظروف الراهنة أقوي مما كانت عليه قبلها أكثر ثقة وتماسكا واستقرارا

Egypt will emerge from these current circumstances stronger, more confident and unified and stable.

(Mubarak's speech, 2 February 2011)

The above examples show the collectivisation strategy used in these speeches. The use of our children, Egypt, people, we... is a strategy employed to set the 'nation' against what Mubarak labelled as the 'mobs and criminals'. By using expressions such as 'our children', 'nation' and 'people', leaders sought inclusivity against those who have been labelled as outsiders, trouble-makers and foreign agents. This strategy of collectivisation and inclusivity, where leaders sought to create an image of a country and leadership against rogue groups or individuals, is intended to drive a wedge between protesters and other citizens, but this strategy failed as protesters united and continued to call for the resignation of their leaders. By rejecting the leaders' strategy of divide and rule, protesters managed to have the upper hand in dictating and driving the agenda forward, which has ultimately led to the overthrow of the three leaders. The protesters' success could be traced back to their awareness of what was happening on the ground and their discourse of unity as a social movement. The lack of trust in their leaders could be considered a reason for not heeding their leaders' call for stability and their warnings for the repercussions of the protests on the security and stability of their countries.

What is noticeable from the above examples is that in the context of conflicts, collectivisation is used to support one's approach against what is often considered the outsider, the enemy or opponent. Such a strategy is utilised to rally support and target opponents as outsiders, who have malicious intentions. In the context of the Arab Spring, some Arab governments have used the collectivisation strategy to gain more support and allow themselves legitimacy by appearing to be inclusive and defending the collective cause of the nation or nations, against 'individual criminals' and 'gangs'. The characterisation and representation of the latter could be said to have been used to tarnish the reputation of the protesters and discredit their demands.

Modality in Leaders' Speeches

There are different categories of modality, which perform different functions. These are:

1. Epistemic modality: 'This is to do with the speaker's/author's judgement of the truth of any proposition' (Machin and Mayr 2012: 187).
2. Deontic modality: 'This is to do with influencing people and events. So if I say "students must do the essay", I am expressing greater influence' (Machin and Mayr 2012: 187).
3. Dynamic modality: 'This is related to possibility and ability, but is not subjective in the manner of the first two modalities' (Machin and Mayr 2012: 187).

The use of modals can be very useful when we seek to understand the level of power speakers possess (Machin and Mayr 2012: 190). In the context of the Arab Spring, this will enable us to understand the type of discourse used and how it shapes power and authority of speakers. The following examples are very revealing of the type of power and authority Arab leaders have displayed in their speeches.

Example 8

العنف ما هوش متاعنا، ولا هو من سلوكنا، ولا بد أن يتوقف التيار

Violence has never been part of our customs, or part of our behaviour. The present tide of unrest should stop.

(Ben Ali's speech, 13 January 2011)

إن هذه الأحداث لا يمكن أن تفل من عزمنا ولا أن تنال من مكاسبنا، بل يجب أن تستخلص جميع الأطراف العبرة منها وان نواصل مسيرتنا بكل ارادة وحماس

These incidents will never break down our determination nor undermine our achievements. Rather, they should encourage all parties to draw the necessary lessons and never detract from the imperative to continue our work with determination and enthusiasm.

(Ben Ali's speech, 13 January 2011)

What is striking about the above examples is that there is less modality in Ben Ali's speeches. Given the nature of the situation, one would expect a wide range of modality to be used, where commands and orders are expressed. However, apart from a few examples of deontic modality, which is expected given the nature of the situation in which these speeches were delivered, there is no example of other types of modality. The interpretation of this is that Arab leaders adopted a calming tone, where they admitted and acknowledged protesters' rights, and this was followed by proposed actions to address the protesters' concerns. It could also be said that Arab leaders have used a reconciliatory tone, deprived of any expressions of command and order, which could fuel protests further. They adopted a conciliatory approach in the way they negotiated with protesters, but this was to no avail as the protests continued undeterred.

The use of deontic modality was present in the first speeches when Arab leaders sought to show their authority and call for the immediate cease of protests. The use of *yajib*, *lābuda* (should) were used to express order and command, but then, as protests grew in number and demands, this strategy shifted and has given way to a style of diplomacy, negotiation and concession, which is unprecedented in the Arabic political discourse when it comes to dealing with domestic issues.

The fact that modality was almost absent in their speeches shows that leaders have been very cautious about the style and tone of their discourses, some of which appeared to be very reasonable, with little menace to protesters. Despite the turbulent times, some of these leaders remained composed and addressed protesters rationally, especially since the threat of clamping down on some protesters failed. This could be described as a new strategy, which shapes the attitudes and behaviour of leaders towards protests and protesters. It has also led to a shift in discourse, ditching the heavy-handed approach and embracing reconciliation and negotiation.

Use of Personification in Speeches

According to Machin and Mayr, 'personification means that human qualities or abilities are assigned to abstractions or inanimate objects'. Personification can be used to conceal real actors. Machin and Mayr (2012: 171) have given the following example for illustration: *Democracy will not stand by while this happens.*

The personification of democracy here aims at concealing the main actors, who are often governments, parties or officials who are responsible for safeguarding and implementing aspects of democracy. 'By personifying democracy (. . .) they are able to hide behind the concept that is generally highly valued by many' (Machin and Mayr 2012: 171).

Sacred and often valued things can be used as unifying factors in a time of conflict. In the case of Arab uprisings, political leaders have personified their countries to conceal their roles and unify people to support them and their agendas. Take for instance, the following examples.

Example 9

أتحدث إليكم في لحظات صعبة يتعرض فيها الوطن لأحداث عصيبة واختبارات قاسية
I talk to you during critical times that are testing Egypt.

اختم عملي من أجل الوطن بما يضمن تسليم أمانته ورايته
I am now absolutely determined to finish my work for the nation in a way that ensures handing over its safe-keeping and banner.

إن الوطن باق والأشخاص زائلون ومصر العريقة هي الخالدة أبدا
The homeland will remain, and people will disappear.

ستخرج مصر من الظروف الراهنة أقوى مما كانت عليه
Egypt will emerge from these current circumstances stronger.

إن شباب مصر هو أغلى ما لديها
Egypt's youth are its most valuable asset.

أنا أعلم أن مصر ستتجاوز أزمتها وستفق من جديد بصدق وإخلاص أبنائها وسترد كيد الكائدين. أعلم علم اليقين أن مصر لن تنكسر إرادة شعبها

I am sure Egypt will overcome its crisis and that its people will never be defeated . . . it will stand on its feet again through the sincerity and faithfulness of all its sons, and it will face plotters.

(Extracts from Mubarak's speech, 2 February 2011)

تونس لنا جميعا، فلنحافظ عليها جميعا، ومستقبلها بين أيدينا فلنؤمنه جميعا

Tunisia belongs to all of us. Let us all preserve it together. Her future lies in our hands. Let us secure her together.

تونس بلادنا الكل، بلاد كل التوانسة، تونس نحبوها وكل شعبها يحبها ويلزم نصونها

Tunisia is a country for all of us, the country of all Tunisians. We love Tunisia. All the people love it, we have to safeguard it.

(Extracts from Ben Ali's speech, 13 January 2011)

In the above examples, the speakers have resorted to the personification of the homeland, emphasising the importance of the nation, flag and its people, in an attempt to rally citizens to support them and their policies. The personification of their countries ('Egypt will overcome', 'Egypt will never be defeated', 'Egypt will face plotters', 'Egypt's youth are its most valuable asset', 'the future of Tunisia' . . .) is designed to conceal the real actor and arouse feelings of love and patriotism against protesters, in the hope of dissuading them from escalating their action further. For instance, Mubarak personified Egypt as an agent that will emerge stronger from the current situation. Egypt has been personified as the mother whose youth are a priceless commodity and she looks forward to seeing them secure her future.

In the example above, Mubarak again personifies Egypt, claiming that she will overcome this crisis. Here Mubarak has personified Egypt as an agent to conceal his own identity and role as president. His personification could be said to have been designed to send out the message that the protests are not against him, but against Egypt, entailing that he is the representative icon of Egypt. The use of motherland and nation is a strategy which is designed to rally people around the flag and against protesters, suggesting that it is Egypt that has been targeted, and not Mubarak and his henchmen. This strategy of hiding behind the sacred and most valued thing for citizens has failed to protect Mubarak and other Arab governments as demonstrations continued unabated.

Resorting to personification to persuade demonstrators and citizens to abandon their protests for the sake of Egypt did not yield any satisfactory results. This could be attributed to the level of protesters' awareness as well as their strong conviction and determination to achieve their goals.

The same strategy was adopted by Ben Ali who repeatedly used Tunisia as a unifying factor, reminding Tunisians of their own country, nation and homeland, in the hope of arousing feelings of patriotism. In the same vein, Gaddafi personified Libya on numerous occasions, giving it a voice with 'Libya wants, Libya will survive, Libya will fight to the end'. The use of Libya as a homeland refers to all Libyans, excluding therefore those who rose against him and his government. This strategy, as mentioned above, is designed to rally Libyans against what he considered to be 'mobs', 'drug addicts' and 'Islamists'. However, as with other leaders, his strategy failed as protests continued to call for his resignation.

Anonymisation in Leaders' Discourse

Anonymisation is common practice in the media, where 'sources' are concealed for different reasons, although some argue that the media uses anonymisation to advance its own opinions and ideologies. The media continues to argue that anonymisation is used to protect sources wishing not to be identified and made public. Anonymity can also be used in cases where speakers are unsure about certain actions, actors or agents. In the Arab Spring context, political leaders' speeches have been full of anonymity as to who was behind the uprisings. It could be interpreted that anonymity was used to create feelings of doubt about protesters and their actions, without being very specific about the main actors behind these protests. The following are some selected examples from the leaders' speeches.

Example 10

ومواطنين شرفاء مارسوا حقهم في التظاهر السلمي تعبيرا عن همومهم وتطلعاتهم، سرعان ما استغلهم من سعى لإشاعة الفوضى واللجوء إلى العنف والمواجهة ، وفي القبض على الشرعية الدستورية والانقضاض عليها

Noble youths and citizens who practise their rights to peaceful demonstrations and protests, expressing their concerns and aspirations, were quickly exploited by those who sought to spread chaos, violence and confrontation.

(Mubarak's speech, 2 February 2011)

أولادنا اليوم في الدار، وموش في المدرسة، وهذا حرام وعيب لأن أصبحنا خائفين عليهم من عنف مجموعات سطو ونهب واعتداء على الأشخاص

Our children are confined at home today, they are not in school. This is totally immoral and shameful, because we have become afraid for their safety, from the acts of violence, looting and attacks perpetrated by small groups of bandits. This is a crime, this is a criminal act, not a protest, and this is sinful.

(Ben Ali's speech, 13 January 2011)

أحداث عنيفة دامية أحيانا أدت إلى وفاة مدنيين وإصابة عدد من رجال الأمن قامت بها عصابات ملثمة أقدمت على الاعتداء ليلا على مؤسسات عمومية وحتى على مواطنين في منازلهم في عمل إرهابي لا يمكن السكوت عنه

Violent incidents, sometimes bloody, which have killed civilians and caused injuries to several officers of the security forces, have been perpetrated by hooded gangs who have attacked public institutions during the night, and even assaulted citizens at home, in a terrorist act that cannot be tolerated.

أحداث وراءها أياد لم تتورع عن توريط أبنائنا من التلاميذ والشباب العاطل فيها

Incidents [were] committed at the instigation of parties who have not hesitated to engage our children among the students and unemployed youth.

إن هذه الأحداث أعمال قلة من المناوئين الذين يغيظهم نجاح تونس

These incidents are the work of a small group of hostile elements who are offended by the success of Tunisia.

(Ben Ali's speech, 10 January 2011)

In the above examples, anonymity has been used on numerous occasions to refer to those who were behind the uprisings. The use of 'groups', 'hands behind', 'acts of a few', 'political forces', 'the work of a small group', conceal real actors, and the reason for this could be twofold: it could be argued that the leaders were vague and broad in their speeches because they did not know exactly who was triggering these uprisings. There were no signs or indications that they had been spearheaded by a political party or a group. The second reason is that anonymity could have been used to minimise the actions of those behind the protests by referring to them in broader terms as 'groups', 'mobs', 'gangs'. Their identity remains concealed, as any identification of these people would make the opposition more visible and would support those calls for allowing the opposition an opportunity to contribute to running these countries. By referring to them as groups, they are stripped of their political identity and political ideas/viewpoints.

As it has been discussed earlier in this chapter, political leaders adopted a strategy of marginalising these groups by presenting them as a threat to the security and unity of their respective countries. This strategy failed, as citizens rejected their government's narrative and discourses and the claims that these uprisings were instigated and driven by a minority few in the pay of foreigners.

Presupposition in Leaders' Speeches

A quick glance at leaders' speeches indicates that presupposition has been used in different contexts to pass a judgement or reinforce a message. Take, for instance, the following examples.

Example 11

أحداث وراءها أياد لم تتورع

Incidents [were] committed at the instigation of parties.

إن هذه الأحداث أعمال قلة من المناوئين الذين يغيظهم نجاح تونس

These incidents are the work of a small group of hostile elements who are offended by the success of Tunisia.

مناوئون مأجورون ضمائرهم على كف أطراف التطرف والإرهاب

Hostile elements in the pay of foreigners, who have sold their souls to extremism and terrorism.

(Ben Ali's speech, 10 January 2011)

The above examples have been taken from Ben Ali's speeches, in which he refers to those who were behind the demonstrations as a 'minority of opposition', who are against the prosperity and success of Tunisia, presupposing that the majority of Tunisians have nothing to do with the uprising. He went even further to qualify the minority and label them as 'extremists and terrorists'.

This presupposes the fact that the majority of Tunisians are law-abiding and that the uprising is the work of extremists. However, this does not square with the fact that millions took to the streets to protest against his government. Are all these people a minority? Are they all extremists?

The way discourse has been constructed here suggests that it is a minority of people who are stirring up these demonstrations, but the presupposition is that the majority of people are innocent people, who are not involved in the protests. It also suggests that these people, contrary to the 'minority of extremists', are genuine and have legitimate concerns, which, in turn implies that the 'minority of extremists' have illegitimate demands.

Although Ben Ali has not named these people, it is presupposed that he was referring to the Al-Nahda, the moderate Islamic party in Tunisia – who won the majority of parliamentary seats in Tunisian post revolution. The way discourse has been constructed here has created a sense of confusion and allowed a large margin for presupposition, which contradicts the essence of the message and undermines Ben Ali's main argument that the uprising is the work of the few, not the majority.

The same approach was adopted in other leaders' speeches where the blame was laid squarely on the few bad apples who wish nothing but destruction to their own countries. But, again, this appeared not to have an effect as uprisings continued to gain momentum and the voices calling for the resignation of Arab leaders got louder and louder.

In the Libyan context, the same approach was used, but Gaddafi's representation of the minority few was very negative. He used degrading attributes such as 'rats', 'cockroaches', 'germs', 'spies', 'sick people', 'drug addicts', and pledged to fight them street by street and house by house. Gaddafi's representation of protesters has been very specific as he labels some of them as 'Qaeda cells' and 'extremists'.

Gaddafi's negative representation of protesters could be said to have been designed to degrade them and cast doubt on their actions. However, like Ben Ali and Mubarak, Gaddafi's strategy of presupposition and singling out groups did not bear any fruit as protests continued and regions started to declare their own opposition to his rule. The situation escalated rapidly and Libya descended into chaos and anarchy, which subsequently led to conflicts between different groups.

Cohesion and Coherence in Arabic Political Speeches

When examining cohesion and coherence across leaders' speeches, one cannot help but notice the great difference between these speeches. While Ben Ali and Mubarak's speeches appear more coherent and cohesive in their structure and argument, Gaddafi's speeches were disjointed, incoherent and lacking in cohesiveness. This could because his strategy was to provide as much information as possible, often with contradictory ideas, thereby undermining the whole argument and making his speeches appear less persuasive than those of Ben Ali and Mubarak. Gaddafi's delivery style and his veering away from the script on numerous occasions created disjointed and incohesive speeches, some of which lasted for more than an hour. It could also be said that the length of Gaddafi's speeches affected their structure and substance, making them less persuasive and less informative, and this could be the reason why his speeches did not get through to protesters.

While some have come to his defence and linked his speeches to his personality, others have sharply criticised the way they were delivered at a time of conflict, when much care should have been given to their structure and delivery. His rambling speeches, with repetitive and disjoint ideas eroded his authority and made him look less persuasive, and this cemented the growing protests across Libya.

Different scholars have linked persuasion to strong arguments and delivery skills. While Gaddafi showed passion and appeared to be energetic, the sporadic content of his speeches and their incoherent delivery could be said to have affected the level of persuasion in his speeches. Repetition and overlexicalisation, although used for emphasis, also made his speeches repetitive and undermined the progression of his ideas and argument in his speeches. His choice of controversial semantics such as 'rats' and 'cockroaches' eroded his authority as some of his speeches appeared to be informal and less persuasive.

Conclusion

This chapter has introduced the reader to a wide range of examples from political speeches in the context of the Arab Spring. We have applied key concepts of discourse analysis to these speeches and shown how these concepts have been utilised to advance ideologies. The practical analysis has also allowed us an insight into the thinking, attitudes and intention in the production of aspects of discourses. The analysis has also enabled us to demonstrate key dynamics in changing discourses. It has taught us that the production of speeches and discourses shape and are shaped by the changing dynamics on the ground. Understanding the production of these discourses will not be complete without understanding the context in which they are produced. We hope this chapter has allowed the reader to make sense of some of the linguistic features found in Arab leaders' speeches during the Arab Spring of 2011.

5

Macro-Analysis of Arabic Political Discourse: The Discourse of Enforcement and Persuasion

In the previous chapter we conducted a micro-analysis of speeches and discourses. We offered some practical analysis and methodological steps for applying different discourse analysis concepts and tools that are vital to understanding the function of discourse.

In this chapter, the discursive practices of two main actors will be examined and analysed. Firstly, Arab leaders' strategies and discourses in response to the Arab Spring will be carefully examined to identify the type and nature of discourses used and the shift in their discursive practices. It will demonstrate how shifts in discourse shape and are shaped by the reality on the ground, and how shifts in the balance of power affects leaders' speeches and discursive practices and their argumentation. Secondly, this chapter will also offer an insight into the discursive practices and strategies of the Arabic public (protesters) during the Arab Spring. It will investigate how they responded to different leaders' discourses and strategies.

Argumentation and Persuasion: Who is to Blame for the Uprising?

The analysis of political leaders' discourses during the Arab Spring suggests a fluctuation and hybridity in terms of argumentation and the strategy of communication used in different speeches. While leaders continue to display strategic shifts in their discourses, the analysis also suggests clear strategic differences in terms of presentation of arguments, notably when considering reasons for the uprisings. While Ben Ali and Mubarak attributed events to a hyper-active gang of youths and also to widespread unemployment, Gaddafi's argumentation, on the other hand, attributed the uprisings to external interference, highlighting the desire of the West to control Libya for economic benefit. He also referred to what he calls the double standards of foreign powers who were against al-Qaeda in other countries (i.e. Iraq), but supported the action of affiliates of Al-Qaeda in Libya. He gave examples of Faluja in Iraq, which was destroyed as American forces were searching for Zarqaoui, while in Libya, he argued, 'they encouraged and supported acts of terrorism'. He continued to argue that these protests were instigated by foreign agents, notably the US. His strategy of taking on the US and other foreign powers was intended to rally people around him in order to crack down on protesters. He also sought to tarnish the protesters' reputation by labelling them traitors and agents for foreign governments.

Example 1a

عملاء اميركا وعملاء ابن لادن وعملاء الزرقاوي
الجرذان والفئران ومدمني مخدرات".

America's agents, Bin Laden's and Zarqaoui's
Rats, mice and drug addicts

Although Gaddafi's speeches adopted a different strategy, it should be mentioned that at the beginning of the conflict other Arab leaders adopted a strategy of targeting and marginalising certain groups, who were blamed for stirring the uprising. This strategy, which will be discussed in the following section, was designed to create disunity between protesters, using the divide and rule strategy.

For Ben Ali and Mubarak, it could be argued that their argument was hybrid and based on the development of events on the ground. Initially, the blame was focused on what they considered a minority of bad apples who had been exploited by foreign powers to create havoc in the country as the following examples illustrate.

Example 1b

مناوئون مأجورون ضمائرهم على كف أطراف التطرف والإرهاب، التي تسيرها من الخارج أطراف لا تكن الخير لبلد حريص على العمل والمثابرة

Hostile elements in the pay of foreigners, who have sold their souls to extremism and terrorism, manipulated from outside the country by parties who do not wish well to a country determined to persevere and work.

(Ben Ali's speech, 10 January 2011)

قوى سياسية سعت الى التصعيد وصب الزيت على النار. استهدفت أمن الوطن واستقراره بأعمال إثارة وتحريض وسلب ونهب، وإشعال للحرائق وقطع للطرقات واعتداء على مرافق الدولة والممتلكات العامة

[Those protests were transformed from a noble and civilised phenomenon of practising freedom of expression to unfortunate clashes, mobilised and controlled] by political forces that wanted to escalate and pour fuel on the fire. They targeted the nation's security and stability through acts of provocation and incitement, theft and looting, arson, blocking roads and attacking state facilities and public property.

(Mubarak's speech, 1 February 2011)

تابعت محاولات البعض لاعتلاء موجة هذه التظاهرات والمتاجرة بشعاراته

I have followed attempts by some to ride the wave of these demonstrations and exploit the slogans.

(Mubarak's speech, 29 January 2011)

However, as protests grew in scope, both leaders changed their argument, acknowledged the status quo and started listening to the protesters' demands and making concessions. Then their argument shifted to blaming members of their own circle in a move to show accountability, but this strategy failed in the face of growing protests. After realising that their approach and persuasive strategies had failed, they both stepped down, with Ben Ali fleeing to Saudi Arabia and Mubarak resigning his post. Their strategy and approach was totally different to that of Gaddafi who continued to blame foreign powers for the uprising.

The strategy of Blame and Denial

As protests reached their climax, Arab leaders resorted to the traditional strategy of divide and rule by targeting some protesters and blaming others for stirring demonstrations and causing violence. They were labelled as 'mobs', 'gangs' and 'foreign agents' as the following extracts demonstrate.

Example 2

حتى نفرق بين هذه العصابات والمجموعات من المنحرفين

Until we isolate these criminal mobs and gangs

(Ben Ali's speech, 10 January 2011)

أحداث وراءها أياد لم تتورع عن توريط أبنائنا من التلاميذ والشباب العاطل فيها. أياد تحث على الشغب والخروج إلى الشارع بنشر شعارات اليأس الكاذبة

Incidents occurred at the instigation of parties who have not hesitated to engage our children among the students and unemployed youth. These parties incite violence and riots, spread slogans of despair, and fabricate misleading and erroneous information.

(Ben Ali's speech, 10 January 2011)

استغلهم من سعى لإشاعة الفوضى واللجوء إلى العنف والمواجهة وفي القبض على الشرعية الدستورية والانقضاض عليها

(. . .) they were quickly exploited by those who sought to spread chaos, violence and confrontation, and to violate the constitutional legitimacy and to attack it.

(Mubarak's speech, 1 February 2011)

إن هذه الأحداث أعمال قلة من المناوئين الذين يغيظهم نجاح تونس بل يسوؤهم ويحير نفوسهم ما تحقق لها من تقدم ونماء

These incidents are the work of a small group of hostile elements who are offended by the success of Tunisia and who are filled with resentment and grievance, because of the progress and development achieved by the country.

(Ben Ali's speech, 10 January 2011)

As Lahlali points out:

> Ben Ali and Mubarak have laid the blame on a minority of protesters who were seen to be manipulated by foreign agents. The strategy of casting doubt on the protesters is designed to portray them as foreign agents who work against their own country's interest. What is striking about this strategy is that the 'perpetrators' are referred to anonymously and described as violent mobs, used and directed by foreign forces. (Lahlali 2011: 4)

This strategy of marginalising, targeting and accusing individuals and groups of treason was designed to shun them and tarnish their credibility as genuine protesters. They have been characterised as 'outsiders', 'gangs' and 'mobs', who wish nothing but harm to their homeland. By positioning them as enemies of their own countries, political leaders have sought to defuse the protests and isolate the main actors who are driving the protest. This strategy is clearly visible in using the dichotomy of Us (the nation) and Them (the enemy of the nation). The use of terminologies and phrases that are rooted in the colonial period is designed to arouse citizens' feelings against any foreign intervention, excluding therefore protesters who have been portrayed as 'mobs', 'gangs' and 'foreign agents'. This discourse of '*intafiḍ*' (rise up against/ protest) has its roots in the era of the struggle for independence, when the discourse was directed at Arab nations to stand against imperialism. More recently, Arab leaders have used a similar strategy with the hope of mobilising and influencing the public to denounce demonstrations and stand against those they label as 'gangs' and 'criminals'. However, this attempt has failed miserably as protests have grown in size and demands, reaching the point of no return, and resulting in the deterioration of security and the eruption of conflict and civil war in some countries.

The strategy of blame, which has been reflected in the binary of Us vs Them, and the negative representation of the other (protesters) as 'criminals', 'mobs', 'gangs' and 'agents' has backfired for two main reasons. Firstly, the protests were spontaneous and people took to the street in genuine protest against the status quo, and by blaming minorities some Arab leaders have undermined the protesters' rights and exacerbated the situation since their actions have fuelled anger. Their actions have given the impression that they are not listening and that they are resorting to the same strategy of divide and rule. This strategy of disunification has rallied protesters and unified them against the regimes as manifested in their slogans and discourses, such as سلمية سلمية *silmiyya silmiyya* (peaceful peaceful). . . مطلبنا واحد *maṭlabunā wāḥid* (we have shared demands). The last slogan is a clear indication of the protesters' unity and consensus over their needs, which seem to reject the blame strategy utilised by the authorities. The second reason for the failure of this strategy is that protesters' demands have not been taken seriously and that the situation escalated when some Arab leaders continued to use the same rhetoric of blame and denial. As protests grew in size and scale, leaders realised the gravity of the situation, and this induced some of them to start offering concessions, including acknowledging people's legitimate right to protest.

Despite efforts to defuse the situation and establish some sort of normality, Arab leaders' call for normality fell on deaf ears. Realising the gravity of the situation, a shift in strategy became necessary. This shift in strategy has given way to a new discourse; a discourse of reconciliation, negotiation and compromise. As protests gathered momentum, spreading across cities and villages, Arab regimes, mainly those of Ben Ali and Mubarak caved in and acknowledged that the status quo was unsustainable and that change was inevitable. Their blame and denial strategy changed and this time around, the blame fell on the cabinet, officials and ministers who had been accused of incompetence and corruption. Cabinets were dissolved and new ones formed, in the hope of calming down protests. However, this move did nothing but fuel protests further (Lahlali 2011). This shift in strategy is apparent in the discourse and speeches of Arab leaders, as the following extracts demonstrate.

Example 3

وأنا فهمتكم، فهمت الجميع: البطال، والمحتاج والسياسي واللي طالب مزيد من الحريات، فهمتكم، فهمتكم الكل.

I understood you all, the jobless, the needy, the political and all those who are calling for more freedom.

(Ben Ali's speech, 13 January 2011)

ونحب نؤكد أن العديد من الأمور لم تجر كيما حبيتها تكون، وخصوصا في مجالي الديمقراطية والحريات، وغلطوني أحيانا بحجب الحقائق وسيحاسبون.

I would like to affirm that many things didn't work the way I wished, especially regarding democracy and freedom. Some around me have sometimes misled me by hiding truths, and they will be indeed be held accountable for that.

ولذا أجدد لكم، وبكل وضوح، راني باش نعمل على دعم الديمقراطية وتفعيل التعددية. نعم على دعم الديمقراطية وتفعيل التعددية.

I clearly repeat that I will support the multi-party system and democracy.

(Ben Ali's speech, 13 January 2011)

أنا مقتنع تمام الاقتناع بصدق نواياكم وتحرككم وأن مطالبكم هي عادلة ومشروعة، والأخطاء موجود في أي نظام ودولة، ولكن المهم الاعتراف بها ومحاسبة مرتكبيها، وأنا كرئيس جمهورية لا أجد حرجاً في الاستماع الى شباب بلادي

I am fully convinced that your intentions and your actions are honest, and that your demands are just and legitimate. Mistakes can be made in any political system and in any state. But, the most important thing is to recognise them and correct them as soon as possible and bring to account those who have committed them. As a president I find no shame in listening to my country's youth.

(Mubarak's speech, 11 February 2011)

نكلمكم لأن الوضع يفرض تغيير عميق.. تغيير عميق وشامل

I address you because the situation dictates deep changes, deep and comprehensive changes.

(Ben Ali's speech, 13 January 2011)

The above examples not only mark a shift in strategy, but are also in stark contrast to traditional political speeches, where there is a clear command, control and unwavering authority. As demonstrations gathered momentum, leaders' political speeches changed in tone and substance. They became more democratic, calling for dialogue, negotiations, reform and the freedom to protest. In the above examples, the words ديمقراطية – حريات dīmuqrāṭiyya/democracy – ḥurriyyāt/freedom (respectively) are repeated several times with the aim of persuading protesters. In the context of Tunisia, some demands were implemented, and took immediate effect, in a move to calm protesters, but as the trust between protesters and the regime eroded, some considered the government move a tactic to suppress their legitimate protests. This loss of trust between protesters and leaders exacerbated the situation, with protesters clinging to their demands, including the overthrow of the regimes. Such an unprecedented shift in the discourse and attitudes of political leaders came as a response to the tide of unexpected protests and their strict demands, some of which were considered red lines and taboo in the Arabic culture. The hardening position of protesters has induced political leaders to change their strategies as reflected in their political discourse. It seems that certain patterns were adopted in all speeches during the Arab spring.

A glance at Arab leaders' speeches since the eruption of the Arab Spring suggests that they have adopted identical themes and strategies in dealing with these uprisings. The following strands were repeated across all speeches:

> Greeting of citizens > Acknowledging the peaceful right of demonstrations > Rejection of violence > Criticism of individuals and groups who are allegedly behind the protests > Denial of violence against protesters > Self-praise and talk about services and sacrifices > Offer of reform and concessions > No presidency for life: ruling out participation in future presidential contests, with the exception of Gaddafi > Resignation/killed.

As Lahlali (2011) points out, strategies shifted along with the situation on the ground, and the balance of power shifted from regimes to citizens.

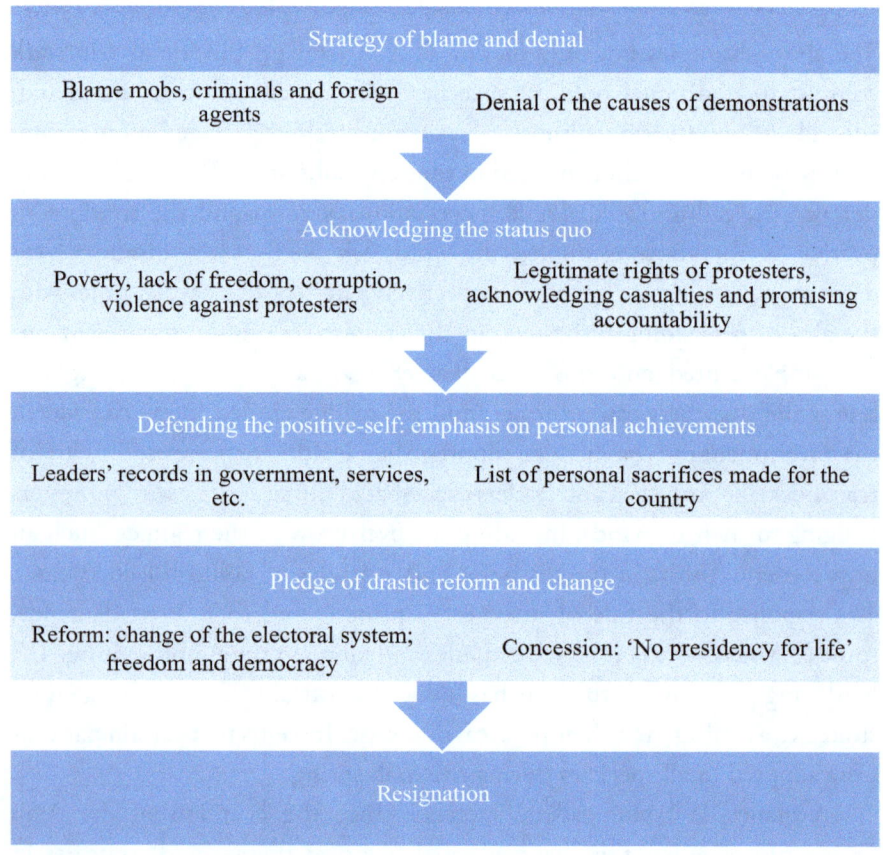

Figure 5.1 Arab leaders' strategy shift

Figure 5.1 shows the shift in the discourse strategies of Arab leaders. These strategies were triggered by the hybrid changes in the political landscape in these countries. As seen in the extracts from Ben Ali's speech in example 2 above, the use of well-qualified Arabic phrases and idiomatic expressions to denounce demonstrations and blame protesters as 'mobs', 'criminals' and 'agents in the pay of foreigners' reflect such a strategy of blame and denial. While there were tangible examples and signs that the economic and democratic situations had become intolerable for ordinary citizens, some Arab leaders continued to deny this and pursued a strategy of pursuit of those 'mobs'.

What is interesting in some of the above examples/extracts is the use of the Arabic phrase 'national security' and the 'protection of the state'. These are phrases which are often employed in time of conflict and crisis to drum up support for regimes and governments. The same strategy has been utilised here to deter citizens from joining protests and warn others that their actions could jeopardise the safety and security of the country. While some Arab leaders pursue a policy of scaremongering, they remain vague in their accusations and do not name or point the finger at those responsible for 'threatening the security of the country'. The use of مناوئون مأجورون *munāwi'ūna ma'jūrūna* (*Hostile elements in the pay of foreigners*) remains very broad as it can be applied to any person or party. One would argue here, however, that in the absence of a clear leadership for these demonstrations, leaders remained generic in their accusations and hence their discourses, which are full of metaphor such as وراءها أياد *warā'ahā ayādin* (*at the instigation of parties*), which could be said to have been designed to alert protesters to the fact that these demonstrations were instigated and stirred by 'invisible agents'. In the absence of leaders and actors to be held responsible for these actions, Arab leaders have resorted to the strategy of '*ta'mīm*' (generalisation), which makes their speeches and discourses vague and unpersuasive.

What the Arab Spring has shown us is that at a time of conflict discourses shift as the balance of power shifts. In the case of the Arab Spring, Arab leaders' discourse shifted when protesters gained the upper hand and their protests became widespread. This shift often allows concessions and a change of dynamics, where the negative other becomes more acceptable and their attributes as well as their actions become tolerable and considered the norm.

The shift also paves the way to concessions and a willingness to change the status quo. It also tells us that the negative other becomes the positive other, while the positive US becomes the negative US. This reverse of attribution and characteristics of individuals and groups is dictated by the change of the social and political landscape.

The examples of Egypt, Tunisia and Libya demonstrate this shift. For instance, the protesters were labelled as 'mobs' and 'criminals', and then became legitimate protesters with the right to stage protests and make demands without fear or intimidation. However, the positive US (leaders), who 'defended and protected the country and who sacrificed so much', become powerless as protests movements swept the Arab world. As the dynamics changed and protests gathered momentum, a sense of equity emerged, and protesters were elevated to the status of negotiators; powerful bodies with demands, and in control.

Situations of conflict have taught us that discourses are not stable entities, but they do shift as the dynamics of the society shift. We concluded that the discourse of powerless people changes as these people gain control, power and authority. The protesters' slogans of '*irḥal*' (leave) is just one tangible example of this power, where protesters demanded the immediate resignation of their leaders. Using the imperative in Arabic is a sign of power, order and command, which is often associated with powerful people, and is accepted and acted upon unquestionably. Despite the changes on the ground, which gave protesters the upper hand, some Arab leaders continued to stick to their guns in a very defiant attitude, as is exemplified in their discourse of defiance, which will be discussed in the following section.

Discourse of Defiance

Unlike other Arab leaders who adopted a discourse of reconciliation, appeal and willingness to negotiate their exit, Gaddafi emerged defiant, threatening and unwavering in his resolve to fight to the last minute. His defiant discourse is expressed through the use of the first person pronoun 'I', which shows his self-pride, determination and exclusivity. Arab leaders often use the inclusive pronoun 'we' to reflect the voice of citizens and nation, but Gaddafi has opted for the '*anā*' (I) to show his power and authority. By praising himself as a 'revolutionary fighter' who is prepared to die for the cause of Libya, he sought to send out the message to his supporters to rally behind him. What is striking about his defiant discourse is the use of religious terminologies, which are intended to show his religiosity and commitment to his faith and his willingness to die as a 'martyr'. The use of 'martyr', 'Mujahid', 'true Muslim leader', 'Salah-al-Deen' are good examples to cite here, as the following example demonstrates:

Example 4

وستكون شهادتي هذه بمثابة صوتي إلى العالم. أنني وقفت في وجه غزو الناتو.. وقاومت الجلافة وقساوتهم وأحبطت عملية الخيانة.. وأنني نهضت في وجه الغرب وطموحاته الاستعمارية.. وأنني مع أخوتي الافارقة وأخوتي الحقيقيين في العالم العربي والإسلامي الذين كنت بمثابة منارة وشعلة نور لهم

ولكن، بغض النظر عن ما قمت بإنجازه، فإنه لم يكن كافياً بالنسبة للبعض. ولكن هناك آخرون كانوا يعرفون أنني بمثابة الابن لجمال عبد الناصر، الزعيم العربي المسلم الوحيد الحقيقي الذي كان لدينا منذ صلاح الدين الأيوبي. الذي سار على خطاه عندما قام بتأمين قناة السويس لصالح شعبه. كما فعلت أنا كذلك عندما أعلنت أن ليبيا هي ملك للشعب الليبي، فأنا حاولت تقليده بهدف الحفاظ على شعبي حراً من هيمنة الاستعمار واللصوص الذين ينهبونا

'Let this testament be my voice to the world, that I stood up to crusader attacks of NATO, stood up to cruelty, stoop up to betrayal, stood up to the West and its colonialist ambitions, and that I stood with my African brothers, my true Arab and Muslim brothers, as a beacon of light.

But, no matter what I did, it was never enough for some, but for others, they knew I was the son of Gamal Abdel Nasser, the only true Arab and Muslim leader we've had since Salah-al-Deen, when he claimed the Suez Canal for his people, as I claimed Libya, for my people. It was his footsteps I tried to follow, to keep my people free from colonial domination – from thieves who would steal from us.'

(Gaddafi's letter, 20 October 2011)

أنا مقاتل ؛ مجاهد ؛ مناضل ؛ ثائر من الخيمة . . . أنا سـأموت طاهرا وشهيدا في النهاية.

'I am a fighter, a revolutionary from tents . . . I will die as a martyr at the end.'

(Gaddafi's speech, 22 February 2011)

Gaddafi used a revolutionary discourse, coupled with a discourse of martyrdom, which other Arab leaders had not used before. His discourse of martyrdom was legitimised by intertextual reference to historical battles and Libyan heroes, and this was intended to mobilise his supporters to fight with him 'to the last drop of blood'. His defiant discourse could be said to have been designed to warn those who wish to oust him that he would not go quietly.

Unlike other leaders, Gaddafi presented himself as the 'fighter', 'revolutionary', the modest leader who lives in a tent, and the religious leader who wished to die as a martyr. Gaddafi's discourse embodies three registers: military, political and religious. These have been carefully selected to portray Gaddafi positively as a powerful leader who 'stood up to crusaders' attacks' and to 'cruelty' and 'betrayal'. However, he unsuccessfully used the politics of bravery, sacrifice and martyrdom and modesty to entice his supporters to continue to fight for him. Although his message was heard loud and clear, most of his supporters deserted him, including sections of his military.

Compared with that of other leaders, it could be argued that Gaddafi's discourse underwent little transition, and despite his offer to allow changes to the political structure to satisfy regions and tribal demands, he showed little remorse and, indeed, little shift in his discourse. He continued his anti-Western rhetoric, defying and challenging demonstrators whom he considered to be 'traitors and agents of foreign powers'.

In the midst of reprimanding and holding people accountable for the uprising, some Arab leaders emphasised their great achievements during their rule, as will be discussed in the following section.

The Discourse of Greatness: The Legacy of the Past

During the Arab Spring, when demonstrations reached their peak and the call for the overthrow of regimes became even louder, some Arab regimes resorted to self-praise and glorification, with the aim of reminding citizens of their positive attributes, services and contributions to their respective countries, highlighting the roles and offices they held as true citizens. The following examples illustrate this clearly.

Example 5

حزني وألمي كبيران لأني مضيت أكثر من 50 سنة من عمري في خدمة تونس في مختلف المواقع: من الجيش الوطني إلى المسؤوليات المختلفة و23 سنة على رأس الدولة، كل يوم من حياتي كان ومازال لخدمة البلاد

I am deeply saddened. I have spent more than 50 years of my life in the service of Tunisia. Serving in different positions, from the National Army, to different decision-making positions, and 23 years at the Presidency. Every day of my life was and will always be devoted to the service of my country.

(Ben Ali's speech, 13 January 2011)

إنني لم أكن يوما طالب سلطة أو جاه ويعلم الشعب الظروف العصيبة التي تحملت فيها المسؤولية وما قدمته للوطن حربا وسلاما كما أنني رجل من أبناء قواتنا المسلحة وليس من طبعي خيانة الأمانة أو التخلي عن الواجب والمسؤولية

I have never wanted power or prestige, and people know the difficult circumstances in which I shouldered the responsibility and what I have given to the homeland during war and during the peace. I am also a man of the army, and it is not in my nature to give up responsibility.

(Mubarak's speech, 2 February 2011)

إن حسني مبارك الذي يتحدث إليكم اليوم يعتز بما قضاه من سنين طويلة في خدمة مصر وشعبها إن هذا الوطن العزيز هو وطني مثلما هو وطن كل مصري ومصرية فيه عشت و حاربت من اجله ودافعت عن أرضه وسيادته

Hosni Mubarak who speaks to you today is proud of the long years he spent in the service of Egypt and its people. This dear nation is my country, it is the country of all Egyptians, here I have lived and fought for its sake and I defended its land, its sovereignty.

(Mubarak's speech, 2 February 2011)

لقد شهدتُ حروب هذ البلد، وعشت أيام الانكسار وأيام النصر والتحرير، وكانت أسعد ايام حياتي عندما رفعت علم مصر فوق سيناء

I lived the days of defeat and occupation, I also lived the days of the (Suez) crossing, victory and liberation.

(Mubarak's speech, 11 February 2011)

The above examples are evidence of the shift in discourse strategies in Arab leaders' speeches. After a blame and denial strategy, where sections of protesters have been blamed for the protests, Arab leaders have moderated their discourses as protests grew in size and scale. They have shown some moderation, coupled with self-praise and positive-self description. As the above examples show, Arab leaders have talked about their contributions and services to their respective countries in an attempt to remind the young generation of the sacrifices they made, and this is designed to rally support around their leadership and presidency. What is striking here is the lack of the title 'president' and the use of the name without a title, which is designed to appeal to the Egyptian people and show that he is an ordinary citizen like them.

In his analysis of Mubarak's and Ben Ali's speeches, Lahlali (2011) commented that by resorting to listing their achievements and the services they had performed, they sought to remind their citizens of their contribution to their respective countries. However, this strategy of appealing to protesters through self-praise, self-sacrifice and services to the country did not bear any fruit. Being unable to win the hearts and minds of the protesters, Arab leaders made the final concession of ruling out their participation in future presidential contests.

As they made these concessions, their discourses shifted to identifying and positioning themselves in relation to historical icons of their respective countries, as will be explained in the following section.

Positioning through History
As their popularity plummeted and the support for their presidency started waning, the three Arab leaders resorted to the strategy of positioning and identifying themselves in relation to the founders of their countries, martyrs, or historical icons.

Ben Ali identified himself as the man who pursued the agenda of reform and continued the legacy of Bourqiba, the founder of modern Tunisia. Ben Ali often referred to his work in relation to Bourqiba's. By aligning himself with Bourqiba, Ben Ali sought to attract Bourqiba's supporters and also bestow on himself a similar style of leadership.

The same approach was adopted by Mubarak. He portrayed himself as the defender of Egypt, who spent years in the service of his country and who won so many battles. He referred to his predecessors as the greatest people who had fought vehemently for their country. He also identified himself with the military, by quantifying the roles and services he performed. Again, this is a strategy used to gain more sympathy from the military and wider Egyptian society.

Gaddafi was another leader who identified himself through the history of his country, Libya. He positioned himself as '*thawrī*' (revolutionary) who 'liberated Libya from foreign powers'. The military coup of 1977, which led to the overthrow of King Idris I, was his key identification feature. On numerous occasions, he referred to what he considered a 'historical moment' in the history of Libya, which brought prosperity to Libya and fair distribution of wealth amongst Libyans. But Gaddafi's association with Libya's history and its icons was not confined to the Libyan post revolution only, but he continued to identify himself in relation to the greatest Libyan freedom fighters, such as Omar Mukhtar, who fought for the independence of Libya.

These three Arab leaders positioned themselves in relation to other respected leaders or icons who had fought, defended or served their respective countries. By identifying themselves with other leaders and icons, they emphasised a 'sense of belonging' to their own countries (Van Dijk 2016), rejecting therefore those voices that were calling for their resignation. However, there were cases where leaders implicitly denounced former leaders. Take, for instance, Libya. Gaddafi was full of criticism for the pre-revolution era during the reign of King Idris I. Gaddafi considered King Idris I to be a 'puppet' of foreign powers, who controlled his regime and 'stole' Libya's oil and wealth for the benefit of their own people. He considered the king to be 'weak' and controlled by foreign powers, and this, according to Gaddafi, was the main reason for the 'Libyan revolution of 1977'.

Apart from portraying themselves as the greatest, who have done so much for their countries, quantifying and qualifying the services they have performed, their achievements and accomplishments, Arab leaders have strategically aligned themselves with renowned historical leaders or founders of their nations. In his speeches, Ben Ali kept referring to Bourqiba as the founder of modern Tunisia. The latter has a special place amongst Tunisians because of his reform and focus on education, especially female education.

Gaddafi constantly referred to Omar Mukhtar, who led the struggle for independence against the Italians. Omar Mukhtar's bravery and leadership won him the support of his generation and future generations. He became an icon of freedom and independence in Libya. The question here is why did Gaddafi refer to Libyan history and Omar Mukhtar in particular? At a time when his nationalism was questioned and his achievements were contested, he resorted to past icons to defend himself as a loyal, patriotic leader who considered himself 'the son of Omar Mukhtar'. Another interpretation could be that he used this historical icon to remind citizens that his country needed someone tough, like Omar Mukhtar. The main reason was to remind Libyans of their own history of fighting imperialism and colonisation. The tacit message here is that if you support the revolution, which is instigated by foreign powers, you are supporting the new occupation of Libya and the prospect of its wealth being depleted by these foreign powers, as the following extracts suggest.

Example 6

وستكون شهادتي هذه بمثابة صوتي إلى العالم. أنني وقفت في وجه غزو الناتو.. وقاومت الجلافة وقساوتهم وأحبطت عملية الخيانة.. وأنني نهضت في وجه الغرب وطموحاته الاستعمارية.. وأنني مع أخوتي الافارقة وأخوتي الحقيقيين في العالم العربي والإسلامي الذين كنت بمثابة منارة وشعلة نور لهم

ولكن، بغض النظر عن ما قمت بإنجازه، فإنه لم يكن كافياً بالنسبة للبعض. ولكن هناك آخرون كانوا يعرفون أنني بمثابة الابن لجمال عبد الناصر، الزعيم العربي المسلم الوحيد الحقيقي الذي كان لدينا منذ صلاح الدين الأيوبي. الذي سار على خطاه عندما قام بتأمين قناة السويس لصالح شعبه. كما فعلت أنا كذلك عندما أعلنت أن ليبيا هي ملك للشعب الليبي، فأنا حاولت تقليده بهدف الحفاظ على شعبي حراً من هيمنة الاستعمار واللصوص الذين ينهبونا

'Let this testament be my voice to the world, that I stood up to crusader attacks of NATO, stood up to cruelty, stoop up to betrayal, stood up to the West and its colonialist ambitions, and that I stood with my African brothers, my true Arab and Muslim brothers, as a beacon of light.

However, no matter what I did, it was never enough for some, but for others, they knew I was the son of Gamal Abdel Nasser, the only true Arab and Muslim leader we've had since Salah-al-Deen, when he claimed the Suez Canal for his people, as I claimed Libya, for my people, it was his footsteps I tried to follow, to keep my people free from colonial domination – from thieves who would steal from us.'

(Gaddafi's letter, 20 October 2011)

The above extracts reiterate Gaddafi's message of fighting imperialism and foreign occupations. His speeches embody the concept of Them vs Us. 'Them' are negatively represented as occupiers, robbers, thieves and crusaders, while he portrays himself as the son of Nasser and Salah al-Deen. By citing their positive attributes he sought to show that he has much in common with these people and that he has the same attributes as those leaders.

Apart from the strategy of appealing to the young generation, these leaders' positive representation of the self is designed to persuade protesters of the qualities and skills that they have acquired during their long service to the country. Their positive attributes include being a 'man of the army', 'devoted', 'committed', 'long years of service', 'made sacrifices'. By reiterating these positive attributes they intend to position themselves against what they called 'mobs', 'criminals' and 'foreign agents', who wish to do harm to their motherland, as discussed earlier. The use of *Inna* and *qad* in the paragraphs, in which personal qualities and attributes have been listed, is very revealing indeed as it emphasises and reinforces these qualities.

What we find significant and interesting as we read the positive self-representation is the association of the self with the military in the three discourses. Several interpretations spring to mind as we read these statements. The first is that it is designed to remind military leaders that they are one of them, seeking therefore protection and support. The second interpretation could be that the association with the military aims to rally public support. In Mubarak's speeches he dwelt on the victories he achieved in Sinai when he was a member of the military, as the following example demonstrates.

Example 7

لقد شهدتُ حروب هذا البلد، وعشت أيام الانكسار وأيام النصر والتحرير، وكانت أسعد ايام
حياتي عندما رفعت علم مصر فوق سيناء

I lived the days of defeat and occupation, I also lived the days of the Suez) crossing, victory and liberation.

(Mubarak's speech, 11 February 2011)

This discourse of winning citizens' hearts and minds is a new phenomenon in the Arab world. While leaders' attributes are promoted by the state-owned media, it's rare to find leaders appealing in desperate tones for support. This soft discourse, which is free of threat or intimidation, is a shift in strategy and discourse, as the new social and political landscapes dictate new practices and discourses that satisfy discontented protesters.

The arguments in these political discourses is that Arab leaders are loyal, faithful and have a track record of serving their country, unlike some of the protesters who are represented as 'mobs', 'traitors' and 'criminals', and whose intention is to cause harm to the nation that these political leaders have built and developed.

While Arab leaders caved in and started making concessions, and making it clear that they had heard and listened to the protesters' demands, the protesters on the other hand continued to reject offers of reform, reconciliation and moderation, calling for the resignation of these leaders, as manifested in their discourses of resistance and persistence. As protests showed no sign of abating, Arab leaders adopted a new discourse of heroism and self-sacrifice for the homeland.

The Discourse of Heroism

As the net became tighter and tighter around them, the leaders' discourse grew in self-praise and recognition of self-sacrifice and services. But what is striking here is the way they portrayed themselves as heroes who had fought for their own countries. They had often built profiles similar to their own national heroes. By referring to such icons as Bourqiba in his speeches, Ben Ali aims to associate himself with the founder of modern Tunisia. Apart from associating himself with Bourqiba, Ben Ali proudly displayed the forty-year service he performed for his country. His shift in strategy and discourse by focusing on his achievements and services could be said to have been designed to boost his popularity and drum up support for his presidency following the decline of his popularity and the waning of support from the Tunisian people. The following extracts from his speeches are concrete examples of his appeals for support and endorsement of his own services.

Example 8

حزني وألمي كبيران لأني مضيت أكثر من 50 سنة من عمري في خدمة تونس في مختلف المواقع: من الجيش الوطني إلى المسؤوليات المختلفة و23 سنة على رأس الدولة، كل يوم من حياتي كان ومازال لخدمة البلاد

I am deeply saddened because I have spent more than 50 years of my life in the service of Tunisia in various positions: from the national army, to various responsibilities and 23 years as head of state. Every day of my life was and will always be devoted to the service of my country.

(Ben Ali's speech, 13 January 2011)

Similarly, Mubarak did not miss the opportunity of reiterating his sacrifices and services for his own country, explicating the work he has done for Egypt since he has joined the army. He proudly highlighted the victories he contributed to, notably the 1973 war with Israel. This was intended to show his heroism in an attempt to win the hearts and minds of those protesting against him. Despite his discourse of heroism and sacrifice, the growing protests forced him in the end to resign his position as president of Egypt. Below are some of the examples which elucidate these services and sacrifices.

إن حسنى مبارك الذي يتحدث إليكم اليوم يعتز بما قضاه من سنين طويلة في خدمة مصر وشعبها. إن هذا الوطن العزيز هو وطني، مثلما هو وطن كل مصري ومصرية، فيه عشت، و حاربت من اجله ودافعت عن أرضه وسيادته.

Hosni Mubarak who speaks to you today is proud of the long years he spent in the service of Egypt and its people. This dear nation is my country, as it is the country of all Egyptians, here I have lived and fought for its sake and defended its territory and its sovereignty.

(Mubarak's speech, 2 February 2011)

لقد شهدتُ حروب هذ البلد، وعشت أيام الانكسار وأيام النصر والتحرير، وكانت أسعد أيام حياتي عندما رفعت علم مصر فوق سيناء.

I witnessed this country's wars. I lived through days of defeat, days of victory and liberation, and the happiest day of my life was when the flag of Egypt was raised over Sinai.

(Mubarak's speech, 11 February 2011)

In Libya, Gaddafi's discourse of heroism is very dominant. There are many references to his revolution in 1977, and how he liberated Libya from what he called 'occupiers'. His 'revolutionary act' made him a hero of Libya, who fought occupiers as did Omar Mukhtar, as the following examples explain; نهضت في وجه الغرب وطموحاته الاستعمارية *nahaḍtu fī wajhi algharbi wa ṭumūḥātihi al'istiʿmāriyya (I stood up to the West and its colonialist ambitions).* وقفت في وجه غزو الناتو *waqaftu fī wajhi ghazwi al-Nitū (I stood up to crusader attacks of NATO).* Gaddafi's discourse was different from other leaders' discourses as it portrays him as an Arab and African leader. In an attempt to attract the support of Arab citizens he associated himself with Gamal Abdel Nasser, the charismatic Arab leader بمثابة الابن لجمال عبد الناصر *bimatābati al'ibni lijamāl 'abd anāṣir (I was the son of Gamal Abdel Nasser).* He also appealed to African and Muslim nations to support him; a move different to other Arab leaders' discourses.

Example 9

وأنني مع إخوتي الأفارقة وإخوتي الحقيقيين في العالم العربي والإسلامي الذين كنت بمثابة منارة وشعلة نور لهم

I stood with my African brothers, my true Arab and Muslim brothers, as a beacon of light.

(Gaddafi's letter, 11 October 2011)

Gaddafi's discourse of heroism could be said to have been orchestrated to rally Libyans, Arabs, Africans and Muslims for his support. More importantly, it was intended to elevate his status and re-establish his authority, which had been eroded by large demonstrations in Libyan cities and towns. Similar to other Arab leaders, his attempt to portray himself as a hero failed and he was subsequently killed by his own people.

What is intriguing about the three cases discussed above is that discourse has been shifted as strategies shifted. In order to defuse the growing protests and the unprecedented call for resignations, the three leaders resorted to the discourse of heroism and empathy as a move to persuade protesters to abandon their demands. However, despite this discourse of heroism, sacrifice and services for the motherland, the protests continued to gather momentum, and subsequently ended these leaders' reigns.

The concluding remark for this section is that discourses can be manipulated to serve ideas, strategies and ideologies. They can also shift depending on the context and circumstances of the producer of these discourses. For instance, in the context of the Arab Spring, a variety of discourses have been produced to mirror the existing reality and circumstances. At the beginning of the uprising, we saw strong discourses which reflected confident leaders who were in charge of the situation, and reprimanding protesters and labelling them as 'agents of foreign powers', 'minority of drug addicts' and 'extremists', but their rhetoric and discourse shifted to a more moderated tone as protests were scaled up. This paved the way to a discourse of reconciliation, moderation and recognition of the status quo, coupled with suggestions and promises for improving the situation. These shifts, which were intended to persuade protesters to abandon their protests, are very visible when some linguistic aspects of these discourses are examined. In the following section we will dwell on how syntax has been employed as a tool for persuasion in Arab leaders' discourses.

Syntax as a Power of Persuasion

A further examination of Arab leaders' speeches suggests that a wide range of syntactic aspects has been adopted in different speeches, although this varies from one speech to the other. This variation of syntax across and within speeches of the same leader is very revealing indeed. In early speeches of the uprising, Arab leaders resorted to short sentences, and information was delivered in a very measured and manageable manner. This could be because Arab leaders were in control and little explanation and persuasion were required. The Arab leaders' explanations were very concise and no further elaboration was provided, suggesting that in early stages of the Arab Spring, they were very confident that they would deal with the situation in the traditional manner, without resorting to further explanation. However, as protests grew in scope and momentum, their discourse changed and so did the syntactic nature of their speeches and discourses. As demonstrations and protests show no sign of abating, Arab leaders realised that much work had to be done to persuade protesters to abandon their protests and return to normality. This act of persuasion found its way into the syntax of leaders' discourses. Contrary to the syntactic nature of their early speeches, Arab leaders adopted a new strategy, where further explanation and elaboration were provided, with long sentences and different clauses to explain, justify and elaborate on decisions and actions taken, and this negatively impacted the syntactic nature of their speeches. Additional examples and further information, which was intended for persuasion purposes, impacted the syntactic nature of their discourse, and rendered it incohesive and at times very repetitive.

The use of dependent clauses in the later speeches of Arab leaders suggests that additional information was provided to explain, clarify and respond to the protesters' needs and demands. This additional information could be said to have been designed to ensure that protesters' concerns were attended to in a very persuasive manner. Apart from the use of repetition and overlexicalisation, Arab leaders resorted to dependent clauses to provide further information and answer protesters' questions in a comprehensive manner.

So what does the above analysis tell us about the use of syntax in discourse during a time of unrest or conflict? As demonstrated above, there was a tendency to keep it short and concise when protests were very small. So most of leaders' speeches and discourses were to the point, demonstrating their confidence and sense of purpose by condemning the protests and the 'minority' of protesters behind them. Little explanation has been provided about these people and the reason for their protests, although in Tunisia it was made obvious that this was in response to the incident of Bouazzizi. It could be suggested here that in the early stages of the uprisings and conflicts, discourses were produced with little elaboration, and this is reflected in the syntactic nature of the text. However, as conflicts grew and spread, the syntactic form of discourses shifted, from short to long sentences, from single Arabic lexical items to repetitive ones, designed to provide further elaboration with the aim of cementing their arguments and dissuading protesters. It has also been remarked that the longer conflicts and uprisings lasted, the longer were the speeches and discourses that were produced to address them. This often resulted in repetition, overlexicalisation, incoherent argument, use of colloquial language, as well as the use of the singular pronoun '*anā*' (I) in Arabic (Abu Hatab 2013). Ben Ali's and Gaddafi's speeches are good examples to mention here. In the case of Gaddafi, one of his last speeches lasted more than an hour and it appeared to be very repetitive, incoherently presented, with much focus on the '*anā*' (the self). Similarly, Ben Ali's last speech was longer, repetitive, used colloquial Arabic and was full of self-praise and the use of '*anā*'. However, in order to fully understand the syntactic nature of Arab leaders' discourses, it would be useful to examine the Arab public (protesters) discourse, compared to that of the Arab leaders. When comparing the two discourses of two different actors in conflict, as in the Arab Spring, it is evident that there were two paradoxical approaches and strategies in the production of discourse. Unlike Arab leaders' discourses, protesters' discourse starts with providing an explanation for the reasons for these protests, often supplemented with imagery. But as protests successfully progressed, the discourse became very concise and in some instances consisted of one or two lexical items, such as '*irḥal*' (leave), *istaqil* (resign) and '*yasquṭi al-ṭāghūt*' (down with the tyrant).

Religious Discourse in Political Speeches

Religion plays a significant part in the everyday practices of Arab nations. Although some of these countries are liberal and adopt liberal laws, the grass roots of these countries are conservative and they tend to heed imams' advice. One would expect that at a time of conflict and heightened tension, Arab leaders would adopt a religious discourse to appeal to those conservative sectors of society, but this was not the case. Several interpretations and explanations spring to mind, one of which is that Tunisia, for instance, has a long history of liberalism, where political Islam has been absent and religion has been confined to mosques. In the case of Egypt, there was a history of conflict between the leadership and the Muslim Brotherhood. These reasons could justify the lack of religious discourse in those speeches. Apart from the religious openings: باسم الله الرحمن الرحيم *bismi Allahi arraḥmānī arraḥīm (In the Name of God, the Merciful, the Compassionate)*, no aspects of religious discourse feature in the leaders' speeches. Some used religion in their speeches for persuasive purposes, but Arab leaders have not used religion to advance their messages; perhaps they felt that the vast majority of their respective countries supported their agendas. In the case of Egypt, it could be that Mubarak's desire was to keep the minority of Coptic Christians on his side. Several interpretations could be offered here, but the conclusion is that Arab leaders remained liberal in their discourses, even when the tide was turning against them.

While religion appeared to be absent in Ben Ali and Mubarak's speeches, Gaddafi's speeches were not free of religious discourse. His repetition of terminologies such as 'martyrdom', 'crusade', 'Jerusalem' are clear indications that he used religion to support his arguments. The fact that he portrayed the uprising as a confrontation between him (his country) and the crusaders was intended to galvanise Libyans, Arabs and Muslims to support him. The following extract illustrates the above point.

Example 10

وستكون شهادتي هذه بمثابة صوتي إلى العالم. أنني وقفت في وجه غزو الناتو.. وقاومت الجلافة وقساوتهم، وأحبطت عملية الخيانة.. وأنني نهضت في وجه الغرب وطموحاته

الاستعمارية.. وأنني مع أخوتي الافارقة وأخوتي الحقيقيين في العالم العربي والإسلامي الذين كنت بمثابة منارة وشعلة نور لهم.

Let this testament be my voice to the world, that I stood up to the crusader attacks of NATO, stood up to cruelty, stood up to betrayal, stood up to the West and its colonialist ambitions, and that I stood with my African brothers, my true Arab and Muslim brothers, as a beacon of light.

(Gaddafi's letter, 20 October 2011)

The use of religion in political leaders' speeches is very modest and is confined to those phrases and terminologies used at the opening of speeches. This comes as no surprise when considering the leaders' historical background and liberal approach. However, what is striking is the use of religion by Gaddafi in framing the uprising in relation to crusades, Islamic groups and other religious symbols. In his case, religion has been used to advance his cause and rally Libyans and Muslims around the Libyan flag to fight what he calls the 'crusade and elements of Al-Qaeda'.

Intertextuality and Persuasion in Leaders' Speeches

As we examine the Arab leaders' speeches, we cannot help but notice reference to the past, mainly the glorious history of the three nations. There is reference to specific historical moments and events. In Egypt, for instance, there was a reference to the victory of 1973 and the sacrifices Mubarak had made since he joined the army. In Tunisia, Ben Ali referred to the independence of Tunisia and his contribution to that. He also highlighted the glorious days of Tunisian independence and the achievement of his government after he took over as leader.

The Arab leaders' use of intertextuality here was designed to link the present to the past, with the hope of strengthening their arguments to win over protesters. However, their discourse of the present-past failed to connect, and this could be because much time had elapsed and there was little recollection of the past amongst the younger generation. The second reason could be that the present situation was so gloomy and the majority of citizens were so dissatisfied, that the argument of the past had little impact.

By using intertextuality, Arab leaders sought to compare themselves with other leaders who were very popular amongst citizens because of their achievements, the struggle against imperialism and the fight for independence. The case of Omar Mukhtar in Libya is a good example to cite here. Gaddafi used the example of Omar Mukhtar on numerous occasions to advance his argument and display patriotism and loyalty to his country.

The same argument was advanced by Ben Ali and Mubarak, but their argument, despite its significance in the history of these nations, was ineffective as protests continued unabated. In terms of language and discourse, the three leaders used what I consider to be a discourse of pride and positive-self. Despite the pressure mounted on leaders because of the continuation of demonstrations, Arab leaders used a very positive tone in reference to the history of their countries and in their assessment of the present situation. The repetitive phrases/nouns of *Ajdādnā'* (ancestors), *shuhadā'* (martyrs)', *abṭāl* (heroes) was designed to establish that link between the past and present, urging protesters to fight those who had fought their ancestors, martyrs and heroes. The strategy here is to derail protests from domestic, social, economic and political grievances to confrontation with the other – here, Western powers.

This confrontation was more explicit in Gaddafi's speeches, and he used it as his main argument against the uprising. He referred to the Libyan revolution of 1977, when Gaddafi and his fellow military men staged a coup against King Idris, calling it the liberation of Libya from Western nations, notably the US, Italy, Britain and France. By going back to history and linking the current uprising to the desire for bringing back Western powers, his intention was to remind Libyans of their own history but also of his 'revolutionary action' against foreign powers. He also reviewed Libyan history, reiterating the struggle of his ancestors against imperialism and other Arab regimes. All this was designed to persuade Libyans to trust and support him. The use of his own family as martyrs, who sacrificed everything for the sake of Libya, was a strategy aimed to rally support, while portraying himself as a true Libyan who would do everything it takes to protect Libya from occupation by foreign powers. This is more obvious in his last speech, aired in his home, which had been destroyed by American and some European air raids. In a defiant speech, he sought again to use the venue to remind Libyans that he had sacrificed a great deal for the sake of protecting Libya from foreign powers.

> أخاطبكم من هذا المكان الصامد؛ هذا البيت في طرابلس ، الذي أغارت عليه «170» طائرة ؛ تقودها الدول النووية الكبرى أمريكا وبريطانيا والحلف الأطلسي. «40» طائرة بوينج ، تزود هذه الحملة بالوقود ، تخطت كل القصور ؛ وكل المنازل ؛ وكل بيوتكم ، كل بيوتكم تركتها ، تبحث عن منزل «معمر القذافي» ، لماذا ؟ هل لأن «معمر القذافي» رئيس جمهورية ؟ لو كان رئيسا لعاملوه مثلما عاملوا رؤساء الدول الأخرى
>
> *I am addressing you from this steadfast place. This house in Tripoli which was raided by 170 planes led by the great nuclear states, America, Britain and NATO. Forty Boeing planes were assisting in refuelling the campaign. They bypassed all the palaces and all the houses — all your houses, they left your houses behind – looking for the house of Muammar Qaddafi. Why? Because he is president of the republic? If he were a president, they would have treated him like they have treated other heads of state.*
>
> (Gaddafi's speech, 22 February 2011)

Gaddafi also listed other historical events outside Libya to strengthen his argument and legitimise any action against what he called الفئران *fi'rān (rats)*, الجرذان *aljurdān (cockroaches)* and مدمني مخدرات *mudminī mukhadirāt (drug addicts)*. By referring to the Russian crisis of 1993, when President Boris Yeltsin and the Russian parliament political stand-off was resolved by military force, and China's attack on the Tiananmen movement in the late 1980s, he sought to build a case that, like any other country, Libya had the right to crack down on these 'minority groups', whose aim is 'the destruction of Libya'. This intertextuality in Gaddafi's speech was addressed to the international community, who expressed concerns over Gaddafi's threat of using violence against his own people.

Intertextuality was one of the most popular features in the leaders' speeches. They resorted to the past to justify and legitimise some of their actions by comparing the current struggle to the struggle against imperialism and the fight for independence. Their discourses contain names, slogans and phrases associated with the fight for independence of their respective countries. For instance, the use of أسلافنا *aslafnā (ancestors)*; 1973 انتصار *intiṣār* (the victory of 1973); عمر المختار Omar Al Mukhtar الحملة الصليبية *alḥamla aṣṣalībiyya* (*the crusade*).

These are a few examples that are designed to link the present to the past, and they are aimed at arousing feelings of patriotism and sense of solidarity with these leaders. However, this has not deterred protesters from continuing with their demands. It could be said, therefore, that intertextuality has been used to revive certain national historical icons and events, with the aim of maintaining national unity. While the leaders' strategy of reverting to the past to celebrate glories and icons did not accomplish its major objective of rallying the nation around them, some of them resorted to the discourse of scaremongering to dissuade protesters from their actions.

The Discourse of Scaremongering

As protests gathered momentum across Arab nations, the regimes were unable to stop them, and they resorted to a discourse of fear, manifested in creating stories that threaten citizens' lives, security, jobs and continuity. This is more evident in Gaddafi's speeches when he alluded to the fact that their protests could invite foreign powers to invade Libya as they did in Afghanistan. By giving the example of Afghanistan, Gaddafi sought to warn protesters that their actions could have unbearable consequences, while Ben Ali and Mubarak warned of the consequences of protests on education, security and economy as the following extracts demonstrate.

Example 11

هل أنتم تريدون أن تأتي أمريكا إليكم، تحتلكم وتعمل لكم مثل أفغانستان؛ ومثل الصومال؛ ومثل باكستان؛ مثل العراق؟!. أيعجبكم هذا؛ أن بلادنا ستصبح مثل أفغانستان

Do you want America to come to you, occupy you and do to you what it did to Afghanistan, Somalia, Pakistan and Iraq? Our country will become like Afghanistan.

(Gaddafi's speech, 22 February 2011)

تألمنا لسقوط ضحايا وتضرر أشخاص، وأنا أرفض أن يسقط المزيد بسبب تواصل العنف والنهب.

أولادنا اليوم في الدار، وموش في المدرسة، وهذا حرام وعيب لأن أصبحنا خائفين عليهم من عنف مجموعات سطو ونهب واعتداء على الأشخاص، وهذا إجرام، موش احتجاج، وهذا حرام.

> We were saddened for the victims of these events and the damage suffered by persons, and I refuse to see more victims as a result of the ongoing violence and looting.
>
> Our children are confined at home today, they are not in school. This is totally immoral and shameful, because we have become afraid for their safety, from the acts of violence, looting and attacks perpetrated by small groups of bandits. This is a crime, this is a criminal act, not a protest, and this is sinful.
>
> (Ben Ali's speech, 13 January 2011)

نعيش معا أياما مؤلمة ، وأكثر ما يوجعنا هو الخوف الذي انتاب الأغلبية الكاسحة من المصريين، وما ساورهم من انزعاج وقلق وهواجس حول ما سيأتي به غدهم ولذويهم وعائلاتهم ومستقبل ومصير بلدهم

> We are living together in difficult times, and what hurts our hearts the most is the fear which has overtaken most Egyptians and the anxiety which has overtaken them regarding what tomorrow will bring for them and their families, and the future and destiny of their country.
>
> (Mubarak's speech, 27 January 2011)

Other leaders (i.e. Syria and Yemen) have also warned protesters of the impact their actions can have on security, as well as the economy and the reputation of their country abroad. They have expressed their concerns over the escalation of violence and the ramifications of this for security. Their discourse of fear has been extended to include the impact of protests on families and children in an attempt to stop children's involvement in the protests. By painting a gloomy picture of the security situation in their countries, Arab leaders have created an environment of fear, where citizens have been invited to choose between security, chaos and disorder.

The use of 'fear', 'anxiety', 'concerns', 'painful days', 'ongoing violence and looting' are terminologies and expressions designed to spread fear amongst citizens about the future of their countries. This spread of fear has been amplified by linking the lack of security to 'mobs' and 'gangs', who 'violently attack people'. The number of casualties has been attributed to 'violence and looting'. This strategy of relating protests to violence could be interpreted as an attempt to tarnish the protesters' reputation and put an end to the continuing protests. However, it appears that the level of awareness amongst protesters hindered this attempt and ensured a continuation of protests at all levels.

While some leaders' strategy of amplifying the impact of protests on security and economy failed, others have resorted to different communication approaches in trying to deter protesters. The use of colloquial Arabic in some of the speeches could be said to have been designed to spread this fear at a higher level, as it broke the traditional norm of formal speeches. Ben Ali, for instance, used it in his last speech, especially when talking about 'violence', 'mobs' and 'gangs'. This is to reinforce his message that the use of violence threatens citizens' lives and their future.

The Discourse of Inclusion

What is striking in the discourse of fear is the use of the inclusive 'we' by Arab leaders, which could indicate that they share the protesters' fear of violence and lack of security, and that they are, like other citizens, very concerned with the situation and very worried about the future. The use of 'we' or prefix '*nā*' suggests that Arab leaders are ordinary people who seem to be genuinely concerned about the well-being of their citizens and families, but protesters and other sceptics would argue that this is a linguistic strategy and a tactic intended to single out and blame some protesters for the uprising. However, this strategy failed to have an impact on protesters as they realised that some leaders resorted to the strategy of divide and rule.

The use of '*awlādnā*' (our children) makes the discourse very personal as it refers to families, the future generation and therefore the future of the country. It suggests that '*awlādnā*' (our children) are very precious and very vulnerable and will need protecting from the 'criminals', 'gangs' and 'mobs' who seek to destroy them. This very carefully selected family discourse is designed to make families rethink their involvement in protests as their action could harm their own children. By addressing families, leaders realised the significance of the family in the Arabic culture, and how their interference could have a knock-on effect on the scale of protests. However, the outcome of the protests in some Arab countries suggests that parents did not heed the warnings, as some parents have other concerns pertaining to their children's future and the long-term prosperity of their respective countries.

While Ben Ali used families and children to dissuade protesters, Gaddafi used the analogy of Afghanistan and Iraq to deter protesters. He reminded Libyans of the conflict in Afghanistan and Iraq, and the destructiveness and the presence of United States in both countries. He used the discourse of negativity and scaremongering to advance his argument of the involvement of what he called people of Bin Laden and al-Qaeda in Libyan protests, which could attract the United States to take action against them as they did in Afghanistan and Iraq. By using this analogy, Gaddafi appealed to protesters but also hoped to persuade the international community that his action was against al-Qaeda and its affiliates in Libya. This strategy sought to remind both the international community and Libyans of the danger al-Qaeda posed in Libya and neighbouring countries. The following is an example from Gaddafi's speeches.

Example 12

أنظروا إلى ليبيا تريد الاستعمار ؛ تريد الانتكاسة ؛ تريد الحضيض
وترون ما يحدث في الصومال، هل تريدون بلادكم، مثل الصومال ؛ مثل العراق؟!. نفس المجموعة التي خرّبت هذه البلدان، هي التي دخلت إلى ليبيا الآن ؛ هي التي تريد أن تُلحق ليبيا بأفغانستان وبالصومال،

Look at Libya, you want colonialism; you want a setback; you want rock bottom. And you see what is happening in Somalia; do you want your country like Somalia, like Iraq?! It is the same group that has sabotaged these countries, which has now entered Libya; they want Libya to be like Afghanistan and Somalia.

(Gaddafi's speech, 22 February 2011)

The use of phrases, such as الاستعمار *isti'mār (colonialism)* ; انتكاسة *intikāsa (set back)* ; الحضيض *alḥaḍiḍ (rock bottom)*; خرّب *kharraba (sabotaged)*; هي التي تريد أن تُلحق ليبيا بأفغانستان وبالصومال *hiya alatī turīdu an tulḥiqa Libya bi Afghānistān wa bi al-Ṣūmāl* (*they want Libya to be like Afghanistan and Somalia*), was designed to spread fear amongst protesters, but his discourse fell on deaf ears as protests continued across Libya. While others may look back and say that part of Gaddafi's discourse and warnings had some truth in them as Libya descended into chaos after he was killed, having a severe impact on the national security and economy, others would equally argue that this could have been prevented if Gaddafi and his government had responded positively to the protesters' demands. Libya descended into civil war, with factions fighting each other and seeking to seize power to fill the power vacuum in the country.

What can be noticed from the sequence of events in Libya, Tunisia and Egypt is that as leaders started losing control, their strategy shifted and they started to moderate their discourses, shifting their arguments to accommodate protesters' demands.

The Discourse of Reconciliation and Command in Arabic Political Speeches

This section aims to examine the discourse of command in the political leaders' speeches and the Arab public discourses from a grammatical perspective. We will look at how the imperative has been used to position oneself against the other, but also how the imperative could serve as an indicator of change when it is unconventionally used by unexpected actors. Traditionally, orders are associated with the hierarchy of power and authority in the Arabic context, but in this section we will argue that during the Arab Spring a shift emerged and that command, power and assertiveness were displayed differently at different stages of the conflict. We will argue that the leaders' use of the discourse of command faded gradually as the Arab Spring progressed and the dynamics of power shifted. The change in the political landscape of the Arab world impacted the production of political leaders' discourse, and as protests grew leaders' discourses were moderated, replacing command and order with conciliation. It should be mentioned, however, that there are some clear differences in the different leaders' discourse. The other shift we aim to examine is the use of protesters' command and orders vis-à-vis their leaders.

When the Arab Spring began, most Arab leaders were caught by surprise and some were unprepared as to how to deal with the wave of protests. At the beginning of the conflict, Arab leaders handled the crisis as they would normally deal with protests, by adhering to their traditional approach of addressing protesters. Linguistically and in their speeches to the nation, the structure and content of Arab leaders' speeches were almost identical, consisting of an introduction, with Islamic greeting and the direct address of citizens, a body content, and a conclusion. In these speeches they sought to demonstrate their power and authority, rejecting the widespread protests and threatening severe punishment for those who had instigated this wide unrest. Threat and menace were explicit in their orders through the use of imperative in Arabic. Take, for instance, the following examples.

Example 13a

العنف ما هوش متاعنا، ولا هو من سلوكنا، ولا بد أن يتوقف التيار. يتوقف بتكاتف جهود الجميع

Violence has never been part of our customs, or part of our behaviour. The present tide of unrest should stop. We must bring it to a halt together.

يزي من اللجوء للكرطوش الحي، الكرطوش موش مقبول، ما عندوش مبرر

Stop using live ammunition. Live ammunition is not acceptable, and is not justifiable!

(Ben Ali's speech, 13 January 2011)

Although commands are associated with power and authority, the above examples, with the exception of Gaddafi, convey little command and order. This is unusual in the Arabic context, where the expectation is to give orders and show leadership and authority by commanding protesters to cease their actions, however, the leaders' speeches display little of this, despite the gravity of the situation. Leaders here have chosen the path of diplomacy rather than threat, command and order, although others would argue that they resorted to this soft diplomacy after realising that protesters had reached a point of no return. However, not all leaders followed an entirely diplomatic style; Gaddafi, for instance, used the stick and carrot approach. He responded to some of the protesters' demands, but remained strict and tough in his speeches, using negative semantic labels, coupled with a clear style of command, with the frequent use of the imperative to explicitly demonstrate his authority as a command-in-chief. His authority was visible in his use of the imperative when ordering the public to take action and stop the 'rats and cockroaches' who wished his country harm, as the following examples show.

Example 13b

اطلعوا بسرعة إلى الشوارع ؛ سيطروا على الشوارع

Get out of your homes, secure the streets.

أطلعوا من بيوتكم اعتبارا من الآن

Get out of your homes now.

(Gaddafi's speech, 22 February 2011)

While Ben Ali's and Mubarak's speeches were gentle in their tone, some of Gaddafi's speeches adopted a confrontational tone, in particular when addressing what he calls 'foreign agents'. His argumentation was based on the threat posed by 'Western powers and extremists', who he thinks managed to mobilise a minority of young Libyans to rebel and take up arms against his government. He argued that these 'rats' and 'cockroaches' were in the pay of foreign agents who wish for the destruction of Libya. He considered these people to be traitors who let their country, leader and ancestors down by conspiring with foreigners against their own country. Gaddafi used historical confrontations with 'colonisers' to cement his argument and portray himself as Libya's leader and defender. His argument was characterised by linking the present to the past, reminding Libyans of their own history and the heroism of their ancestors who defeated great powers, indicating that they should rise up and protect their country. However, while narrating the past triumphs of Libyans, he took the opportunity to threaten those who sought to challenge his power and authority. This is exemplified in the language and discourse utilised in his speeches, some of which was introduced earlier.

Ben Ali and Mubarak, in contrast, adopted a conciliatory soft approach, but were firm when addressing protesters. They were not as confrontational as Gaddafi, but they expressed concerns over the security and safety of the country and its people. However, their carrot and stick strategy, manifested in a gentle tone and a clampdown on protesters, did not deter the latter from pursuing their demands. Despite the difference in the nature and delivery of their political discourse, the three Arab leaders failed to persuade protesters to abandon their actions. This eventually led to the overthrow of the three presidents, with one being killed and two stepping down. The outcome is also very revealing and reflects the nature and type of discourses delivered by these leaders. Gaddafi's confrontational and challenging discourse sprang from his desire to fight to the last minute those who sought to overthrow him, and he did until he was killed by his own people.

Another difference in the leaders' speeches is the length of each speech. Gaddafi's speeches are very long, compared with those of Ben Ali and Mubarak. The length of his speeches could be said to have affected the substance and argument of his discourse. As discussed in Chapter 4, the cohesion and coherence of his speeches suffered immensely as ideas appeared disjointed and sentences and paragraphs were incohesive. This lack of cohesion and coherence negatively impacted his argument, which was vital to persuading protesters to call off their demonstrations.

Although there is a difference in the style and delivery of political speeches, it could be argued that most of the speeches were conciliatory and were designed to win over the Arab public and protesters. This is a shift in terms of discourse of Arab leaders, where tradition dictates that they are the source of power and authority. With the exception of Gaddafi, who also showed a degree of moderation, Arab leaders' speeches are diplomatic in nature, showing a degree of respect and humanity. But what was the protesters' reaction and how has this been reflected in their discourse? Did it reflect the tradition of respect and loyalty to leaders? Or did it mark a shift in its style and substance? To answer these questions, we will examine some of the protesters' statements and slogans. Take for instances the following slogans.

Example 14

"ثورة ثورة. . . حتى النصر"

Revolution until triumph.

"وصبرنا سنوات ولم يتبق إلا ساعات"

The long endurance will come to an end in a matter of hours.

"الشعب يريد محاكمة الرئيس القاتل"

People would like to bring to trial the dictator (murderer/killer president).

"محاكمات فورية للمسؤولين عن قتل شهداء الثورة، محاكمات عاجلة للفاسدين وسارقي ثروات الوطن."

Immediate trial for those responsible for the killing of the martyrs of the revolution, and for looting the wealth of the country.

"ويسقط مبارك العميل"

Down with Mubarak, the puppet.

"وصامدون حتى يرحل الطاغية"

Persevering until the downfall of the tyrant.

"ويسقط الفرعون والزبانية"

Down with pharaoh and tyrant.

"يسقط الطاغوت"

Down with the tyrant.

"وصامدون حتى يرحل الطاغية"

Persevering until the downfall of the tyrant.

The above examples mark a shift in the discourse of protesters. Traditionally, citizens are very loyal, polite and respectful to their leaders. However, during the Arab Spring this attitude changed and protesters become very vocal and critical. Their criticism and reprimand exceeded all cultural boundaries and broke taboos that had long been held and respected. The call upon leaders to resign, to depart, to be brought to justice is unprecedented in the Arab public discourse. What is intriguing is the negative attributes attributed to some of the leaders. The use of 'ṭāghūt' (tyrant), '*phir'awn*' (pharaoh) is a clear example of this change in the public discourse.

As Lahlali (2014: 8) pointed out, 'in Arabic literature, Pharaoh is a symbol of tyranny, aggression and dictatorship. This, again, reveals quite lucidly the strong feelings of discontent among the Egyptian people against Mubarak.' The widespread negative slogans, coupled with imperatives such as *irḥal* (leave) are good examples of this shift in discourse. It shows that power and authority shift when political and social dynamics shift. The fact that these negative attributes have been uttered reflects the protesters' confidence and power as the traditional political state structures started to crumble. Protesters became more audacious, and dared to challenge the system that had been considered sacred for many years. The fact that protesters chose the Arabic verb *irḥal* rather than, for instance, *idhhab* or *inṣarif* (go, leave) indicates their determination to see their leaders leave once and for all.

The above examples are tangible evidence, therefore, that public discourse underwent a shift during the Arab Spring, and that the discourse of loyalty, respect and obedience can be replaced with a discourse of criticism, reprimand and accountability. Again, it should be reiterated that this is a new phenomenon in Arabic culture and political discourse, but the reason for this shift can be traced back to the changes in the social and political landscape that swept most of Arab countries during 2011. These changes in protesters' discourse intensified the pressure on Arab leaders who, in turn, changed their discourse, and showed some flexibility and reconciliation, coupled with concessions. The following section will consider the discourse of concession as a last resort for leaders in Egypt, Tunisia and Libya.

The Discourse of Concession: The Last Throw of the Dice

As their authority started eroding and waning, leaders started making concessions, including promises of radical reforms in the social, economic and political domains. However, their abrupt change of strategy was ineffective, as protesters remained sceptical about their move. Realising the scale and gravity of protests, leaders resorted to talking of their acts of heroism and years of service to demonstrate the sacrifices they had made for their respective countries. This served as a reminder that they were citizens too, who had worked hard for their countries and who deserved to be treated with dignity and respect. Their appeals and tales of their own services, records in offices and sacrifices did nothing to stop the ever-growing protests. Faced with this dilemma, the leaders threw their last dice and made concessions, promising not to put themselves forward for future elections, confirming that this was their final term of office. They hoped such announcements would prove popular amongst protesters, but in fact they fell on deaf ears as the demonstrations continued. The discourse of 'no presidency for life' failed and with it ended the presidency of both Mubarak and Ben Ali.

Example 15

ونحب نكرر هنا، وخلافا لما أدعاه البعض، أني تعهدت يوم السابع من نوفمبر بأن لا رئاسة مدى الحياة، لا رئاسة مدى الحياة، ولذلك فإني أجدد الشكر لكل من ناشدني للترشح لسنة 2014 ، ولكني أرفض المساس بشرط السن للترشح لرئاسة الجمهورية

I would like to reiterate here, contrary to what some claim, that I pledged on 7 November 1987 that there would be no lifetime presidency, no lifetime presidency. So I again thank those who called on me to stand in 2014, but I refuse to touch the age condition for candidates for the presidency of the republic.

(Ben Ali's speech, 10 January 2011)

وأقول بكل صدق وبصرف النظر عن الظرف الراهن، أني لم أكن أنوي الترشح لفترة رئاسية جديدة وقد قضيت ما يكفي من العمر في خدمة مصر وشعبها

I will say with all honesty – and regardless of this particular situation – that I did not intend to seek a new term as president, because I have spent enough of my life in serving Egypt and its people.

(Mubarak's speech, 2 February 2011)

The conclusion from this is that the shift of discourse from authoritarian to one of moderation and concession, did not deter protesters from staging their protests. This could be attributed to the lack of trust in regimes and the fear of returning to the status quo. What is remarkable as we examine the discourse of concession is that it was used gradually, reflecting the scale and degree of this concession as protests grew, as demonstrated in Figure 5.2.

The diagram shown in Figure 5.2 summarises the order and scale of leaders' concessions. In some societies, these concessions are sufficient to calm down voices and protests because they would be considered genuine. However, in the context of the Arab Spring, this unexpected shift in the leaders' discourse and position created both a sense of confusion and a lack of trust. The scale of concession offered made protesters think that this was a tactic designed to defuse tension and thwart protests. So, although there was a clear shift in discourse on the part of Arab regimes, the recipient of this discourse displayed no shift in position and adopted even a bolder stance by calling for the immediate resignation of these leaders. Although there was nothing to suggest that the leaders would not honour their promises, protesters poured cold water on their concessions and continued to reiterate their popular slogan of '*irḥal*' (leave).

The question to be asked here is: why did protesters decline these concessions? And why there was no shift in their position? Answering these questions

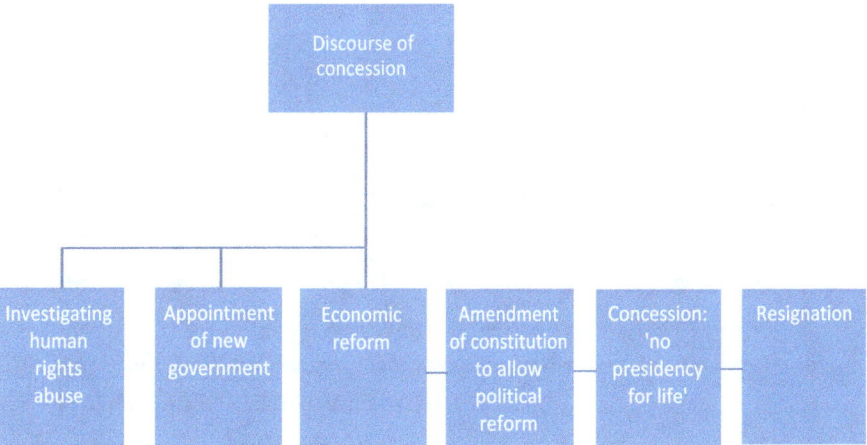

Figure 5.2 Discourse of concession: types and degrees of concession

requires an examination of the protesters' discursive practices. What we have seen is a shift in discourse in terms of their rights and demands. It shifted from a discourse of passive consumers to one of active recipients, where the truth is spoken to those in power. This is a new phenomenon in the Arabic political culture, where norms and practices necessitate absolute loyalty and obedience. This shift in practice and discourse mirrors the shift in the social and political context, where protesters appeared to be challenging the status quo. Their resilience and persistence put significant pressure on leaders who continue to shift their argument and make concessions to protesters, in the hope that demonstrations would abate.

Shift in Argument

Scholars of Arabic political discourse would generally agree that there is a rigid structure for these speeches, which often has a top-down approach delivery, where information and commands are given, and often with clear instructions. Some of these speeches embody the characteristics of praise for the achievement of leaders, and they are frequently designed for external consumption. This type of argument adheres to the rules of persuasion through the use of tangible examples and explicit practices such as national gains and achievements. However, during the Arab Spring this strategy shifted and arguments become apparent even when dealing with domestic issues, or when the discourse was designed for local consumption. The following are examples from leaders' speeches.

Example 16

وأنا ما زلت مُصرا على أن البترول الليبي، يجب أن يكون لليبيين ؛ أنتم لم تعد عندكم ثقة في اللجان الشعبية، خلاص؛ خذوا البترول في يدكم، وتصرفوا فيه؛ حتى لا يقول أحد أنك أخذت حصتي. كل واحد يأخذ حصته، أنت حر

I do insist that Libyan oil must be for the Libyans. You no longer have confidence in the people's committees; take oil and make use of it the way you like, so no one can claim his share has been taken. Each can take his share. You are free.

(Gaddafi's speech, 22 February 2011)

أنا مقتنع تمام الاقتناع بصدق نواياكم وتحرككم وأن مطالبكم هي عادلة ومشروعة، والأخطاء موجودة في أي نظام ودولة، ولكن المهم الاعتراف بها ومحاسبة مرتكبيها، وأنا كرئيس جمهورية لا أجد حرجاً في الاستماع الى شباب بلادي

I am fully convinced that your intentions and your actions are honest, and that your demands are just and legitimate. Mistakes happen in any system or state but what is important is to recognise them and hold those responsible to account. As the president of the republic, I am not embarrassed to listen to the young people of my country.

(Mubarak's speech, 11 February 2011)

وأنا فهمتكم، فهمت الجميع: البطال، والمحتاج والسياسي واللي طالب مزيد من الحريات، فهمتكم، فهمتكم الكل.

I understand you all: the jobless, the needy, the political and all those who are calling for more freedom. I understand you, I understand you all.

(Ben Ali's speech, 13 January 2011)

As the above examples demonstrate, this shift in the structure of political speeches recognises the other (i.e. demonstrators) as recipients of discourse and powerful stakeholders who need to be persuaded and taken seriously. The fact that Arabic political speeches embody this type of negotiation, discussion and argument suggest that recipients become highly valued and regarded as partners in the decision-making. Again, this is a new shift in the political culture in Arab societies, where leaders are traditionally trusted with decision-making and implementation of policies.

In the above examples, Arab leaders sought to negotiate their way through a well-structured argument, which starts with acknowledgement of protesters' demands, but moved to explain the reasons for the status quo, admitting guilt/responsibility and apologising for it, before offering resolutions to the problem. This looks like a typical political speech, but the only difference is that this is new. It is rare in the Arabic political culture for political leaders to admit and apologise for their shortcomings. But what is striking is their determination to hold senior officials accountable for what happened. While this sounds reasonable and could be applauded in some contexts, in the Arabic context this sounds unusual as it is not the custom to reprimand officials in public. The following example demonstrates vividly this unusual approach.

Example 17

ونحب نؤكد أن العديد من الأمور لم تجر كيما حبيتها تكون، وخصوصا في مجالي الديمقراطية والحريات، وغلطوني أحيانا بحجب الحقائق وسيحاسبون.

I would like to affirm that many things didn't work the way I wished, especially regarding democracy and freedom. Some around me have sometimes misled me, by hiding truths, and they will be indeed be held accountable for that.

ولذا أجدد لكم، وبكل وضوح، راني باش نعمل على دعم الديمقراطية وتفعيل التعددية. نعم على دعم الديمقراطية وتفعيل التعددية.

I clearly repeat that I will support the multi-party system and democracy.

(Ben Ali's speech, 13 January 2011)

أنا مقتنع تمام الاقتناع بصدق نواياكم وتحرككم وأن مطالبكم هي عادلة ومشروعة، والأخطاء موجود في أي نظام ودولة، ولكن المهم الاعتراف بها ومحاسبة مرتكبيها، وأنا كرئيس جمهورية لا أجد حرجاً في الاستماع الى شباب بلادي

I am fully convinced that your intentions and your actions are honest, and that your demands are just and legitimate. The mistakes can be made in any political system and in any state. But, the most important thing is to recognise them and correct them as soon as possible and bring to account those who have committed them. As a president I find no shame in listening to my country's youth

(Mubarak's speech, 11 February 2011)

نكلمكم لأن الوضع يفرض تغيير عميق.. تغيير عميق وشامل

I address you because the situation dictates deep changes, deep and comprehensive changes.

(Ben Ali's speech, 13 January 2011)

The above examples demonstrate clearly the shift in argument and discourse. Ben Ali and Mubarak as well as Gaddafi conceded that demonstrators have a case and acknowledged that the current status quo ought to change, proposing different ways forward, which marked a complete shift in their strategy and discourse. The acknowledgment that there are issues that need addressing stands in sharp contrast to their initial reaction that protests are illegitimate and that protesters are agents in the pay of foreigners. This shift in argumentation and discourse came about as protests intensified and the calls for resignation got even louder. It could be said that leaders moderated their speeches and discourses in the face of growing protests. The gist of this is that when the pressure on leaders intensified, they caved in and their concession to the protesters' demands became more evident. This suggests that discourse can shift depending on the circumstances and context. We have noticed that leaders moderated their discourses as the pressure mounted because of the number and the intensity of protests. Their moderation gave way to concessions, recognition and acknowledgement of what they initially denied at the beginning of the uprisings. This indicates that positions shift as the political and social variables shift, which in turn leads to a shift in discourse, as the following examples demonstrate.

Example 18

أنا مقتنع تمام الاقتناع بصدق نواياكم وتحرككم وأن مطالبكم هي عادلة ومشروعة، والأخطاء موجود في أي نظام ودولة، ولكن المهم الاعتراف بها ومحاسبة مرتكبيها، وأنا كرئيس جمهورية لا أجد حرجاً في الاستماع الى شباب بلادي

I am fully convinced that your intentions and your actions are honest, and that your demands are just and legitimate. Mistakes can be made in any political system and in any state. But, the most important thing is to recognise them and correct them as soon as possible and bring to account those who have committed them. As a president I find no shame in listening to my country's youth.

(Mubarak's speech, 11 February 2011)

نكلمكم لأن الوضع يفرض تغيير عميق.. تغيير عميق وشامل

I address you because the situation dictates deep changes, deep and comprehensive changes.

(Ben Ali's speech, 13 January 2011)

The above two examples are in stark contrast to the leaders' speeches at the beginning of the uprising. Their discourses then showed signs of threat and menace for those who were behind the uprisings. Their tone was strict, authoritative and contained aspects of order and command. However, this changed as the political and social dynamics changed on the ground, which explains the shift to a more moderate and conciliatory discourse. The diagram in Figure 5.3 summarises this shift in relation to different stages of the conflict.

The diagram in Figure 5.3 summarises the strategic shifts of Arab leaders during the conflict. However, these shifts reflected those of the protesters as the conflict progressed. Change in meaning and style shaped and were shaped

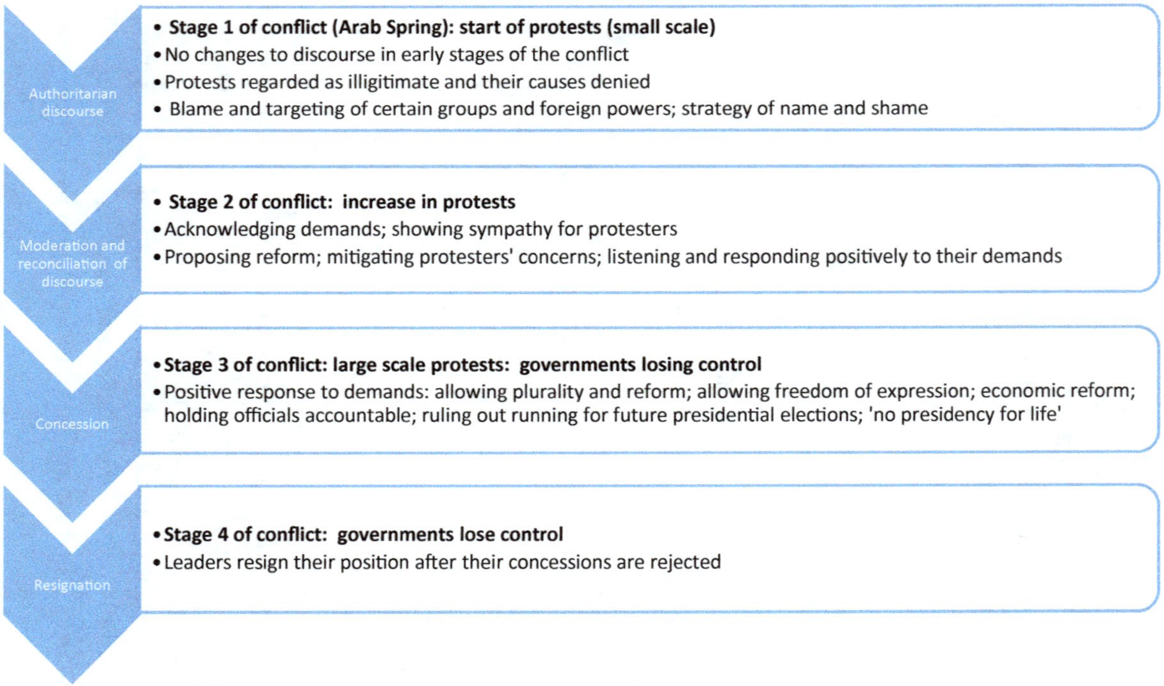

- **Stage 1 of conflict (Arab Spring): start of protests (small scale)**
  - No changes to discourse in early stages of the conflict
  - Protests regarded as illigitimate and their causes denied
  - Blame and targeting of certain groups and foreign powers; strategy of name and shame

- **Stage 2 of conflict: increase in protests**
  - Acknowledging demands; showing sympathy for protesters
  - Proposing reform; mitigating protesters' concerns; listening and responding positively to their demands

- **Stage 3 of conflict: large scale protests: governments losing control**
  - Positive response to demands: allowing plurality and reform; allowing freedom of expression; economic reform; holding officials accountable; ruling out running for future presidential elections; 'no presidency for life'

- **Stage 4 of conflict: governments lose control**
  - Leaders resign their position after their concessions are rejected

Authoritarian discourse → Moderation and reconciliation of discourse → Concession → Resignation

Figure 5.3 Shifts in discourse in relation to the stages of the Arab Spring

by the discourse of both leaders and protesters. The model in Figure 5.4 in the following section summarises these shifts in relation to the different stages of the conflict, arguing that during any conflict there is a shift in discourse from key actors but these shifts depend on the balance of power and the outcome of the conflict.

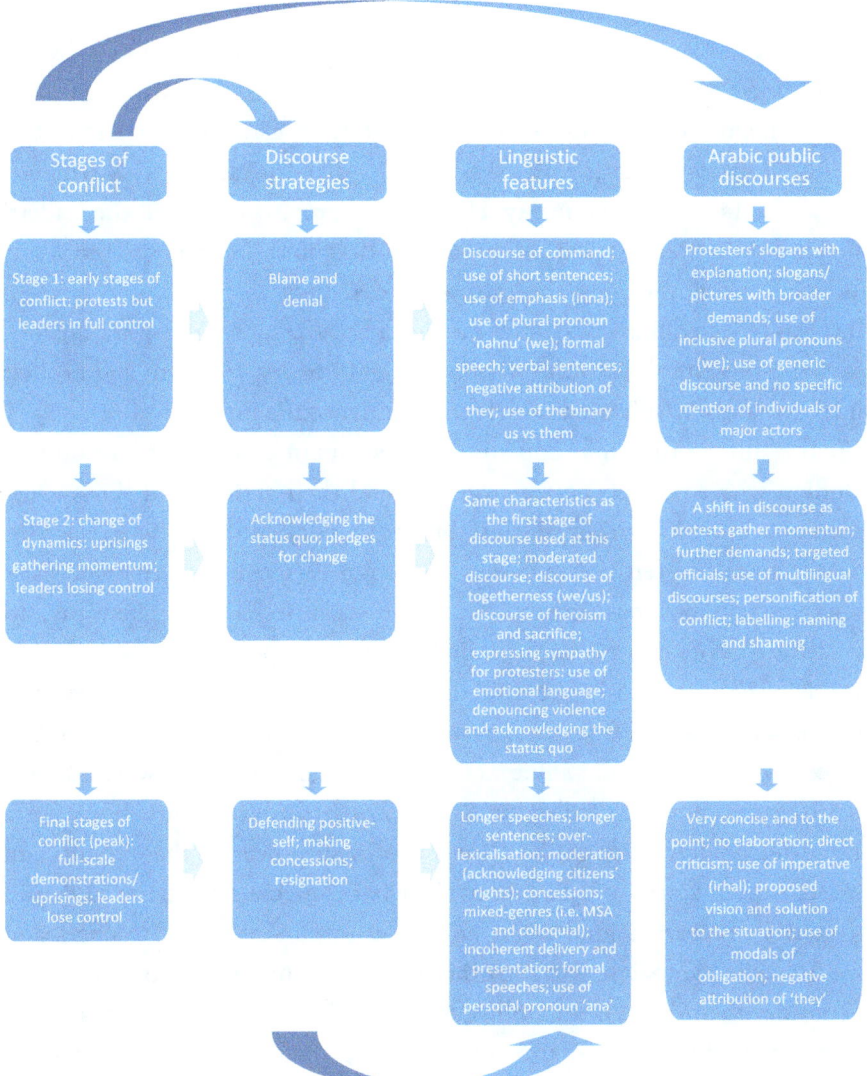

Figure 5.4 The shift in discourse strategies of Arab leaders and the Arab public during the Arab Spring

Analysing the Shift in Discursive Strategies during Time of Conflict: A Model

Figure 5.4 shows key shifts in the discursive strategies of different actors in the conflict, taking the Arab Spring as a case study. It introduces key shifts and contextualises them in relation to different stages of the conflict, highlighting the production of discourse of different actors and how it varies during the course of the conflict.

Figure 5.4 summarises the stances of both leaders and protesters. While Arab leaders' discourse starts with a firm affirmation of the status quo and blames the minority few for the stirring of protests, using menace and threat, the public discourse starts with a broad call for demonstrations, with demands that are connected to the reality. However, as protests escalated, the leaders' speeches shifted and so did the protesters' discourse. Leaders showed a soft approach, acknowledging the protesters' demands and promising change. This was reflected in the way their discourse became more apologetic. In contrast, the protesters' discourse was upbeat and became very firm and explicit in its demands, as mirrored in the frequent use of the imperative.

The shift in discourse and strategies occurs in contexts of tension and conflict, where powerful actors often defend their actions and show a justified and united front, expressing their power and authority as key actors. However, as the tension increases and counter-arguments emerge, these powerful actors change strategy and lean towards lessening the tension and conceding to the opposition, be it public, media or politicians. This concession is often mirrored in the discourse of these actors. A tangible example to give here is the 2020 tension between the UK government and the public concerning A level results. Due to Covid-19, A level students were not able to sit exams, but the results for mock exams conducted by schools were submitted as alternative grades. The government processed these results and lowered the majority of them to avoid what they consider to be 'inflation of grades'. Lowering grades did not go well with students, teachers and parents, who campaigned against this action, calling for the government to reconsider their decision and reinstate teachers' original grades. Initially, the government showed no sign of reconsidering their decision and defended their action and the system, considering it robust and fair. However, as the campaign grew and much pressure was put on the government, the latter conceded that there was an error and that school teachers' original grades would be reinstated.

This change in decision was shaped by the discourse used by ministers who apologised for the stress and anxiety caused by this decision. The government U-turn supports our hypothesis that people in power often tend initially to strongly defend their own actions, but because of relentless pressure they negotiate and concede their positions. This change in decision and stance shapes and is shaped by the reality on the ground and the discourse employed. This supports our claim that discourse strategies of powerful actors during conflicts and tension do shift as the balance of power shifts.

Cognition in Arabic Political Discourse

Mental Processes in Arabic Political Speeches

Machin and Mayr (2012: 107) divided mental processes into three categories: '"cognition" (verbs of thinking, knowing or understanding), "affection" (verbs of liking, disliking or fearing) and "perception" (verbs of seeing, hearing or perceiving)'.

Adopting these categories in the analysis of political speeches will allow us an insight into 'the feelings or states of mind of certain participants' (Machin and Mayr 2012: 107). In the case of Arab leaders it will help us gain an insight into their emotions and mental status during one of the most recent turbulent periods in the history of Arab nations, a period which took everyone by surprise. Their speeches will help us understand their actions, reactions and decisions, as well as their position vis-à-vis the uprising.

In his last speech of the uprising, the late Ben Ali, former president of Tunisia, showed his mental state while recognising and understanding what was happening on the ground, as well as the motives behind the uprising. The following examples illustrate this.

Example 19

وأنا فهمتكم، فهمت الجميع: البطال، والمحتاج والسياسي واللي طالب مزيد من الحريات، فهمتكم، فهمتكم الكل، لكن الأحداث اللي جارية اليوم في بلادنا ما هيش متاعنا، والتخريب ما هوش من عادات التونسي، التونسي المتحضر، التونسي المتسامح.

I have understood you all, the jobless, the needy, and the political, all of those who are claiming more freedom. I have understood you. I have understood each one of you. But the events taking place in our country are not a part of us. Destruction is not part of the Tunisian tradition, the civilised and tolerant Tunisian.

(Ben Ali's speech, 13 January 2011)

إنني أعي هذه التطلعات المشروعة للشعب، وأعلم جيدا قدر همومه ومعاناته

I am aware of the legitimate aspirations of the people, and I know their concerns and suffering. (Mubarak's speech, 29 January 2011)

The above examples demonstrate Ben Ali's and Mubarak's cognitive status towards the uprisings. They both showed a good understanding of the situation and a recognition of the protesters' needs and demands. This process of understanding protesters' discontent is evident in Ben Ali's acknowledgement that he 'understood' their demands and needs. By reiterating protesters' different needs, Ben Ali sought to send out a message of acknowledgement and support, demonstrating therefore his awareness of the need of people from different walks of life. However, the repetition of phrases, such as 'I understood you', is very revealing as to his mental status. In Arabic, repetition is often employed to reinforce and emphasise a message, but in this context it is used as a plea for sympathy and support. This of course is very telling when considering Ben Ali's emotional status and feelings as a president at a very difficult time for him. It shows a degree of weakness and vulnerability which could be very challenging to his authority as the Arabic political culture associates power and authority with strong political leaders. However, Ben Ali's and Mubarak's cognitive phrases show their fragile emotional status. And this could be said to be the reason behind the shift in the discourse used as it departs from the tradition of top-down approach. One could also come to the conclusion that discourse shapes and is shaped by human emotions and feelings, irrespective of their position and status.

The above examples utilised different synonyms to express the same emotions and feelings of understanding, acknowledgement of the issue and awareness of what is happening.

The use of the three Arabic verbs أعي وأعلم وفهمتكم *a'ī wa a'lam wa fahimtukum (I know, I'm aware of and I understood you)* convey the same meaning of knowing and understanding, but differ in terms of register and eloquence. It seems that Mubarak used a high register to express his mental status, compared to Ben Ali, who used a lower register related to Tunisian colloquial Arabic. This shift to a local variation shows that Ben Ali was affected emotionally and used a low register to communicate with the wider Tunisians, maximising his chances of cutting through a large proportion of the Tunisian population, including those illiterate people who may not be able to access Modern Standard Arabic. However, others would interpret this shift as a sign of weakness, as MSA is often associated with education, authority and a level of intellect. By breaking this linguistic norm, most of the observers considered Ben Ali's move as a tactic to show that he was an ordinary citizen like Bouazzizi, whose action triggered the uprisings across Tunisia and the Arab world. While communication with ordinary people is a good approach, using a low register to communicate with Tunisians caused some eyebrows to rise as to the motives behind this strategy, which others considered a sign of desperation and the last throw of dice to rescue his presidency.

In the case of Mubarak, his high register gave him authority and portrayed him as the commander-in-chief, despite the widespread demonstrations. His choice of cognitive phrases such as أعي وأعلم / *aʿī wa aʿlam* (I know/ I'm aware of) shows that he was fully aware of the situation and the events surrounding him. His choice of these verbs was designed to persuade demonstrators that he had sufficient knowledge and insight into what was happening, without lowering the bar of the eloquence of his speech.

While leaders showed that they understood and acknowledged the situation in different degrees of Arabic register, their emotions and feelings were made explicit to their citizens. The following section will carefully examine the mental processes of Arab leaders through affection.

Affection in Arab Leaders' Political Discourse

During their speeches, leaders displayed mixed emotions as to what was happening at the beginning of the uprising. Initially, there was denial and condemnation of what was happening, laying the blame squarely on rogue individuals and 'mobs' whose aim was to create 'chaos and disorder'. However, as uprisings gathered momentum this attitude changed, and so did the mental status of Arab leaders. Following the heavy interference of the police and subsequent casualties, Arab leaders changed their discourse, showing sympathy with protesters and denouncing violence against them. The following are examples of this affection.

Example 20

تألمنا لسقوط ضحايا وتضرر أشخاص، وأنا أرفض أن يسقط المزيد بسبب تواصل العنف والنهب

We were saddened for the victims of these events and damage suffered by persons, and I refuse to see more victims as a result of the ongoing violence and looting.

وأسفي كبير كبير جدا، وعميق جدا، وعميق جدا

My sadness is deep. My sadness is deep and profound, very deep and very profound.

حزني وألمي كبيران

My sorrow and pain are great.

ونحب نؤكد أن العديد من الأمور لم تجر كيما حبيتها تكون

I would like to affirm that many things didn't work the way I wished.

(Above extracts from Ben Ali's speech, 13 January 2011)

وأسفت كل الأسف لما أسفرت عنه من ضحايا أبرياء من المتظاهرين وقوات الشرطة

I deeply regret the loss of innocent lives among protesters and police forces.

(Mubarak's speech, 28 January 2011)

وإذ نعرب عن بالغ أسفنا للوفيات والأضرار التي نجمت عن هذه الأحداث

We express our regret for the deaths and damage generated by these incidents.

(Ben Ali's speech, 10 January 2011)

نعيش معا أياما مؤلمة وأكثر ما يوجعنا هو الخوف الذي انتاب الأغلبية الكاسحة من المصريين

We are living together painful days and the most painful thing is the fear that affected the huge majority of Egyptians.

(Mubarak's speech, 2 February 2011)

The above examples express a degree of remorse and feeling of sadness to what had happened, as demonstrated in the following expressions: 'I deeply regret', 'we feel sad for the fall of casualties', 'our sadness . . .', 'I fear . . .'. Apart from the regret and expression of sadness, Arab leaders expressed fear of what was happening, fear for the future of their respective countries; fear for the security of their countries and fear for their own future.

Although it is not made clear, one could read from these speeches that the leaders' fear of the deteriorating security situation in their countries was a fear for their own future and positions, as the collapse of security would lead to the collapse of their own rule – which is what happened eventually. However, their speeches focus on the people and the impact the lack of security may have on their position as leaders. So by utilising expressions of affection such as fear, regret, sadness, these leaders sought to align themselves with the wider public. The use of attributes such as 'sad', 'sadness', 'regret' are designed to show the leaders' state of mind and well-being, and reflect their sympathy for what was happening.

Mental Process and Expressions of Perception

The feeling of affection, described above, coupled with the leaders' perception of how things were progressing is very revealing indeed. It not only shows the leaders' emotions and feelings, but also depicts their mental processes as they witnessed these uprisings unfolding, as in the following examples.

Example 21

لقد تابعت أولا بأول التظاهرات وما نادت به

I have been closely monitoring the protests and what they were asking for.

(Mubarak's speech, 29 January 2011)

ونحن نواصل الإصغاء إلى مشاغل الجميع ونسعى إلى معالجة الوضعيات الجماعية والفردية

We continue to be attentive to the concerns of all. We are working to address the collective and individual situations.

(Ben Ali's speech, 10 January 2011)

The above examples demonstrate the leaders' perception of what was happening through verbs and expressions of perception. The use of لقد تابعت أولا بأول التظاهرات *laqad tābaʻtu Awalan bi awalin attaẓāhurāt* (*I have been closely monitoring the protests*), ونحن نواصل الإصغاء إلى *wa naḥnu nuwāṣilu al-iṣghāʼa ilā* (*we continue to listen*); شاهدنا *shāhadnā* (*we saw*) display a sense of anxiety exemplified in verbs such as 'we monitored the situation closely'. This suggests that the leaders were in full control and were closely monitoring what was happening, but it also expresses a sense of fear and anxiety. The use of these expressions is intended to show their authority in order to erode the protesters' confidence and deter those who might be considering joining the protests, but this strategy failed and the protests continued, regardless of the last-minute speeches, some of which were full of emotion and feelings of empathy.

The above examples are concrete evidence of the mental state of these leaders and their emotions as protests grew and gathered momentum. While they show a sense of authority and command, they also express a degree of fragility and vulnerability as things started to derail.

Conclusion

This chapter has explored the discursive strategies used by Arab leaders and the Arab public in the context of the Arab Spring. It has been established that Arab leaders made use of a wide range of strategies following the change of circumstances during the Arab Spring. It is evident from the analysis that a shift was witnessed in leaders' discourses as events progressed and social and political dynamics changed. Arab leaders showed a degree of flexibility and conciliatory discourse throughout the Arab Spring. Although their discourses started with rejecting and denying the causes of the Arab Spring, protests increased and were widely supported. This induced Arab leaders to recognise the situation and offer concessions to calm the protests and gain a return to normality. However, their moderate discourses and their concessions did nothing to stop the waves of protests that swept Arab streets. They failed to appease protesters and eventually decided to resign their positions, with the exception of Gaddafi who continued to fight for his position until he was killed by people of his own country. The Arab public, on the other hand, witnessed a strength in their position. Their voice became stronger and so did their discourse of reprimand and criticism of their leaders. The Arabic political taboos of loyalty and allegiance to leaders were broken.

6

Arabic Political Discourse and Politeness Strategies

This chapter will examine the concept of politeness in the context of the Arab Spring. It will look at the politeness strategies in different speeches, statements and slogans, examining shifts in these strategies and discourses. This chapter will provide an explanation for these changes by contextualising them in the wider social, political and cultural context.

Politeness and Arabic Discourse

Language is a means of communication and interaction, through which people express themselves to others. Some are direct, while others are indirect. Speakers aim to be polite and cooperative and to maintain a positive face. In the words of Blum-Kulka and Hamo (2011: 152), 'for Brown and Levinson politeness is the intentional, strategic behaviour of an individual that is meant to satisfy self and other *face wants* in case of threat'. The desire to satisfy and maintain a positive self-image motivates and contributes to a meaningful social interaction, where the positive face is maintained.

Similarly, Fraser (1975: 13) defines politeness as 'a property associated with an utterance in which, according to the hearer, the speaker has neither exceeded any rights nor failed to fulfil any obligations'. In dealing with politeness strategies, we'll adopt some of Brown and Levinson's strategies, which are:

1. Bald On-record: this occurs when the speaker shows no desire to minimise the threat to the hearer's face. The use of imperatives in the Arabic context, for instance, could be considered face-threatening.
2. Positive Politeness: this is designed to minimise the threat to the hearer's positive face by recognising the hearer's needs.
3. Negative Politeness: this is 'the basic claim to territories, personal preserves, rights to non-distraction – i.e., to freedom of action and freedom from imposition'. It is the desire of the speaker to maintain a safe distance from others.
4. Indirect Strategy: the speaker often hints or uses connotations to deliver a message without being direct in their request.

While in the Arabic culture positive politeness is the most prevalent, as speakers are usually very keen to be positive and polite, the slogans of the Arab Spring protesters show the opposite. Protesters used bald on-record strategies and were direct in their requests without fear of embarrassing or upsetting the hearer. In the next section, we will analyse some of the slogans to demonstrate how politeness, which is part and parcel of the Arabic culture, has been flouted in most cases, and given way to impolite discourse. It is part of the Arabic culture that speakers demonstrate a positive communication strategy, where the self and the other are respected and represented positively. Elders and people in power are treated with respect and politeness, and leaders are expected to be supported and defended at all costs. This culture of respect and allegiance is deeply rooted in the Arabic culture and any deviation from this could be considered a sign of breaking cultural norms. The significance of maintaining a positive face is highly desirable in the Arabic culture. In pre Arab Spring demonstrations and protests, for instance, leaders were always praised and hailed as heroes, while the brunt of the anger would be directed at governments or ministers, but even this was done in a very reasonable manner. However, all these traditional norms witnessed a shift during the Arab Spring of 2011. The politeness strategy of respecting leaders and elders has been replaced with a culture of reprimand and accountability, suggesting therefore a new shift in the Arabic culture and its discourse, as will be demonstrated in the coming sections.

Slur in the Arabic Culture

In the Arabic culture, insulting someone is regarded as abhorrent and a sign of disrespect and impoliteness. The action is often blamed on the family for not bringing up their children in accordance with the norms of the society. This falls within the family code of practice, where children and young people are supposed to be taught to respect leaders and elders, as well as parents. By rebelling against these norms, young people demonstrate their rejection of the family and society's code of practice, which is part of the cultural norm of most Arab countries. Families are often held responsible for their children's action. In the Arab leaders' speeches there are numerous examples of leaders calling upon families to interfere and stop their children from participating in protests or taking up arms against the state and the regime. The following is an example from Gaddafi's speeches:

Example 1

من بكرة ؛ . . .كل النساء اللائي عندهن أولاد يطلعن بسرعة، والتي عندها أخ ؛ تطلع بسرعة، والتي عندها قريبها والتي حبيبها ؛ تطلع بسرعة. والرجال الذين عندهم أولاد ؛ يطلعوا بسرعة، والأمهات والأخوات والبنات ؛ كلهن يطلعن بسرعة إلى الشوارع.

From tomorrow (. . .), all wome, who have boys get out quickly, those who have brothers, get out quickly, and those who have a relative or lover, get out quickly. Men who have boys get out quickly; mothers, sisters and girls, all of you get out to the street.

(Gaddafi's speech, 22 February 2011)

As the above example demonstrates, the family has social responsibility and authority and this is deeply rooted in the social norms of Arab societies; parents and leaders remain responsible for the actions of their own family, and they are looked upon very badly if their children do not behave and act in accordance with the established norms. Their discourses should largely adhere to these norms, some of which are loyalty and allegiance to leaders.

The deviation from these norms could be considered a sign of rebellion. However, during the Arab Spring, reprimanding, belittling and insulting leaders was very explicit and replaced the long-standing culture of respect and tolerance.

Although it could be argued that this rebellion against social norms was temporary and came as a response to exceptional circumstances, the scope of this rebellion reveals the level of empowerment and awareness of protesters, as exemplified in their slogans, some of which were very critical of leaders. Protesters' and, indeed, citizens' desire for change continued to trigger protests and demonstrations, which in turn highlighted the plight of demonstrators and their desire for a real change.

The following slogan is a good example of this shift in the discourse of protesters as it includes orders and commands in the form of imperative* ارحل: كفاية عليك جدو وبابا *irḥal: kifāya ʿalayk jaddū wa bābā* (Leave: enough: father and grandfather). This slogan, which summarises Mubarak's long reign, is a tangible example of the protesters' defiance and determination to express their own demands and rights. The protester's slogan here indicates that he has known no other president in his life, except Mubarak, considering him a father and a grandfather, an indication of the long term of his presidency. Although the slogan looks innocent in its content and includes no reprimand, it presupposes the implicit criticism of being a president for so long. By referring to Mubarak as a father and grandfather, the protester sought to emphasise the president's long reign, explicitly requesting his 'departure', using the popular verb *irḥal* (leave).

While Egyptian protesters were very moderate in their slogans, Libyan protesters were very audacious. The following example demonstrates this vividly (Figure 6.1).

The slogan seen in Figure 6.1, which calls Gaddafi a criminal, is very courageous. The protester, who holds the image while showing his face, calls for the departure of Gaddafi, using the popular Arabic imperative verb of *irḥal*. This is unprecedented in the history of Arabic protests as the default is

---

* Available at <http://arab-librarians.blogspot.com/2011/02/blog-post.html> (last accessed 8 April 2021).

Figure 6.1 Protester holding image of Gaddafi demanding his departure

to respect leaders, but calling a leader a 'criminal' is a clear shift from a passive discourse to a discourse of empowerment and emancipation, which is visible in this type of slogan. It would have been unthinkable a few years back to call an Arab leader a 'criminal', a very high charge, which broke Arabic norms. However, the Arab Spring has empowered protesters and opened the door for such a change in discourse.

Two key issues emerged in this regard: the emancipation of the self from the fear and intimidation that some protesters may felt subject to, and the realisation of protesters' rights to hold their leaders accountable for what they do. The second issue is that whenever there is collective solidarity, there is a change in discourse to reflect this solidarity, and in the case of the Arab Spring this is exemplified by the use of the binary Us vs Them discourse, discussed in Chapter 4. By creating this binary, protesters have managed to position themselves as the opposition, rejecting the status quo and calling for political, economic and social change, including the overthrow of some of the leaders, as the example seen in Figure 6.2 demonstrates.

Figure 6.2 Yemeni protesters calling for the departure of the president

Figure 6.2 shows slogans that demand the departure of the late Yemeni leader, Abdullah Saleh. These slogans are similar to those of Egypt and Tunisia. The same slogans were reiterated in different protests across different Arabic countries, with key messages such as 'leave'.

Some of these slogans adopt a harsh tone and style, showing that the days of fear and intimidation have long gone. This suggests that protesters have become bolder in their slogans, targeting and challenging their leaders. Yet again, this is a clear example of the shift in discourse in the Arabic context. This shift would not have happened were it not for their collective empowerment, coupled with a full awareness of their rights and obligations. This collective endeavour and political awareness instilled confidence in the protesters who took on their own leaders and continued to call for their overthrow in different languages and in a variety of ways, as will be discussed in the following section.

Politeness in Multilingual Slogans

While Arabic was the main language used for protests, other languages were also used to express concerns. For instance, the slogans seen in Figure 6.3 were written in different languages, but they contain the same message delivered in Arabic slogans. Again, the discontent of the protesters has been expressed in different languages, appealing to different audiences. The use of English

Figure 6.3 Multilingual call for the departure of Mubarak

and French could be said to have been designed to alert the international community to the protesters' demands. Figure 6.3 demonstrates this vividly.

As mentioned earlier, the use of multilingual slogans is very revealing indeed; it shows that these revolutions were led by the middle-class youth who have mastered different languages. In Figure 6.3, Modern Standard Arabic, French and English have been used to call for the departure of Mubarak.

Multilingual slogans also show the level of criticism levelled against leaders, which demonstrates the shift in politeness strategies employed by protesters who have resorted to belittling, reprimanding and holding leaders accountable for their actions. These unprecedented social and cultural changes stand in direct contrast to the deeply rooted values of respect, loyalty and allegiance to leaders.

Thus, the above examples demonstrate the protesters' shift in discursive practices and attitudes towards their own leaders. In the slogans seen in Figure 6.3, protesters used the imperative and called on Mubarak to leave in different languages. The analysis has also shown a clear shift in terms of politeness strategies when addressing Arab leaders. The fact that protesters used 'lā buda' (you have to), 'degage' (leave), 'go out' (leave) shows their determination and commitment to removing Mubarak from power. This shift mirrors the political, social and cultural shift in Arab society during the Arab Spring. It also shows the level of political and social activism which has swept Arab countries, with vibrant and dynamic protesters opposing the status quo in their countries and calling for the resignation of their leaders. This dynamism has changed the protesters' discourse from that of recipients and consumers to producers of discourse, but this production is underpinned by political and social changes, which found their way into these slogans.

Breaking Social and Cultural Taboos

As mentioned above, there are certain cultural taboos that were religiously adhered to and respected, and any attempt to break or violate these taboos could be considered a rebellious act against society and its cultural norms. However, some of these rules have been violated, and the traditional displays of loyalty and allegiance have been replaced with those of rebellion, with leaders being reprimanded, named and shamed with all sorts of negative labels. The strategy of maintaining a positive face for the self and the other has been replaced with a strategy of negativity and reprimand. The Arab Spring slogans are a good example of this shift in discourse and behaviour in the Arab world. The use of slogans such as *irḥal* (leave), for instance, is a clear violation of the Arabic culture, as the use of the imperative towards elders and leaders is associated with disrespect and contempt. The following examples from the Arab Spring clearly demonstrate another shift in discourse and politeness strategies in the Arabic culture.

Example 2

"ثورة ثورة.. حتى النصر"

Revolution until triumph.

"الشعب يريد محاكمة الرئيس القاتل"

People would like to bring to trial the dictator (murderer/killer president).

" محاكمات فورية للمسؤولين عن قتل شهداء الثورة، محاكمات عاجلة للفاسدين وسارقي ثروات الوطن."

Immediate trial for those responsible for the killing of the martyrs of the revolution, and for looting the wealth of the country.

"وصامدون حتى يرحل الطاغية"

Persevering until the downfall of the tyrant.

"ويسقط الفرعون والزبانية"

Down with pharaoh and tyrant.

"يسقط الطاغوت"

Down with the tyrant.

"وصامدون حتى يرحل الطاغية"

Persevering until the downfall of the tyrant.

الحرية تنادي فلبي النداء

Answer the call for liberty.

أخرج فإن الفساد ظهر في البر والبحر، اللهم وفق كل حر على تحرير هذا البلد المنكوب

Take to the street to demonstrate against the corruption, which has plagued the nation. We should liberate this afflicted society.

..وهو أسوأ نظام في التاريخ، وربما أسوأ من فرعون. لقد كان لفرعون كرامة لكن هذا الرجل وأزلامه لا كرامة لهم.

And his [Mubarak's] is the worst regime in the history of Egypt, it is worse than Pharaoh's. At least, Pharaoh had some dignity, but the current regime and its henchmen have none.

The above slogans mark a clear shift in the deeply rooted politeness strategies in the Arabic culture. The fact that these slogans contain harsh criticism of some Arab leaders, calling upon them 'to leave', 'to resign' and 'to be brought to justice' is a new phenomenon in the Arabic culture. Naming them 'murders', 'oppressors' and 'tyrants' shows the scale and scope of the fallout, and also the cultural shift shaped by these slogans. From an Arabic perspective, protesters have used an impolite strategy to express their feelings of discontent and resentment of the status quo. Such feelings have given way to new politeness strategies, which depart from the long-held traditional ones, mentioned above.

To sum up, it appears that the long-held tradition of respect has been dismantled and replaced with strategies of criticism and reprimand, deviating therefore from the long tradition of respect for leaders. This shift in discourse could be attributed to the shift in the social and political landscape of Arabic countries. As the scope and scale of protests gathered momentum, this emboldened protesters and empowered them to take on their own leaders, which they did, judging by the wide range of negative slogans directed at leaders (Figures 6.1, 6.2 and 6.3), and the subsequent resignation and flight of some of these leaders.

So What was Behind this Abrupt Change, and Why Was It Now?

Answering these questions requires further analysis of the social and political landscape. Historically, and after the independence of most Arab countries, there was always a dominant party that had ruled for years. With the hegemony of a single party system, Arab citizens had become used to certain narratives and discourses from these party leaders as well as governments. These discourses consisted of legitimising, supporting and promoting the social and political activities undertaken by governments and officials, while the dissenting voice in some countries remained muted. While economic grievances remain one of the reasons for such uprisings, protesters expressed a desire for social and political reforms. As protests grew in scope and demand, protesters became very confident and empowered to take on their own leaders in an unprecedented turn in the history of Arab societies. So this 'violation' of the cultural and political norms could be said to have been generated by the emancipation and empowerment of these protesters whose voice was marginalised by the governing elite. While some would argue that this marginalisation was unintentional because of the political and social systems in place, others continued to lay the blame on governments.

Whichever side of the argument you may be on, the fact is that these protests were triggered by decades of economic malfunction in some of these countries. This leads us to conclude that social and political change can be generated by awareness and empowerment of key stakeholders who have the desire and willingness to change. This empowerment, and political and social changes, shape and are shaped by discourses (Fairclough 1992).

Politeness in Leaders' Speeches

The analysis of Arab leaders' speeches during the Arab Spring suggests that most of them employed a strategy of positive politeness, thereby ensuring that their speeches were received positively without any face threatening. Using positive attributes to describe protesters, recognise their rights to protests, and acknowledge their demands, are good examples of showing willingness to respond positively. Although some negative attributes were used in some leaders' speeches, these were directed at a 'minority of protesters' who were accused of perpetuating 'acts of violence'. While some Arab leaders hoped to keep the majority of protesters on their side by showing willingness to listen and respond positively to their demands, their face-threatening behaviour, especially when addressing some groups during the protests, turned other protesters against them.

However, as we continue to examine speeches of different leaders, one cannot help but notice that Arab leaders adopted different strategies in addressing their people. For instance, Gaddafi's strategy was bald on-record and he threatened to use violence against protesters, if they do not cease their actions. His directness and his negative attribution to protesters is a clear example of this as the following examples demonstrate.

Example 3

نحن لم نستخدم القوة بعد ، والقوة تساند الشعب الليبي . إذا وصلت الأمور إلى حد استخدام القوة ، سنستخدمها وفقا للقانون الدولي ووفقا للدستور الليبي و القوانين الليبية . من الغد أو من الليلة ، تخرجون كل المدن الليبية والقرى الليبية والواحات الليبية التي هي تحب (معمر القذافي)، لأن «معمر القذافي» هو المجد .

We have not used force yet. And [armed] force is to support the Libyan people. If it reaches a point where we have to use force, then we will use it, in accordance with international law and the Libyan constitution and laws. Starting from tomorrow, by God, starting tonight even, all Libyan cities, towns and oases that love Muammar Qaddafi should go out – because Muammar Qaddafi is glory.

(Gaddafi's speech, 22 February 2011)

Gaddafi's politeness strategies, characterised by its bald on-record directness, could be blamed for the heightened tensions with protesters, which escalated protests and ended up in confrontation. Gaddafi's impolite style was mirrored in his very negative attributes and his desire to criticise and infuriate protesters through the use of negative attributes, some of which were very offensive. But one could argue here that this directness in Gaddafi's politeness strategies came at a time when protesters had defied the state, challenging Gaddafi's authority and power.

What can be observed from Gaddafi's speeches is that he was direct in his style and tone and his semantics constituted a departure from what is known in Arabic as '*khiṭāb al-qā'id*' (the speech of the leader), which is often designed to appeal to the nation, and promote policies and strategies in a more structured and acceptable discourse. Phrases such as 'dear citizens', 'my sons and daughters', 'my children', 'our children' are often employed to appeal to the nation and show respect as well as appreciation to the audience. This genre of discourse is very rigid in its structure and often very carefully scripted to show the authority of the leader. Compared to other Arab leaders, Gaddafi violated some aspects of Arabic political speech/discourse, both in terms of the structure, substance and the use of lexis or semantics. His speeches departed from the rigid structure of traditional speeches as the language used does not reflect the authority of a leader who is supposed to conduct himself in a professional and respectful manner. The context of the delivery and production of speeches are often vital to determining the type and nature of discourse. One could also argue here that in the context of conflict, speakers are compelled to adopt different formats and structures, which reflect the reality and feeling of the speaker. These sentiments find their way to the text of these speeches, and this explains the angry tone of some of them, notably Gaddafi's, contrary to other leaders' speeches which were more balanced in their approach, despite the difficult and unusual circumstances under which they were delivered.

The question remains: why this disparity in leaders' speeches? While it is very challenging to give a comprehensive answer to a pressing question, this disparity could be attributed to the character of individual leaders. In his speeches, Gaddafi described himself as the revolutionary man whose main objective was to defend and protect Libya from foreign aggression, little did he know that the main opposition consisted of his own citizens who protested against his rule and eventually brought him down.

Apart from politeness or lack of it, it could be said that Arabic political speeches during times of conflict adopt different strategies, reflecting the speakers' characters, their ambitions, services and emotions. Apart from Gaddafi's strategies discussed above, other speeches have displayed a level of flexibility, where conversation and negotiation with citizens took place. For instance, Ben Ali's speeches are good examples of positively responding to protesters' demands by showing signs of a willingness to change things and act on protesters' 'legitimate demands'. This could be described as a moderate discourse, where a window of discussion and conversation with citizens was opened, but was rejected outright by protesters who emerged to have the upper hand in what was happening.

Politeness and the Tribe

What is striking about the different political speeches delivered during the Arab Spring is the intertextual reference to historical glories and the significance of the national heroes as well as tribal leaders. Speeches displayed a very polite tone, full of praise for historical events, leaders and martyrs. It could be argued here that this is part of the leaders' strategy of showing respect and appreciation for the history of tribes and their leaders, and is designed to allure some of the tribes to support the regime. In the context of Libya, for instance, the use of attributes such as أبطال '*Abṭāl*' (heroes), أوفياء *Awfiyā*' (loyal), شهداء '*shuhadā*' (martyr), أمجاد '*Amjād*' (glories), أهل الكرم '*ahal al-karam*' (people of generosity) is intended to show a positive face towards tribal leaders and communities who have contributed to the defence of Libya. This discourse of praise and commendation was produced to persuade tribes, communities and their leaders that the speaker had nothing but admiration for them and their ancestors. This politeness strategy, which springs from the Arabic culture of glorifying and paying tribute to key heroes and communities, could be designed to establish a truce with those tribes/regions that rose against their leaders. By recognising the tribes' history and their leaders, speakers expressed their respect and sought to maintain face. In Gaddafi's speeches, for instance, he specifically named tribes and historical Libyan icons in a move to show his admiration for their contribution to the history of Libya.

Example 4

نحن أجدر بليبيا من تلك الجرذان وأولئك المأجورين ، من هم هؤلاء المأجورين المدفوع لهم الثمن من المخابرات الأجنبية ؟!، (. . .) هؤلاء ليس عندهم قبائل ، فالقبائل الليبية ؛ قبائل شريفة ومجاهدة ومكافحة ، تتقاطر عليّ في هذا الشهر .
كل القبائل من البطنان ؛ إلى الجبل الغربي ؛ إلى فزان، كلهم يهتفون هتافا واحدا . . . ، إيطاليا قبّلت يد ابن الشهيد شيخ الشهداء «عمر المختار» ، وهذا مجد ما بعده مجد ليس لـ «المنفه» فقط ؛ ولا للبطنان فقط ؛ ولا لبنغازي فقط ؛ بل لليبيين وللعرب وللمسلمين

We are more worthy of Libya than those rats and hired people. Who are those hired people? Those people do not belong to any tribe; because Libyan tribes are honourable fighters. They have all come to me this month.
All those tribes from Butnan, to the Nafusa Mountains, to Fezzan, they are all chanting the same slogan (. . .). Italy kissed the hands of the son of the martyr – Omar Mukhtar – and this is such a glory that no glory compares to it, and not just to the Maafah tribe, not to the Butnan, and not for Benghazi only, but for all Libyans, Arabs and Muslims.

(Gaddafi's speech, 22 February 2011)

In the Arabic culture, this type of recognition is considered a gesture of politeness. Tribes remain the cornerstone of some Arabic countries and any disrespect to them and their leaders could lead to confrontations with governments. Politeness is very significant here as it ensures that tribes and their constituents are in support of the state and its leader. This explains the different politeness strategies displayed during the Arab Spring, the most popular of which is the narrative that promotes the glorious history, the 'martyrs' who have sacrificed themselves for the independence of their nations. This genre of politeness strategy is intended to win over tribes and communities, but more importantly it sought to link the present to the past, with the hope of rallying support and uniting different communities under the umbrella of one nation and leader. However, as mentioned earlier, speakers and leaders displayed different politeness strategies when addressing protests and protesters. They often used unpopular terminologies and expressions that violate Arabic culture ethics and norms of addressing the other. Gaddafi's speeches embody clear examples of this type of 'offensive' lexis, directed at protesters who have been labelled as 'mice', 'cockroaches', 'drug users' and 'traitors'.

As mentioned above, Gaddafi's strategy of appealing to tribes by recognising their historical past was intended to drum up support and rally some of these tribes to combat the growing protests. His praise of the tribes and key families was designed to give them the prominence to be able to support and stand by his side. His repetition of 'family' several times in his speeches was aimed at elevating and highlighting the significance of those families, with the hope that his appeal could rally them behind his leadership; however, despite the praise and acknowledgement of their status, some of these families could not turn the tide of protests directed at him.

Discussion

Two main politeness strategies emerged in the leaders' speeches during the Arab Spring. The first strategy was one of maintaining face and being positive when addressing the nation, the tribe, communities or leaders. This was often well articulated and a variety of Arabic politeness expressions were used for this purpose. The second strategy was the use of negative face and bald on-record strategy, mainly directed at those protesters who explicitly and visibly called for the downfall of the leaders. We have given examples from Gaddafi's speeches, in which he was explicitly critical of protesters, using some very negative expressions and phrases.

The strategy of divide and rule as reflected in leaders' politeness strategies backfired to a certain extent, as protests continued to call for the resignation of the leaders, even at a time when leaders sought to show praise and a positive face towards protesters.

What does all this tell us about Arabic politeness in the context of conflict? We learnt that speakers used two different strategies. The first was designed to maintain and gain face by showing signs of cooperation and collaboration with recipients. In the case of the Arab Spring, this appeal was directed to different religious groups, tribes, elders and communities, as they are regarded key stakeholders in Arab societies. The second strategy was confrontational and negative, and directed against some protesters, mainly those accused of steering protests. So one could argue here that at a time of tension and conflict in the Arabic context, politeness – a very deeply rooted value – was flouted, violated and no longer tagged to the Arabic culture.

Antonyms and Politeness in Leaders' Speeches

According to Palmer (1983: 94), 'the term ANTONYMY is used for "oppositeness of meaning"; words that are opposite are ANTONYMS. Antonymy is often thought of as the opposite of synonymy' (Palmer 1983: 94).

One of the main characteristics of politeness strategies in Arab leaders' speeches is the use of antonyms to express their opposition to protesters, while acknowledging and recognising the legitimate right of others. It has also been used to show the positive self and the negative other. Take the example of Gaddafi. He shows positive face when he talks about the history of Libya, its sacrifices, its heroes and martyrs, showing great respect and admiration for these people. His praise for Libyan heroes and martyrs reflects his positive strategy of appealing to the Libyan people in an attempt to rally his supporters. On the other hand, he used antonyms to discredit those he considers to be 'mobs' and 'foreign agents', employing therefore a strategy of reprimand and criticism. He used lexical items such as 'mobs', 'drug addicts', 'mice', 'cockroaches', 'traitors', 'foreign agents' to describe this group of people, contrary to the positive lexis used when describing his supporters. So, it could be argued here that antonyms have been used to polarise protesters. We have seen in previous sections and chapters that Arab leaders resorted to the strategy of divide and rule, which failed in most cases, as evidenced by the continuation of protests and subsequent overthrow of some leaders.

Why Antonyms in Leaders' Speeches?

There is no clear-cut answer to this question, but it could be interpreted as a strategy to show negative attribution to the other. For instance, in some of Gaddafi's speeches he was very positive and full of praise for those who supported him, but used antonyms to negatively describe the opposition and protesters who targeted him.

As I write this book, a second wave of protests has erupted in other Arab countries. Widespread protests in Algeria, Lebanon and Sudan continue to call for the resignation of their presidents. The leaders of these countries have adopted the same strategy of recognising protesters' legitimate demands, but used antonyms to critique the opposition and what they consider a minority of 'bad apples', who have been accused of instigating these protests. As for protesters, they have adopted the same approach and strategy as used in the first wave of protests. Their slogans are identical to the 2011 slogans, but their tone appears to be more balanced and less aggressive than those used in the Libyan protests and others. The slogans call for the resignation of their regimes, but they break no taboos, maintaining positive face for the president, ensuring a discourse of dignity and respect.

Conclusion

In this chapter, we have examined the concept of politeness in the context of the Arab Spring. We have analysed different speeches and protesters' slogans, concluding that different politeness strategies were used during the Arab Spring. It has also been concluded that there was a shift in the use of politeness in the protesters' speeches, suggesting therefore a shift from the long-established Arabic culture of respecting leaders and elders to a more questioning and reprimanding style. This shift, as explained above, stems from the level of empowerment and awareness of the protesters, which replaced feelings and attitudes of fear and caution.

Apart from the strategies used and the identified shifts in the politeness strategies of the Arab public, there was a degree of discrepancy as to the leaders' use of politeness strategies. It appears that Gaddafi was very direct and bald on-record compared to other Arab leaders. His criticism of those behind the protests was very direct and explicit. The same applies to other leaders' speeches, where there was direct criticism for certain anonymous groups who had been accused of instigating the protests.

7

Arabic Islamic Political Discourse

In Chapters 4 and 5 we examined the micro- and macro-analysis of the discourse of the Egyptian, Libyan and Tunisian leaders, as well as public discourse, while in Chapter 6 we studied politeness strategies of the leaders and protesters. In this chapter we will examine the discourse of Islamic parties post Arab Spring. The landslide victory of most Islamic parties in post Arab Spring elections in Egypt and Tunisia took many observers by surprise and revealed their popularity in these countries. The study of their discourse will facilitate a good understanding of the dialectical relationship between them and the wider public. Since these parties form or have formed part of the government in these countries, we consider them part of the political system. The question to be answered here is: has the social and political landscape led to a change in the discourse of Islamic parties in these countries? Answering this question necessitates a thorough examination of the discourse of these parties post Arab Spring. A comprehensive analysis of their discourses will be offered with a clear focus on the main aspects and features, which constitute these changes. The chapter focuses on Al-Nahda and the Freedom and Justice Party (FJP) in Tunisia and Egypt respectively. A CDA approach, mainly Fairclough's (1995a) framework of language and social change, has been adopted for the analysis of the data, which has been collected from speeches, statements and slogans made by these parties.

The Arab Spring and Islamic Parties

The Arab Spring has changed the fabric of Arab societies and their political landscape. Islamists who had been marginalised from political life with a very limited say in the running of their countries, found themselves contributing to the debate and discussion. This post Arab Spring popularity resulted from disillusion with the old elite, parties and faces that had held power for so long, offering little to improve their livelihood. Islamists were seen to have a clean hand, to be transparent and anti-corruption. This was a valid reason for people in Tunisia, Morocco and Egypt to overwhelmingly elect some of these parties. In Morocco, for instance, and following the Moroccan constitutional reform, the Justice and Development Party (PJD) secured the majority of votes in the legislative elections, which saw the first Islamic party leader in Morocco to lead the government. The PJD is considered a moderate Islamic party which campaigned for social justice and anti-corruption. This victory was unprecedented in the history of Moroccan politics, as it revealed a wider Moroccan feeling and attitude towards a moderate Islamic party, which has shown willingness to co-exist with other progressive parties (i.e. liberals, leftists, etc.). In fact, the Moroccan system of government, post 2011, has been praised by many political observers and has been considered a model for co-existence, where parties, irrespective of their political agendas agree on a programme that meets citizens' aspirations.

In Tunisia, the Al-Nahda Party won a landslide victory in the first parliamentary elections to be held in Tunisia, post the demise of Ben Ali (Amin 2012). Their victory, which was free and democratic, made Al-Nahda the first Islamic party to form the government in the history of Tunisia. However, their celebration did not last long as they had to hand over power and called for fresh elections, following protests concerning the state of the economy. The recalled election saw them lose their first place to Nidaa' Tunis, a coalition of several parties, but this did not deter Al-Nahda from taking part in the new government as a minority party.

In Egypt, Islamic parties won a landslide victory (Amin 2012) and Morsi was elected as President of the Republic, but his victory was short-lived and his term ended abruptly following demonstrations that led to a military interference after 'Morsi was given an ultimatum offering his resignation, but refused and a coup by the army became a reality' (Seeberg and Shteiwi 2014: 3–4). The ousting of Morsi met with a wall of silence from some Western countries, which was interpreted by others as implicit endorsement of the coup, and this was reflected in statements such as, 'the EU did not officially name the ousting of Morsi a coup' (Seeberg and Shteiwi 2014: 4).

'The military coup' in Egypt set the democratic process back and it had visible repercussions on the political and media landscape. The plurality and dissonance of perspectives were replaced with monolithic parties and media outlets, which restricted discussions and limited plurality. A repetition of the situation post-1952 revolution could be seen in the post-2013 military coup. Post 1952 saw 'the pluralistic and vibrant media scene . . . replaced by a much more monolithic and restrictive media environment after Egypt achieved independence' (Khamis 2011: 1160). Since the military coup of 2013, political activism and the media in general have been very strictly regulated, resulting in limited freedom of expression and political plurality in Egypt. In other Arab countries, the demise of regimes has paved the way for a multiplicity of political views from different groups. This has contributed to the emergence of 'alternative and opposition public spheres' (Jakubowicz 2007: 137) 'which reflect a wide array of conflicting currents of thoughts, including leftists, secularists, Islamists, and feminists, among others' (Khamis 2011: 1171). This diversity has itself contributed to a rich media landscape, which was absent in the past. While this diversity is very important for a healthy democratic society, it could be risky in an insecure environment with poor governance as this could create competitive agendas, often leading to violent confrontations because of competing views and perspectives. Take for instance Libya post Gaddafi, which descended into chaos giving rise to some very extreme groups, culminating in armed confrontations. It has also contributed to the creation of mini states, with tribal and regional affiliations.

The scenario of post 1952 in Egypt seems to be repeating itself post 2013. Pre 2013, which started with 'the granting of a relatively wider margin of freedom and pluralization in both the political and media domains, ended with very strict and restrictive measures against his political opponents and their publications' (Khamis 2011: 1160). These restrictive measures, which were visible post 1952, as Khamis has asserted, were duplicated in the post-2013 military takeover.

The emergence of some Islamic parties as dominant post Arab Spring took most observers by surprise; observers who devoted time and energy to analysing the new political and social landscape in some of these countries. The speeches of the leaders of Islamic parties were monitored and their actions were closely analysed in order to determine their political ideologies and their impact on what have been characterised as 'secularist states'. Different opinions have been expressed in relation to the outcome of post Arab Spring democratic elections. There are those who have encouraged the process and expressed their desire to see the process take its course, and those who have displayed concern as to how these Islamic parties will interact with other parties and the international community. The prejudices of 'the dogmatic nature' of these parties and the assumption of their inability to co-exist with others has paved the way to debates about the conformity of Islamic parties agendas with democracy.

The victory of the Al-Nahda party and the Muslim Brotherhood in Tunisia and Egypt respectively has induced others to delve into the ideological orientation of these parties and the impact of the implementation of their ideologies. Leaders' speeches have been monitored and analysed closely to determine the direction of travel for these parties. In this chapter we will examine some of these speeches and, where possible, compare and contrast them with pre Arab Spring speeches for the same leader. This comparison will allow us to examine any shift in discourse, and consider whether these leaders moderated their speeches once in power. Fairclough's (1995b) framework will be adopted for the study of these speeches. A textual analysis of some of these discourses will be conducted and contextualised in relation to the ideologies and policies of these parties.

The Arab Spring: Al-Nahda Discursive Practices

Al-Nahda: A Historical Background

The arrival of the Al-Nahda party onto the political scene in Tunisia was unprecedented, given the long history of its marginalisation. Its victory in the first democratic election took everyone by surprise, both inside and outside Tunisia. By securing the majority, Al-Nahda had to form the first Islamic government in the history of Tunisia and North Africa. However, this government was short-lived and had to resign following protests on its performance, although some would argue that these protests were political and were staged to bring down Al-Nahda. However, Al-Nahda's political moderation, both in terms of policies and actions on the ground, has allowed the party to continue to play a vital role in the Tunisian political landscape. This moderation is manifested in the party's discourse of *al-wasaṭiyya*, which reflects a moderate stance, contrary to other Islamic parties who have rigidly adopted a traditional Islamic political discourse. In this section, the speeches of Al-Nahda leaders will be examined to reveal their type and nature, and the shift of their discourses, if any.

Despite the exile and repression of some Islamic parties, their willingness to participate in the political landscape and their desire to lead governments remained strong throughout the 2000s. This was evident in the strong performance of the Egyptian Muslim Brothers in the 2005 legislative elections (Covatorta and Merone 2015: 29). The 2012 parliamentary and presidential elections were further evidence of this surge of Islamic parties, not only in Egypt but in Tunisia as well. This victory could be attributed to their 'successful electoral campaigns', which were meticulously planned and efficiently run, and supported by a strong media campaign, which helped to mobilise voters (Covatorta and Merone 2015: 29).

Their success encouraged media and experts to zoom in on their policies, questioning their pragmatism and flexibility in dealing with a wide range of social and political issues. In the context of Al-Nahda, it was observed that the party adopted a pragmatic stance. For instance, it agreed to a constitution where there is no reference to *Sharīʿah*, but supported justice and liberty as fundamental Islamic values. Such action triggered criticism of the party by those who claim that Al-Nahda has been stripped of its core Islamic values and that there is little Islamic left in the party (Covatorta and Merone 2015: 32). However, Al-Nahda's response was that the main principles of the party are justice and liberty, which are regarded as core Islamic values. It should be mentioned here that Al-Nahda's actions since the overthrow of Ben Ali's regime demonstrate their pragmatism, pluralism (Covatorta and Merone 2015: 36) and desire to co-exist with other ideologically different parties. Their formation of a coalition government, despite their sweeping victory, is tangible evidence of their willingness to compromise. Al-Nahda's action is mirrored in their discursive practices, as will be discussed in subsequent sections.

To borrow Covatorta and Merone's words, 'the Tunisian Al-Nahda still claims to be an Islamic party that has been able to fulfil the Islamic project by subscribing to a political system that enshrines liberty and justice. (. . .) Al-Nahda represent the furthest point of ideological evolution towards a coincidence between liberal-democracy and Islamism' (2015: 38–9). The suppleness of Al-Nahda, contrary to other Islamic parties in the Arab world, has helped during the transition period and has brought everyone together, avoiding the political fallout that occurred in other Arab states.

Al-Nahda's participation in the political process is evident in its full participation in the legislative elections, which have been characterised as free and fair elections. It has also taken part in drafting the Tunisian new constitution, which 'enshrines individual freedoms and boasts a very lively and plural civil society' (Cavatorta 2018: 243). Its commitment to the new political process is in sharp contrast with its past, which saw the party play 'a prominent role in Tunisian politics, albeit from a position of illegality' (Cavatorta 2018: 244). Many observers attribute Al-Nahda's success and its integration into the Tunisian political system to its leader Rachid Al-Ghannouchi, who is a renowned Muslim intellectual and who has displayed a level of pragmatism in dealing with challenging political and ideological issues post 2011. These new changes have transformed Al-Nahda 'into a pillar of new liberal democratic system' (Cavatorta 2018: 244). Its transformation would not have taken place were it not for its flexibility and sense of responsibility, which put the national interest before the party's interest, making it less radical in terms of ideology, and this made Al-Nahda 'fully integrated and a reliable member of the current political system' (Cavatorta 2018: 245).

Since 2011 Al-Nahda has demonstrated a willingness to fully integrate into the political system. For instance, at its tenth congress the party decided to separate its religious and political activism. This decision has allowed the party to focus on its 'political agenda and economic vision' (Cavatorta 2018: 245). This move of separating the party from its original movement could be said to have been designed to address criticism of using religion to mobilise Tunisians against other parties. It has also been designed to distance itself from 'extremist acts' witnessed in Tunisia and other parts of the world.

But, more importantly, this move reflects the desire of Al-Nahda's leadership to fully integrate in the political scene and engage with other secular parties, without being hampered by the religious wing of the party.

Al-Nahda's move emulated the Moroccan PJD model of separating the party from its original movement. 'In March 2015, Al-Nahda invited leaders from the MUR and PJD to discuss the Moroccan model of separation between da'wa and politics, and a few months later adopted the same division of labour' (Masbah 2018: 140).

As mentioned above, Al-Nahda was not the only Islamic party to find itself engaged in the political process. Following Tunisia, in January 2011 mass demonstrations hit Egyptian cities, culminating in the downfall of its president, Hosni Mubarak (r. 1981–2011). The resignation of Mubarak paved the way for a new political system, with 'new constitutional provisions [which] temporarily broadened political participation and bolstered freedom of assembly and demonstration between January 2011 and June 2013' (Drevon 2018: 261–2). The new constitution resulted in fair and free parliamentary and presidential elections, which were dominated by Ḥizb al-Ḥurriyya wa al-'Adāla (Freedom and Justice Party, FJP) (Joya 2018: 89). This was unprecedented in Egyptian history, especially because the Muslim Brotherhood had been marginalised for so long, and denied the opportunity to participate in the Egyptian political system. This marginalisation pushed the movement to work underground and focus on social services. This included 'offering charity programmes and social services to rural and impoverished urban areas of the country' (Joya: 90), especially when the state budget shrank and was unable 'to continue to provide adequate social services' (Joya: 90).

The FJP victory was short-lived as rounds of demonstrations against the FJP prompted the military to interfere and end Morsi's rule. This happened as 'opposition to President Morsi escalated in Spring 2013 and climaxed on 30 June, when mass protests organised throughout the country demanded his resignation. On 3 July, an army-led coalition suspended the Egyptian constitution and removed Morsi from power' (Drevon 2018: 266).

Joya attributed the demonstrations against the FJP to the party's failure 'to consider the demands of the uprising for social justice, jobs and democracy' (2018: 102). Others have considered the issue of diversity and political participation, blaming the FJP for a lack of moderation when gaining power. Zollner (2018: 160), for instance, concluded that 'there is no case supporting the 'participation-moderation' thesis'. While this could be a reason, others have argued that the FJP has followed the political process and won free and fair elections, and the instruction from the electorate is to govern and make a difference to the livelihood of impoverished Egyptians.

While the FJP has shown little flexibility in terms of moderation and participation in the political process, it could be said that most of the Islamist parties in the Maghreb have demonstrated a level of pragmatism and moderation in their political participation. In this respect, Masbah (2018: 137) posits that the PJD is an example of an Islamist party that has adopted pragmatism, considering 'political interest as more important than ideology'. This level of pragmatism and moderation is evident in the discursive practices of their leaders. Masbah (2018) attributes the PJD's success to their flexibility, as dictated by the Moroccan political landscape, where cooperation with different stakeholders is necessary in order to form a government.

Another reason for PJD's success is what Masbah (2018: 139) referred to as 'latent secularisation', meaning the process by which 'an Islamist party (1) quits its religious mother organisation, (2) divides its religious activities from its political ones and (3) explicitly recognises its 'mundane' nature, which means that its political activities are based on rational calculations rather than purely religious objectives'. Realising the significance of this divide, Al-Nahda, as mentioned earlier, adopted the same policy in 2015 to ensure that its political party is fully integrated in the political system and engaged with other parties. However, despite Al-Nahda being able to form a 'coalition [government] in Tunisia, its popularity suffered anyway because of its own mistakes and the difficult situation that it faced in political, economic and security terms. The result was the loss of its popularity in the parliamentary elections of October 2014' (Dalacoura 2018: 295).

Despite its dwindling popularity, according to Wolf (2018: 216), Al-Nahda leaders have shown a spirit of 'reconciliation and compromise', which renders accusations of extremism and their being a 'solo' religious party obsolete.

The Discourse of Al-Nahda

Having introduced Al-Nahda and its political aspirations, as well as the circumstances of its rise, the following section will examine the main characteristics of some of the speeches of Al-Nahda's leaders. It will closely analyse their structure and substance, as well as their political agenda. The main impetus here is to verify the extent to which moderation in the political process shapes and is shaped by leaders' discourses, if any. It will also allow us an insight into the type and nature of Al-Nahda's political discourse post 2011. The focus will be on analysing both culture-specific and politics-specific terminologies to identify the new direction of Islamist leaders' discourses. This section will seek to answer the following question: What are the main characteristics of the speeches of Al-Nahda's leaders?

Before Al-Nahda entered the political process, its speeches were characterised by a wide range of culture-specific expressions, reflecting the speaker's frame of reference. Some of these speeches and discourses could not escape quotations from the Quran and Hadith, which were used to support and justify leaders' arguments, therefore giving their speeches a religious connotation. These speeches start with Islamic greetings and end with a verse from the Quran or a saying from the Hadith of the Prophet Mohammed. While this is acceptable within the prism of Arabic political discourse, the emphasis on religion in every aspect of the speech has been questioned by the opposition to Al-Nahda. Although such a practice is acceptable to the party and its affiliates, it has been criticised by liberal and secular parties for using religion to advance their agenda. However, Al-Nahda's post-Arab Spring discourse, as will be demonstrated later on, changed immensely as it deviated from religion-based discourse to what can be described as a 'liberal' political discourse. This shift in discourse emanates from the change in the political structure of the party. As mentioned earlier, in 2015, Al-Nahda decided to separate its *Da'wa* and politics and focus on political matters without being influenced by its *Da'wa* wing. This process allowed Al-Nahda a shift in its discourse, where the focus centred on secular terminologies, veering away from religion-based discourse. This new shift has allowed Al-Nahda to operate as part of a coalition government and to work with secular and liberal parties. But it has also helped Al-Nahda to position itself as a democratic party, fully engaged in the political process and dealing with political matters that were in the past the agenda of secular parties. It could be argued here that this marks a shift in Al-Nahda's traditional, religion-centred discourse. This shift cannot be considered in isolation from the social and political change in Tunisian society post 2011. In fact, it mirrors to a full extent this change, as evidenced in the speeches of Al-Nahda leaders. This new shift is in stark contrast to their traditional discourse, which, as mentioned earlier, is very conservative and deeply rooted in the Islamic register. This is even more the case in speeches that are designed for local and constituency consumption. However, the speeches and discourses that were designed for external consumption tended to adopt a new style and completely different register, promoting liberal and democratic values. While this is feasible as every discourse has its target audience, critics of Al-Nahda have considered it a political hypocrisy, where different messages and often conflicting ones are delivered to different audiences, with the sole aim of pleasing and appeasement, and this makes Al-Nahda's rivals question the integrity and reliability of the party and its discourses.

While Al-Nahda's discourse interacts with the Tunisian society, notably the secularist elements of it, its conservative critics consider Al-Nahda's strategy a deviation from the main Islamic principles and they believe that Al-Nahda has nothing Islamic about it. This has been evidenced by the linguistic shift in discourse, where the focus is more on democratic issues such as human rights, freedom, liberty and justice; although Al-Nahda argues that these are Islamic values that need to be promoted and implemented, providing different justifications for their listing. Some of these discourses are carefully designed to appeal to specific audiences. This pragmatism could be said to have allowed Al-Nahda to interact with different stakeholders, both in Tunisia and beyond. Although this interaction has fascinated outsiders, it has irritated some supporters, who feel that the party has deviated from its core values and principles. The question that poses itself in this regard, however, is: why such a change? Having witnessed the collapse of other Islamic parties (i.e. Ḥizb al-Ḥurriyya wa al-'Adāla in Egypt), Al-Nahda realised that its survival is connected to its flexibility and open policies, which interact and respond to the political landscape and the demands of the Tunisian people, who are highly informed and aware of their rights and obligations. Such a strategic move has gained Al-Nahda friends and admirers among secularists and liberals in Tunisia and beyond.

Al-Nahda's strategy was unprecedented in the Arab World as it has managed to establish that democracy is a process and a system that can be embraced by Islamic parties, without any conflict with their Islamic values. The question here is whether this shift in strategy and political orientation shapes and is shaped by Al-Nahda's discourse. To this end, the following section will examine Al-Nahda's political speeches with a view to answering the following sub-questions:

1. How do they address the public sphere?
2. How much space does the religious register occupy in these speeches?
3. How do they position themselves vis-à-vis the public and other political parties in Tunisia?
4. What international discourse has been adopted in their speeches?
5. Has the new social and political landscape led to a change in the discourse of Islamic parties in these countries?

By answering these questions, we should be able to understand not only the characteristics of these discourses and their specifications, but also their ideological nature, the progressive nature (or lack of it) of their producers and their relevance to the wider national political landscape. We should also be able to understand the shift in discourse in these leaders' speeches, compared to their pre-2011 speeches. More precisely, it should allow us to contextualise these discourses within the political process of respective countries, linking them to the participation-moderation concept to see if participation in the political process has induced some of these leaders to moderate their discourse when it comes to crucial political issues.

Al-Nahda Discourse: Democracy, National Interest, Reconciliation and Security

Endorsing Democratic Values
One of the most noticeable features of Al-Nahda's discourse has been its endorsement of the democratic process, emphasising that its Islamic values are compatible with democracy and can be effortlessly implemented and integrated into the political process. Its focus on freedom, liberty and human rights issues is a key example of its willingness to engage in the democratic process.

This pragmatic approach has facilitated its interaction with other democratic forces in Tunisia, notably secularists and liberals. In his speech to the party, the leader of Al-Nahda emphasised the importance of the democratic process and the legitimacy that parties and governments receive through the ballots. He called upon the opposition to respect the voice of the Tunisian people and their choices, and said that Al-Nahda would continue to respect these choices and would not hesitate to stand down if the majority of Tunisian people voted for it. He refered to the will and legitimacy of the people in selecting their own government, as demonstrated in the following examples.

Example 1

الحكومة جاءت بإرادة شعبية ديمقراطية ويمكن تغييرها (. . .) والشرعية تؤخذ بصناديق الاقتراع والحكومات في الديمقراطية لا تأتي إلا بالانتخابات

The government was democratically elected and can be changed, as legitimacy and democracy are achieved through elections.

(Al-Ghannouchi's speech, 3 August 2013)

حركة النهضة انتخبها التونسيون ولهم الحق في أن يبقوها أو أن يخرجوها من السلطة وسوف نقبل بذلك.

لقد عزّزت التشريعات الجديدة مكاسب التونسيات والتونسيين في مجالات عديدة منها الحريات الفردية والعامة من خلال قانون مناهضة العنف ضد المرأة وقانون مناهضة التمييز العنصري وقانون المصالحة.

The Al-Nahda party was elected by Tunisians and they have the right to keep it or to remove it from power, and we will accept that.

The new legislation has strengthened the gains of the Tunisian people in many areas, including individual and public liberties as manifested in the laws on violence against women, the equality act and the reconciliation act.

(Al-Ghannouchi's speech, 3 August 2013)

هؤلاء الانقلابيون هاربون من الاحتكام لصناديق الاقتراع لأنهم جربوها ولم تعطهم الشيء الكثير

These supporter of the coup are fleeing from the ballot boxes because they tried it and did not give them much.

(Al-Ghannouchi's speech, 3 August 2013)

What is striking about Al-Ghannouchi's speeches is the frequent reference to elections, democracy, legitimacy and transparency. The democratic register is heavily present in his speeches, which indicates his party's endorsement of the process of democracy. His linking of 'democratic governments' to 'ballots' is yet again another example of Al-Nahda's claim of supporting the democratic process, although some might argue that this is often the case when these parties are popular, and they often reject democracy when it goes against their interests. Although this is beside the point, the fact of the matter is that Al-Nahda has mastered the game and has shown total readiness to play, without any fear of being rejected by the electorate. Al-Nahda's new discourse could be attributed to a host of reasons, the most important of which is its leader Al-Ghannouchi and his intellectual approach to modernism, where moderation, co-existence and democracy are central to his message.

The other aspect of Al-Nahda's discourse is its denunciation of violence in all its forms. Their denunciation of violence against women is often reiterated in Al-Nahda's leadership speeches and discourses. The new legislation on domestic violence was designed to protect women, as will be discussed later in this chapter.

So what does all this tell us about Al-Nahda's discursive practices? It should be noted here that Al-Nahda's discourse bears a resemblance to discourses of other secular and liberal parties. Besides its content and substance, it has used similar terminologies and jargon in its discourse of democracy. Its opponents will continue to argue that Al-Nahda has mastered the political game and that it shows moderation and openness to its opposition, but internally Al-Nahda remains as conservative as it has ever been. Away from these criticisms, it could be said that Al-Nahda has successfully navigated itself from the difficult political turmoil that has gripped Tunisia. The party's ability to remain a key player in the Tunisian political landscape could be traced to the lessons learnt from the downfall of the FJP in Egypt. The Egyptian experience allowed Al-Nahda to moderate its approach towards its opposition, culminating in giving up power for the sake of the national interest and unity.

National Interest and Unity
Another key theme in Al-Nahda's discourse is the emphasis on the national interest and the importance of safeguarding national unity. In his speeches

Al-Nahda's leader continued to emphasise that the national interest came before his party's interest. This justifies, for instance, the resignation of Al-Nahda from the government, despite being elected with a vast majority, in order to allow for a national government to address the issues being raised by the opposition. Al-Nahda has actively demonstrated its discourse of national unity and national interest, exemplified in the following examples from Al-Nahda's leader.

Example 2

نحن نبشر بالوحدة الوطنية والمصالحة

We advocate national unity and reconciliation.

ستبقى النهضة ملتزمة برفض منطق الهيمنة والإقصاء، حريصة على الشراكة والتوافق والوحدة الوطنية، مهما كانت نتيجة الانتخابات الرئاسية والتشريعية القادمة ومهما كانت نتيجة النهضة.

Al Nahda will remain committed to rejecting the logic of domination and exclusion, and is keen on partnership, harmony and national unity, irrespective of the outcome of the upcoming presidential and legislative elections, whatever the outcome for Al-Nahda.

وان الحركة ستواصل تحمّلها لمسؤولياتها الوطنية، وحرصها أن تبقى دائما جزء من الحل، تعمل من أجل تقريب وجهات النظر والبحث مع كل الفاعلين السياسيين والاجتماعيين عن توافقات جديدة لحل الأزمة في إطار الدستور وعلى قاعدة المصلحة الوطنية

Al-Nahda will continue to shoulder its national responsibilities and is keen always to remain part of the solution, to work towards bridging differences and working with different parties for conciliatory solutions to resolve the crisis within the framework of the Constitution and on the basis of the national interest.

لن تجدوا منا إلا التمسّك بخدمة المصلحة الوطنية والتعاون في ذلك مع الجميع، حيثما كانت مصلحة تونس

We will only be able to uphold the national interest and cooperate with everyone for the sake of Tunisia.

(Above extracts from Al-Ghannouchi's speech, 3 August 2013)

What is striking about the above examples is Al-Nahda's explicit discourse in relation to safeguarding the Tunisian national interest. A positive discourse of national unity and reconciliation has been expressed, rejecting 'the logic of domination and exclusion, keen on partnership, harmony and national unity'. The discourse of 'national responsibility, the national interest, collaboration' features strongly in Al-Nahda's speeches. Indeed, it could be said that Al-Nahda has been very aware of the Tunisian political landscape and the diversity of parties, their agendas and ideologies, some of which were in opposition to Al-Nahda's. In order to accommodate this dissonance of perspectives, Al-Nahda's leaders chose to focus on reconciliation, national unity and national interest.

Call for Reconciliation
Apart from the discourse of national unity and national interest, one of the key messages of Al-Nahda and its leader since the Jasmine Revolution has been 'al-muṣālaḥa' (reconciliation) between all parties and groups in Tunisia. The phrase al-muṣālaḥa al-waṭaniya (national reconciliation) is used repeatedly and in almost every speech and on every occasion. In terms of discourse, the repetition of al-muṣālaḥa is not unintentional and could be said to be part of the strategic discourse of Al-Nahda, which is designed to demonstrate that Al-Nahda is a peaceful party that puts the interest of the country and its people above its own interests. The discourse of al-muṣālaḥa al-waṭaniya, which gained Al-Nahda friends and respect in Tunisia and beyond, has been very effective as demonstrated by the huge support it has attracted, and the realisation that the fragile transition period necessitates a new strategy of healing, sharing and co-existence. Contrary to what happened in Egypt, where the Muslim Brotherhood (MB) had adopted a totally different approach by opting for self-governance, Al-Nahda was more willing to co-govern with other parties.

Despite the challenges facing Tunisia at the beginning of its transition, the pragmatism of Al-Nahda and its discourse of reconciliation as well as its willingness to accommodate others ensured that Al-Nahda did not commit the same mistake as the FJP in Egypt. The fact that the FJP had decided to govern on its own without the participation of other parties created a hostile environment and created enemies for the party, leading to the downfall of the FJP and its president, Mohammed Morsi.

The following examples from Al-Nahda's discourses demonstrate this strategy of reconciliation.

Example 3

نحن دعاة مصالحة وطنية في هذه البلاد، نريد لتونس أن تتصالح مع نفسها، مع دينها، مع شعبها.
نحن مع مصالحة وطنية شاملة، نريد لتونس أن تتصالح مع تاريخها، والنهضة حلقة في تاريخ تونس.
نحن نمد أيدينا للتفاوض والحوار دفاعا عن وحدتنا الوطنية. نحن نرحب بكل من يريد أن يشارك في السلطة للتسريع في المسار الانتقالي.

We are advocates of national reconciliation in this country; we want Tunisia to reconcile with itself, with its religion and with its people.
We support a comprehensive national reconciliation; we want Tunisia to reconcile with its history and Al-Nahda is part of the history of Tunisia.
We extend our hands for dialogue and negotiation in defence of our national unity. We welcome all those who wish to join the government to accelerate the transitional process.

(Al-Ghannouchi's speech, 3 August 2013)

In the above examples, the use of 'we', with reference to Al-Nahda, is followed by phrases showing Al-Nahda's willingness and desire for national reconciliation as exemplified in نحن دعاة مصالحة وطنية *Naḥnu duʿātu muṣālaḥa waṭaniya* (we are advocates of national reconciliation).

The emphasis on reconciliation is linguistically apparent in the repetition of مصالحة *muṣālaḥa* 'reconciliation' in different Arabic forms, i.e. noun and verb تتصالح *Tataṣālaḥ* (to reconcile) – (reconciliation) *muṣalaḥa* مصالحة. This is rare in Arabic political speeches, but here it is employed to express strong emphasis. In the above example, Al-Nahda directly linked dialogue and negotiation to 'defending national unity'. This strategic thinking as mirrored in the discourse of Al-Nahda is a clear indication of the party's new strategy and discourse of 'national unity'. The discourse of national unity, reconciliation, dialogue and negotiation allowed Al-Nahda to portray itself as a progressive party, a claim which has been contested by its opponents who consider Al-Nahda to be dogmatic, and wrapped in a different colour. Al-Nahda's call for reconciliation and national unity was supported by their denunciation of violence and call for a peaceful means for resolving challenging matters.

Denunciation of Violence

Crucial to reconciliation and national unity has been the message of peace and co-existence, as well as the denunciation of violence. In his speeches, Al-Ghannouchi insisted on the peaceful nature of Al-Nahda, denouncing violence and reiterating the significance of working and living in harmony with other stakeholders and parties, irrespective of their perspectives/differences. He emphasised the importance of the national interest and the prosperity of the country and its people, which is the sole responsibility of all parties including Al-Nahda. Of importance to this national interest and unity is the democratic process which ensures peaceful transition, away from any acts of violence or confrontation. It could be said here that Al-Ghannouchi's speeches are carefully orchestrated to send out the message that Al-Nahda believes in democracy and is willing to participate in the process, respecting other parties and movements which may hold different perspectives and viewpoints. In his reconciliation speech in August 2013, Al-Ghannouchi rejected acts of violence and anything that could lead to conflict among Tunisians, calling for dialogue, negotiation and reconciliation.

It could be remarked here that Al-Ghannouchi's speeches/discourses mark a clear shift in the party's movement from being suspected as 'the enemy of democracy' to advocating it; from the party's self-interest to the national interest and unity; from the hegemony of one party and its single rule to full participation in a coalition government, irrespective of the results.

This reassurance to the public, political parties and the international community marks a new shift in Al-Nahda's strategy. It was designed to send out the message that they are not power-hungry, but a party that can be satisfied with partial representation in a national coalition that would protect the Tunisian national interest. The repetition of '*tashārukiyya*' (partnership) is designed to hammer the message home that Al-Nahda is willing to form a coalition and co-exist with other parties, irrespective of their ideologies and differences. Such a spirit of sharing and willingness to engage with others, no matter how different they are, is key to stability, defeating therefore any thoughts of conflict.

Example 4

وبالرغم من حملات الملاحقة الأمنية والتشويه الإعلامي ومحاولات اتهام النهضة وقياداتها بالإرهاب، فقد أنصف القضاء الأجنبي النهضة في كل القضايا التي رفعناها اليه ضد كل من افترى علينا فرية العنف والإرهاب

Despite the campaigns of prosecution, media distortion and attempts to accuse Al-Nahda and its leadership of terrorism, the foreign judiciary did justice to Al-Nahda in all the cases we lodged against those who have accused us of violence and terrorism.

(Al-Ghannouchi's speech, 27 October 2018)

The above example shows Al-Nahda's determination to defend its peaceful nature and its discourse of dialogue and negotiation, rejecting accusations of violence and terrorism. Al-Nahda sought to show here its tolerant and peaceful nature, which was supported by the foreign judiciary who vindicated the movement from these allegations, as reiterated in Al-Ghannouchi's speeches. This discourse of peace and reconciliation is shaped in Al-Nahda's action towards different stakeholders. However, the opposition accused Al-Nahda of double standards as manifested in its usage of different discourses for different audiences and purposes.

Analysis of Al-Nahda's Speeches

In this section we intend to examine the type of discourse delivered by leaders of Al-Nahda, with a particular focus on the language register and the type of lexis employed. We will also examine certain themes and strands that are prevalent in these speeches and which could mark a shift.

Progressive Discourse or a Tactic?

As discussed above, and contrary to what observers expected, Al-Nahda displayed a level of flexibility and openness, expressing the desire to collaborate and co-exist with others. There was a fear that Al-Nahda would establish *Sharī'ah* and that it would curb freedom of expression which could have knock-on effect on human rights issues, notably the rights of women, but this fear subsided as Al-Nahda passed new laws in support of women and public freedom. Its acceptance of the constitution without the mention of *Sharī'ah* could be considered an example of Al-Nahda's shift in approach when handling issues of importance for the Tunisian people. As discussed earlier, Al-Nahda's discourse of national interest, reconciliation, co-existence and respect for freedoms and liberties could be taken as indicative examples of its progressive nature, even though others may question Al-Nahda's strategy and its practice in reality.

More importantly, Al-Nahda's discourse reflects the party's willingness to participate and contribute to the running of the country. The insistence on championing liberties and human rights issues has in particular gained the party friends inside and outside Tunisia, although others would argue that this is a strategy used to mobilise the public and aimed at refining Al-Nahda's image abroad.

The following examples demonstrate this level of openness and modernism in the party's thinking.

Example 5

لقد عزّزت التشريعات الجديدة مكاسب التونسيات والتونسيين في مجالات عديدة، منها الحريات الفردية والعامة من خلال قانون مناهضة العنف ضد المرأة وقانون مناهضة التمييز العنصري، ومنها المحاسبة والشفافية من خلال قانون التصريح على المكاسب وقانون المصالحة . وتمثّل هذه التشريعات ضمانات إضافية وآليات جديدة تساعد على بناء مجتمع العدل والحرية والمساواة وتكافئ الفرص ، الذي بشّرت به ثورة الحرية والكرامة.

The new legislation has strengthened Tunisians and their gains in many areas, including individual and public freedoms through the Anti-Violence against Women Act and the Anti-Apartheid Act, including accountability and transparency through the Declaration on Benefits Act and the Reconciliation Act. These legislations represent additional guarantees and new mechanisms that help build a society of justice, freedom, equality and equal opportunities, which was heralded by the revolution of Freedom and Dignity.

The above examples illustrate the type of discourse used by Al-Nahda concerning key policy issues pertaining to public freedom, women and human rights. It could be argued here that these examples are a clear indication of Al-Nahda's new discourse when it comes to these matters. The passing of laws of championing women's rights, equalities and liberties was used by Al-Nahda to argue their progressive nature, rejecting the claims that they are anti-women and anti-equality. Al-Nahda's new discourse of women's rights, equality, liberty and freedom becomes very explicit post Arab Spring. Al-Nahda's measures, highlighted in the above examples, could be said to have been designed to reflect Al-Nahda's progressive discourse and outward-looking nature. Al-Nahda continued to argue that this new discourse is embedded in the Islamic values of the party and that this does not contradict core Islamic values. The following section will examine Al-Nahda's political discourse in relation to its Islamic register.

Al-Nahda and Islam: Religious Register in Al-Nahda's Discourse
Before dwelling on Al-Nahda's discourse in relation to its Islamic register, it's vital to consider the following key aspects of Al-Nahda's discourse post Jasmine Revolution, which have been reiterated by Al-Nahda's leaders on numerous occasions in an attempt to show the party's change and reform since it ascended to power. These are: (1) discourse of modernisation and willingness to engage, participate in and contribute to the democratic process with confidence and without any feeling of inferiority; (2) discourse of liberalism wrapped in Islamic values; (3) discourse of inclusiveness, openness and outward thinking; (4) discourse of national interest and the right of citizens.

These four aspects constitute a new framework for the analysis of Islamic political discourse, where a secular approach has been married with Islamic values to address key challenging issues, which are often regarded as pillars of modernism. Al-Nahda's framework when looked at carefully could be considered an argument advanced against claims that Islam and democracy are incompatible and therefore Islamic parties/movements such as Al-Nahda have no room for this process. This reinforces Al-Nahda's claim that the party is democratic and Islamic, rejecting the claim that you can only be one or the other.

As an Islamic party, it is expected that its discourse will be religion-oriented. It is expected that quotations from the Quran and Sunna will be its main pillars, and that its terminologies and concepts will be in line with the party's Islamic frame of reference. However, a preliminary examination of Al-Nahda's speeches suggests the contrary. There is a dearth of key Islamic concepts and phrases in its political discourse, as there is a total absence of quotes from the Quran or Hadith. What is striking is that Al-Nahda's new discourse has little in it that could distinguish it from other secular/liberal parties. Its past discourse of *khilāfa*, *shar'Allah* and *shūrā* has been replaced with modern democratic concepts such as democracy, human rights, equality and gender.

Apart from the *basmalla*, the Islamic opening of speeches, there is little religious register. Traditionally, Islamic parties would heavily cite the Quran or Hadith to support their argument, making their discourse religion-oriented, but Al-Nahda post 2011 has deviated from this tradition and adopted a secular and liberal approach with less focus on religion and more on the democratic process. This is clearly manifested in the terminologies and concepts used. As argued above, this could be due to the new direction taken by Al-Nahda at its fifteenth national congress, where the party was split into two wings: the *Da'wa* wing and the political wing. The latter has allowed the party to focus on the political and social issues that matter most to Tunisians. Its discourse, then, mirrors its new approach and justifies the shift from religion-based to secular and liberal, where Islamic traditional concepts have been replaced with modern democratic concepts.

To explore the above claims and counter claims, we will examine a range of linguistic features such as repetition, inclusive 'we', metonymy, passive voice and implicit representation strategy in Al-Nahda's discourse.

Reiteration/Repetition in Al-Nahda's Discourse

Although reiteration and repetition are acceptable features in Arabic discourse and are often used for emphasis, as discussed in Chapter 6, Al-Nahda's leaders have used it to hammer home their message and persuade the audience of their own argument, as well as political stance. Key concepts and terminologies of importance to their target audience are often repeated. Take, for instance, the following example.

Example 6

الشرعية، انتخابات ، مصالحة وطنية، التشاركية، المصلحة الوطنية، الديمقراطية، الشباب،

Legitimacy, elections, national reconciliation, partnership, national interest, democracy, youth.

The repetition of these key terminologies could be designed to show that Al-Nahda is committed to the democratic process, which ensures the safe transition of democracy and establishes unity and harmony among different political stakeholders in Tunisia. The term 'national interest' has been repeated on numerous occasions to show that Al-Nahda's main priority is the unity of the country and its interest. Al-Nahda was very skilful in using repetition for the sake of persuasion by focusing on key concepts that constitute the core of its political and social message. However, what is striking about Al-Nahda's message is the absence of a religious register in its speeches. While the expectation is that Al-Nahda would use religion to persuade its audience to subscribe to its message, in most of its political discourses this element has been absent. This could be because these speeches have a particular audience in mind, mainly Tunisian political parties, organisations and the international community. The level of repetition of non-religious concepts could be traced back to the social and political context of the delivery of these speeches. For instance, in his August 2013 speech, entitled 'National reconciliation', Al-Ghannouchi used repetition to persuade the audience of his party's intention to participate in and contribute to any discussion and debate that would serve the national interest. He also revealed his party's willingness to co-exist with other parties and participate in the democratic process, without any feeling of superiority or dominance. But the most striking feature is his repetition of the terms 'democracy' and 'democratic process', 'elections' and 'legitimacy'. This is designed to show that Al-Nahda is a democratic party that is willing to participate and accept the rules of the game, and could be used to persuade those who might doubt the intention of Al-Nahda and its full commitment to the democratic process. Despite its popularity and potential dominance of the elections, Al-Nahda's repetition of التشاركية *attashārukiyya* (partnership) was intended to lessen its opponents' fears and reassure other political parties in Tunisia that Al-Nahda is committed to forming a coalition government, representing those parties that share similar agendas. This came at the time of the counter-revolution in Egypt where the FJP was deposed and accused of dominating the political scene and being unwilling to accommodate other political views.

It could be said that Al-Nahda learnt a lesson from the Egyptian experience and showed flexibility and tolerance in dealing with opposition parties or groups in Tunisia. By reiterating national reconciliation it aimed to send out the message that the party was willing to reconcile and work with others. So the repetition of the above concepts and terminologies tells us that

Al-Nahda's discourse is often carefully thought out and intended to reassure the public and international community that the party is agile in its approach, putting the national interest front and centre. This key message rendered Al-Nahda a key national player whose aim and intention was to serve the national interest and unity, as was reiterated in Ghanouchi's speeches discussed above. The desire for a unified national front and reconciliation for the sake of national interest leads us to examine Al-Nahda's inclusive and exclusive strategy through the use of its discourse.

Inclusiveness and Exclusiveness in Al-Nahda's Discourse
At the heart of its message of national unity and reconciliation is the discourse of inclusivity. In their speeches Al-Nahda's leaders have used the inclusive pronoun 'we', often referring to Tunisia and Tunisians. The repetition of نحن *naḥnu* (we) on numerous occasions in speeches is designed to show the wider representation of Al-Nahda and its inclusive approach when addressing Tunisians and Tunisian political parties. Several interpretations spring into mind here: first, it shows that Al-Nahda sought to demonstrate that it is part and parcel of Tunisia and Tunisian society, refuting any suggestion that its loyalty lies beyond Tunisia. So the repetition of 'we' could be said to have been used to address those who allege that Al-Nahda's affiliation lies outside Tunisia. The constant repetition of 'we' could also be interpreted as Al-Nahda's attempt to show its affiliation to Tunisia and its integration as part of the Tunisian society. This inclusivity in discourse could be designed to serve as a reminder that Al-Nahda is a Tunisian political party that is part of the Tunisian political landscape. The use of the inclusive pronoun 'we' could also be interpreted as an attempt to gain support and rally Tunisians behind the party.

Al-Nahda widely adopted the inclusive 'we' when addressing the Tunisian people, but addressed the party's affiliates using '*nahḍawiyūn*' and '*nahḍawiyāt*' in reference to the affiliation of its supporters and party members. This clear distinction in some of Al-Nahda's speeches shows the party's communicative strategy, as matters reserved for the party are addressed to the party members while other matters are addressed to the wider Tunisian society, often using the inclusive pronoun 'we'. The matters that are addressed to the wider Tunisian society are often broad, but relevant to Tunisians, such as democracy, liberty, freedom and reconciliation, in which the inclusive pronoun is repeatedly used. However, matters related to the party are addressed to the membership of the party, such as the following example where Al-Ghannouchi congratulated party members on their success and achievement.

Example 7

أيتها النهضويات، أيها النهضويون، يحقّ لكم أن تفخروا بحزبكم وبانتمائكم إلى مشروعه الوطني الجامع الذي دقّقه المؤتمر العاشر وحدّد معالمه الكبرى وقبل به، وأقبل عليه الكثير من التونسيات والتونسيين ومنحوه ثقتهم في الانتخابات

Oh Al-Nahda affiliates. You should be proud of your party and your affiliation to its comprehensive national project, which was examined by the Tenth Congress and defined its great features and accepted it, and was endorsed by many Tunisians in the elections.

(Al-Ghannouchi's speech, 27 October 2018)

The above example was solely directed to Al-Nahda's members, and congratulates them on their achievement. Apart from the use of 'we' in his speeches, Al-Ghannouchi would directly address Tunisians as أيتها التونسيات، أيها التونسيون *ayuhā al-Tūnusiyūn, ayatuhā al-Tūnusiyāt* (oh Tunisians). This is part of the party's reaching-out strategy, where it sought to communicate with the wider public, and to keep Tunisians informed about matters of interest to them such as services, employment and confidence in the government, as the following example demonstrates.

Example 8

إن خدمتكم وتحسين ظروف عيشكم هي أساس شرعية وجود الأحزاب السياسية وتنافسها في نيل ثقتكم. في الانتخابات، تختارون بإرادتكم الحرة من تجدون فيهم المصداقية والكفاءة والقدرة على تحقيق وعوده. لقد شرّفتمونا بمنحنا ثقتكم في كل الاستحقاقات الانتخابية، وآخرها الانتخابات المحلّية، وأعطيتمونا الفرصة لخدمتكم عبر برامجنا ومشاريعنا. من جهتنا لن ندّخر جهدا في ذلك، وسنمكّن ممثّلينا في المجالس البلدية من الدعم والاسناد الكافيين

Serving you and improving your living conditions are the main reasons for the existence of political parties and their competition in gaining your trust in elections. You choose with your free will who you find credible, able and capable of fulfilling these promises. You have honoured us with your confidence in all elections, the latest of which is the local elections and you have given us the opportunity to serve you through our programmes and projects. We will spare no effort in this and we will enable our representatives in the municipal councils to support you.

(Al-Ghannouchi's speech, 27 October 2018)

Apart from the inclusive 'we', Al-Nahda used the second plural pronoun in addressing citizens to make a direct appeal and also to establish a direct link with citizens such as لخدمتكم *likhidmatikum* (to serve you) - ظروف عيشكم *ẓorūfu 'aychikum* (living conditions) ثقتكم *thiqatakum* (your trust). By linking the livelihood of citizens to the services provided by the party, Al-Nahda aims to show their commitment to improving their living conditions. The direct address through the use of the second plural pronoun is designed to establish a direct communication link with the wider Tunisian public. While Al-Nahda showed the desire and willingness to serve the Tunisian people, it was also very critical of its opposition, as will be discussed in the following section.

From the above analysis it is clear that in their representation of the self, Al-Nahda and Al-Ghannouchi produced what I call a discourse of 'our people'. These were referred to as our 'crowd', '*nahḍawiyūn*', '*tūnusiyūn*', preceded by the possessive pronoun 'our' in a show of strength, whenever there is a large crowd. But 'our' is not a simple pronoun that can be used in any context; it is intended here to send out the message that Al-Nahda is Tunisian and has its own people who form the fabric of the Tunisian society. It could also be used to signal that Al-Nahda enjoys a wide support among Tunisians, including its own party members. This dichotomy of 'our' reminds us of Van Dijk's binary of 'Us vs Them'.

While Al-Nahda may not have the intention of separating its own people from the remainder of Tunisian society, its discourse suggests that distinction, unintentional as it may be. Polarisation in politics does happen, but it can be a risky business, as it could harm any prospect of unity and reconciliation and alienate the very people it seeks to attract. After all, this is in stark contrast to the discourse of unity, reconciliation and national interest, which Al-Ghannouchi and other members of Al-Nahda have produced and advocated. Could this conflicting message reflect the 'double discourse' which

Al-Nahda is accused of, as discussed earlier in this chapter? The use of 'our' reflects the one-sided discourse of the party where 'our' people are presented in a positive manner, adopting all attributes that reflect this positivism.

The Other in Al-Nahda's Discourse

Al-Nahda adopted a discourse of mutual respect for its opponents and competitors. As we go through examples of these discourses, we notice the conciliatory tone, treating all parties with dignity and respect. While this is clear in its discourses, its opponents would argue that it is a strategy to show that Al-Nahda is an outward-looking party, seeking co-existence with all other political parties that hold different perspectives and ideologies. These parties were presented as representative of fellow citizens who happened to have different perspectives, and were not considered to be enemies of Al-Nahda; rather, they were regarded as key partners in the democratic process. While showing a positive attitude towards political parties, Al-Ghannouchi was very critical of those who opposed Al-Nahda and called for its marginalisation, as shown in the following example.

Example 9

هؤلاء الانقلابيون هاربون من الاحتكام لصناديق الاقتراع لأنهم جربوها ولم تعطهم الشيء الكثير

These supporters of the coup are fleeing from the ballot boxes because they tried it and did not give them much.

لسنا مشروع انقلاب ولا حرب أهلية ولا فتنة نحن نستن بسنة نبينا "و ما أرسلناك الا رحمة للعالمين " نريد أن نكون في هذه البلاد كالاسمنت يجمع التونسيين .

We are not a coup, nor a civil war, nor a sedition; we follow our Prophet's path: 'We have only sent you [Prophet] as a mercy to humanity.' We want to be in this country like a cement that brings together Tunisians.

نحن لا نتمنى الشر لمعارضينا وإنما نتمنى لهم الخير فكلهم أبناء تونس، نحن نبشر بالوحدة الوطنية والمصالحة

We do not wish evil for our opponents, but we wish them good; all of them are the sons of Tunisia. We preach national unity and reconciliation.

هذا الحشد العظيم هو رسالة واضحة للإنقلابيين بانهم لن يمروا ولن نترك الثورة المضادة ولا الحكومة المضادة

This great crowd is a clear message to the supporters of the coup that they will not succeed, and we will allow neither counter-revolution nor counter-government.
(Above extracts from Al-Ghannouchi's speech, 3 August 2013)

Although Al-Ghannouchi has displayed positive attributes when describing political parties, in some cases he referred to opponents of Al-Nahda as 'coupists' who attempt to stage a coup against the legitimately elected Al-Nahda, according to Al-Ghannouchi. By using the Arabic word '*inqilābiyūn*' (coupists), he refers to those supporters of the 'military coup' in Egypt which saw the overthrow of Morsi and the Muslim Brotherhood, emphasising Al-Nahda's position of rejecting counter-revolutions and being a peaceful party with the aim of bringing Tunisians together. His rejection of Tunisian civil war and any attempt to depose the government were clear in his employment of 'counter-revolution' and 'counter-government' discourse. His desire for reconciliation is evident in his message: he wishes good and no evil to his opposition as they are Tunisians, and he aims for reconciliation and national unity. Al-Ghannouchi's discourse combines both firmness and elasticity; firm that the counter-revolution should not prevail and flexibility in his willingness to have national unity and reconciliation.

This discourse of Al-Nahda marks again a shift in the strategy of dealing with national crises and the way forward, bearing in mind different stakeholders in Tunisia. This strategic shift of embracing the other and putting the national interest first, gained Al-Nahda, as discussed earlier, popularity in Tunisia and beyond. It has been seen as the facilitator rather than the dominant party that sought to govern alone.

Al-Nahda's discourse could be characterised as 'reconciliatory', 'moderate' and 'confrontation free'. This type of discourse, which seeks to enhance democracy and co-existence in Tunisia, is still in its infancy and requires time to become fully fledged, as will democracy and the democratic process in Tunisia. It should be pointed out here that Al-Nahda has brought a new way of thinking to the process where liberty and freedom are key concepts in its new discourse. The fact that Al-Nahda, as discussed earlier, managed to separate the politics from the *Da'wa* has facilitated the process of integration into the political process and has allowed the party to deal with those key issues that matter most to electorates. It could be argued here that Al-Nahda's discourse is influenced by Western concepts, brought back and adopted by some of its leaders who spent most of their exile in Western capitals, such as Al-Ghannouchi who lived most of his life in London. The fact that its discourse contains more diplomatic and democratic concepts is very revealing of the party and its strategy for survival in Tunisia.

The other shift in discourse is the emphasis on democracy and the right of people to elect their representatives. In his speech on national unity and reconciliation, Al-Ghannouchi used the huge crowd to boast the wide support his party enjoys across Tunisia. The fact that Al-Ghannouchi repeated 'this crowd' more than once is a good example of how Al-Nahda uses its popularity to claim legitimacy and push forward its political and social agenda. In rejecting the attempt to overthrow the Tunisian government, Al-Ghannouchi used the crowd to advance his argument that Al-Nahda will not be marginalised as long as the party continues to be popular throughout Tunisia.

Representation of the Self
Al-Nahda has been presented as a peaceful and democratic party, whose main aim is national unity, reconciliation and co-existence. It portrays itself as a legitimate party representing a wider section of society. In its discourse it is represented as the safeguard of democracy and national unity. Its leaders wish to portray Al-Nahda as the party that came to defend the freedom and liberty of Tunisians, following the Jasmine Revolution. In its own discourse, the party represents itself as the 'God-fearing party' when addressing its members and supporters in Tunisia, but for outside consumption it is represented as a democratic Islamic party that has adopted liberal views in line with its Islamic frame of reference. This dual representation has brought some criticism to Al-Nahda and it has been accused of dual messages, as well as flip-flopping. The following section will look at some of the criticism of Al-Nahda's approach and its discourses.

While Al-Nahda's speeches are delivered with a Tunisian audience in mind, and matters that are of concern to the Tunisian people, other speeches, however, are designed for the consumption of the international community, where democracy, human rights, freedoms and liberties constitute the key message. It represents a sort of reassurance for the international community that Al-Nahda is committed to the democratic process and is willing to work with different stakeholders in Tunisia and beyond. It also serves as a reassurance that the interests of some of these countries are protected and will not be impacted by any government formed by Al-Nahda. It should be said here that Al-Nahda was very successful in its communication strategy, and this helped the party to push back claims and allegations of anti-democracy.

The global discourse of Al-Nahda has not only allowed the party to reach out to supporters beyond Tunisia, but has enabled it to establish communication with different parties outside Tunisia. This successful communication strategy has given the party more visibility and enabled others to gain access, which has culminated in a good understanding of the party's strategic direction and its political ambitions, as well as its way of thinking.

Criticisms of Al-Nahda and its Discourse

Despite Al-Nahda's promotional discourse and self-praise, its critics see the party as having multiple discourses for multiple audiences. They claim that Al-Nahda lacks clear principles and strategies to govern its discourse. In the absence of these strategies they accuse Al-Nahda of pleasing and appeasing the audience by addressing people with what they like to hear, thereby violating some of their own values and principles. For instance, it has been noted that there is a discourse for the party members, a discourse for the Tunisian people, and a third discourse for an external audience. The critics of Al-Nahda often use this to send out the message that Al-Nahda has no principles and that it is flip-flopping when it comes to sensitive political matters. Al-Nahda has unequivocally rejected these allegations as false and designed to tarnish the party's reputation.

While its critics continue to unpick Al-Nahda's main weaknesses and its deficiencies, the party continues to rally its supporters, challenging its critics through a programme of social and cultural support. This support is clearly manifested in the party's discourse, but with the split of the party from its Daʻwa wing, this support is envisaged to increase as the main functions of its Daʿwa is to promote social and cultural activities that are in line with the party's core values and principles. For its critics, Al-Nahda uses religion to recruit Tunisians to the party, exploiting religion for political and ideological gains, a charge refuted by Al-Nahda.

While the Tunisian revolution has allowed the formation of a new political landscape in Tunisia and has culminated in fair and transparent democratic elections, the political success of Islamists in Egypt did not last long, as the FJP was ousted from power following protests against the party, which culminated in the overthrow of Morsi and his government. The following section will dwell on the Freedom and Justice Party (FJP) discourses, practices, weaknesses, errors, challenges and successes during their short-lived governance.

Ḥizb al-Ḥurriyya wa al-ʿAdāla, Freedom and Justice Party (FJP), Egypt

This section will examine the main discourses of the FJP and its leaders. We aim to examine how its discourses shape and are shaped by the political and ideological orientations of the party. We will seek to examine whether there is any shift in its discourse post 2011.

In its first participation in the 2011–12 elections, Ḥizb al-Ḥurriyya wa al-ʿAdāla won the majority of seats in both the lower and upper house in Egypt. These were regarded as 'free and fair' elections (Joya 2018: 89). The party's victory culminated in securing the post of the president, when Mohammed Morsi defeated his rival Ahmed Shafiq in one of the fairest and most transparent presidential elections. However, this victory was short-lived when the party and its President have been ousted from power. The overthrow of Morsi's government has been attributed to several factors, including 'their failure to offer a progressive vision of the economy' (Joya 2018: 89).

The ousting of Morsi from the office by the military triggered much analysis and debate as to the reasons for his overthrow. While some people blame the military, others have laid the blame on the ability of the MB/FJP to deal with the economic situation post 2011. Joya (2018: 89) asserted that the FJP sought to accommodate other parts of the ruling class, but 'their strategy was not supported by Mubarak-era capitalists or the military'. She goes on to argue that the

MB encountered challenges 'pertaining to social justice and political rights as well as the economy in the post-uprising period' (Joya 2018: 89).

The tension between the MB and the state is not new, but rooted in history and goes back to the 1950s when the MB fought against the existence of imperialism on Muslim lands. After independence, the MB became enemy number one of the state, following an attempted assassination on Nasser, which led to the execution of Qutb in 1954, followed by a total ban on MB activities until 2011 (Joya 2018: 94). While underground, the MB started 'pursuing informal politics through its charitable work, which facilitated the dissemination of its political message' (Joya 2018: 94).

When the FJP took power it was faced with relentless, notably economic, challenges. 'In February 2012, Egypt was faced with a budget deficit, a balance of payments deficit and depleting foreign reserves' (Joya 2018: 96). This economic hardship escalated further as the MB became fully consumed by the power struggle between the party and the military. This tension increased when 'the military sought to curtail the growing influence of the Islamists' (Joya 2018: 100).

Apart from the political power struggle, scholars have attributed the economic stagnation to the party's economic strategy, which focused on 'short-term economic goals rather than long-term economic development strategy' (Joya 2018: 100).

The lack of trust and suspicion of the MB heightened tensions between the military, other parties and the MB. This lack of trust could be attributed to the long years of wear and tear between the party and the Egyptian government.

> The Brotherhood were seen as power-grabbers rather than power-sharers. Morsi's November 2012 decree, granting him powers over the courts, turned many in the Egyptian judiciary against him. By December 2012, public anger against the MB turned into mass protests by women, Coptic groups and liberals. The media turned against the Brotherhood after the Palace protests of December 2012 when Brotherhood supporters shot a journalist. (Joya 2018: 101)

These protests were a golden opportunity for the military to intervene and remove the 'Morsi administration from office in July 2013' (Joya 2018: 101).

For its critics, the MB made numerous errors of judgement when dealing with the economic and political situations in Egypt. Economically, as mentioned above, there was no long-term strategy that would encourage investors and small and medium businesses. They also failed to 'resolve the imbalanced power relationship between labour and capital' (Joya 2018: 101). Politically, contrary to Al-Nahda in Tunisia, the MB 'underestimated the power of competing elites and did not think of power-sharing as an option to stay in power' (Joya 2018: 101). And finally, the MB made no attempt to restructure the institutions of the state to remove any elements of the authoritarian nature of these institutions (Joya 2018: 101). This posed a challenge to the MB as elements of the previous regime remained in place, impeding the new government's work. At the societal level, the MB has been criticised for not taking 'demands of the uprising for social justice, accountability and reform seriously' (Joya 2018: 101).

However, these criticisms were refuted by the MB, calling them fabricated reasons to cover the illegitimate overthrow of Morsi's government, which had been in the planning since the FJP took power following the Egyptian revolution in 2011.

The 2010–12 uprisings and subsequent elections, which saw the arrival of Islamic parties to power has made these groups the central focus of scholars and media experts alike. Their willingness to participate in free and fair elections and their desire to govern has presented scholars with opportunities to re-examine and reassess these groups' strategies and decision-making. Their success has 'generated important empirical and theoretical discussions of their pragmatism and inspired noticeable calls for innovative methodological approaches including cross-country and micro-level studies' (Drevon 2018: 258).

A great deal has been written about the political participation of Islamic parties and groups in the political process post 2011; however, little has been written about these groups' discursive practices and discourses, and how they are shaped or reshaped by the political process. The analysis of discourse would allow researchers to examine more closely the notion of moderation-inclusion through the prisms of discourse. As discourses are the product of certain beliefs and ideas, the analysis of Islamic parties' discourses would elucidate their current beliefs, allowing researchers to make conclusions about any shift (or lack of it) in discourse that culminates from the participation in the political process. The analysis of Al-Nahda's discourse demonstrates its ability to shift from a Da'wa discourse to a political discourse that accommodates different stakeholders with different opinions and perspectives. It has also shown that the party's discourse reflects its strong desire for national unity and reconciliation, putting the national interest before the party's interest, as is evident in Al-Ghannouchi's speeches and discourses. Its discourse has also revealed the moderation-inclusion strategy in Al-Nahda's decision-making and its political processes. While social scientists have concluded that Al-Nahda has changed the way Islamic parties are portrayed, others have considered Al-Nahda to be an exception in its discourses and participation in the political process. However, the question remains: could the phenomenon of Al-Nahda be rolled out to other Islamic groups/parties in the region? In the following sections, the MB's discursive practices will be studied carefully, and comparisons made with Al-Nahda's practices in order to determine whether this is a new phenomenon across the Arab world or an exceptional case pertinent to Al-Nahda.

A great deal has been written about the MB pre and post Arab Spring, but few studies, if any, have examined its discourses during and post Arab Spring, which this section aims to do. Now that we have introduced the MB and the challenges it faced when it ascended to power, it would be very useful to examine the discourse of its leaders pre and post Arab Spring, in order to identify its strategy, the type and nature of its discourse, and how it shapes and is shaped by the party's ideological orientation.

FJP Discursive Practices

Religious Register

In his first speech to the nation, the most noticeable change in Morsi's discourse was his focus on the religious identity of his citizens. Instead of addressing them as Egyptians, or citizens, he opted for a religious categorisation of Egyptians as Muslims and Christians. While some may argue that this was a good strategy that sought to welcome and appreciate citizens from all backgrounds and faiths, others argue that it divided the country along religious lines, and created tension between different groups. The following is an example from a speech of Morsi's speech to illustrate this.

Example 10

أيها المسلمون في مصر أيها المسيحيون في مصر أيها المواطنون الكرام

O Muslims and Christians in Egypt, dear citizens.

(Morsi's speech, 29 June 2012)

The speaker here could have used '*muwāṭinūn*' (citizens) on its own as it is representative and accommodates people from all backgrounds and faiths. By using 'Muslims and Christians', he has made the religious register very explicit, denoting a shift from his predecessor's speech, but a continuity of the genre of discourse delivered by the MB and its leaders. While the mention of religious identity is a recognition of different faiths and ethnicities in Egypt, it could be interpreted as an unintentional attempt to divide the country along religious lines, which could have long-term repercussions for the interaction and integration of different groups and communities.

The opening of Morsi's speeches with a Quranic verse reflects the traditional nature of his speeches. The use of phrases such as *basmala* and the Quranic verses are key components of traditional speeches and this has been the practice in most Arab leaders' speeches. The use of verses from the Quran is often designed to summarise the content of the speech or, at times, give a sense of what will be covered in the speech, strengthening therefore the message. What is different in Morsi's speeches is the substantial use of religious texts, notably when addressing social and cultural matters pertinent to citizens. This could be due to Morsi's desire to appeal to his electorate who have given him their support.

Apart from the reference to Muslims and Christians, the use of *ashshar'iyya* (legitimacy) has been repeated several times, indicating that Morsi has been democratically elected by the majority of Egyptians and that their choice and voice should be respected and protected. The fact that Morsi refers to 'legitimacy' is very revealing. It outlines his recognition of the political process and democracy, and his appreciation of the electorate, who have given him their voices/votes. However, some argue that this is in sharp contrast to his attempt to amend the law to grant himself more powers. As discussed earlier, this created a sense of trepidation among the opposition, who accused him of exploiting his position. These accusations by politicians and civilians deterred

Morsi from carrying out his amendments, but trust in his ability to respect the democratic process was eroded.

The Other in FJP Leaders' Discourse

In his victory speech, Morsi sought to rally citizens behind him, reiterating the message that he is president of all Egyptians, irrespective of their faith and political leanings, but this was undermined by the introductory line in his speech, in which he made specific mention of Muslims and Christians. This was regarded by others as a divisive and faith-oriented discourse. In his speech, Morsi reiterated his willingness to work with all Egyptians, irrespective of whether they are his supporters or opposition, as demonstrated in the following extract.

Example 11

سأتواصل مع الجميع ولا أفرق بين مؤيدين ومعارضين.
جئنا برسالة سلام لا نعتدي على أحد ولكننا قادرين بالجميع أن نرد بل نمنع أي عدوان علينا من أي جهة كانت سنصنع معاً أيها الأحباب المواطنين وأيها الشعب الكريم مفهوماً جديداً للعلاقات الخارجية مع الجميع ونمد أيدينا إلى الجميع

I will interact/work with all, and do not differentiate between supporters and opposition.

We have brought a message of peace that we are not attacking anyone, but we are able to prevent any aggression against us. We will work together, beloved citizens and honorable people, with a new concept of external relations with all.

(Morsi's speech, 29 June 2012)

At the beginning of his tenure, Morsi's speeches were conciliatory, with the aim of unifying the country under his own rule. He would often refer to the national interest, unity and reconciliation. But all this had to change when protests grew against him, demanding his resignation. The following extract demonstrates this shift.

Example 12

لم يدخر أعداء مصر جهداً في محاولة تخريب التجربة الديمقراطية. لقد قادونا إلى دائرة من العنف والتشهير والتحريض والتمويل وكذلك اللعب بالنار في مؤسسات ذات أهمية حيوية. من المعروف أن بقية أولئك الذين استفادوا من النظام السابق يجدون صعوبة في رؤية مصر تنهض حقًا ـ شعبها وجيشها وقوات الشرطة معًا.

إن النظام الإجرامي القديم سوف يفعل ما يريد ويوظف أولئك الذين يعملون في الأجهزة الأمنية ويحميهم. في وقت لاحق كانت هناك انقسامات وحسد وانشقاقات بين الناس وبعض رجال الأمن ، وأحيانًا حتى تشويه المؤسسة

Egypt's enemies have spared no effort in trying to sabotage the democratic experiment. They have led us into a cycle of violence, defamation, incitement and financing, as well as playing with fire in vitally important institutions. It is well known that the rest of those who benefitted from the former regime are finding it difficult to see Egypt truly rise up – its people, army and police force all together.

The former criminal regime would do whatever they wanted and employ those from the security apparatus and protect them. Later on there were rifts, envy and splits between the people and some of the security men, and sometimes even the distortion of the institution.

(Morsi's speech, 26 June 2012)

The other in the above example is described as 'Egypt's enemies' whose main aim was to 'sabotage the democratic experiment', insinuating that they are undemocratic. They have also been presented as the people who are responsible for the chaos that Egypt witnessed, and they have been labelled as 'criminals'. This direct negative representation of the other (i.e. the opposition), reflects the disappointment and frustration of Morsi for what was happening in his country. His words were very direct and undiplomatic in his description of the opposition. The other has also been described as corrupt. Although Morsi did not name any names, his discourse was addressed to Mubarak and his people. The use of lexis such as 'violence', 'defamation', 'incitement' and 'criminals' are strong negative attributions, directed to the old regime.

While the Egyptian opposition and old regime have been represented negatively in Morsi's discourse, the international community has been impartially represented. There is no mention of specific countries, but there is a reassurance to the international community that Morsi's government will respect and adhere to 'international charters and conventions and agreements that Egypt has signed with the world'. Although it is not clearly stated here, the reference in the last part of this quotation is to Israel and the agreements signed with Egypt. The following examples demonstrate the MB's international relations strategy, as exemplified in Morsi's discourse.

Example 13

نحافظ على المعاهدات والمواثيق الدولية، لقد جئنا برسالة سلام إلى العالم. سنحافظ على الالتزامات والاتفاقيات المصرية مع دول العالم.

We will maintain international charters and conventions and the commitments and agreements Egypt has signed with the world.

(Morsi's speech, 25 June 2012)

The above extracts highlight three key issues: (1) the discourse of peace and unity, (2) the discourse of mutual interest and respect, (3) the discourse of foreign policy and a law-abiding nation. These three aspects of discourse could be considered the key framework for the FJP's national and international discourse.

Reconciliation and Unity

One of the discursive features and recurrent themes in FJP's discourses are reconciliation, unity and national interest. Like Al-Nahda, Morsi emphasised that national interest is above everything else and should come before the party's interests. The reference to social cohesion and unity is another theme occurring in Morsi's speeches. This discourse of the loyalty to the nation, not the party, could be said to have been designed to reassure the opposition who may have concerns about his leadership.

Example 14

مصر للمصريين جميعا، كلنا متساوون في الحقوق، وكلنا علينا واجبات لهذا الوطن، وأما عن نفسي فأنني ليس لي حقوق وإنما علي واجبات

Egypt is for all Egyptians; all of us are equals in terms of rights. All of us also have duties towards this homeland. As for myself, I don't have rights. I only have duties.

اننا كمصريين مسلمين ومسيحيين دعاة حضارة وبناء

We Egyptians, Muslims and Christians, are advocates of civilisation and development.

أدعوكم أيها الشعب المصري العظيم، أهلي وعشيرتي، لتقوية وحدتنا الوطنية الشاملة ولتمكين الأواصل بيننا

I invite you, the great Egyptian people ... to cement bonds amongst us, to strengthen our comprehensive national unity.

الوحدة الوطنية هي السبيل الآن للخروج بمصر من هذه المرحلة الصعبة والانطلاق نحو مشروع شامل نحمله جميعا، لنهضة وتنمية مصرية حقيقة، ولتوظيف حقيقي لكل مواردنا.

National unity is the way to lift Egypt out of the present situation and to embark upon a broad project of renaissance, one that is truly Egyptian, leading to real development of our resources.

(Morsi's speech, 29 June 2012)

The above examples reveal the MB discourse post presidential democratic elections. The emphasis on national unity and Egyptian nationalism is evident in the use of lexis such as 'homeland', 'Egypt is for Egyptians', 'we Egyptians', 'comprehensive national unity'. The use of such a discourse could be said to be designed to rally Egyptians to support the new democratically elected president and to encourage unity and social cohesion. This discourse of unity is often followed by the discourse of '*muṣālaḥa*' (reconciliation), which was repeated in many of Morsi's speeches in an attempt to rally support. The use of collaboration and coalition is a tangible example of Morsi's wish to bring different parties together, but his critics would argue that those were empty words, as Morsi failed to accommodate others in his government. This discourse of one nation and one voice was tested when opposition parties called for protests and demonstrations against Morsi and his government.

Example 15

وسأعمل معكم جميعاً على أن نكون شركاء في هذا العمل الوطني ونوسع الثقة بيننا ونعظم التوافق والائتلاف

I will work with all of you to be partners in this national work, to expand trust between us and to maximise the consensus and coalition.

وسأعمل معكم في كل لحظة من ولايتي الرئاسية على بقاء النسيج الوطني متماسك قوي وسوف أغلب مصالح الوطن العليا على كل ما دون ذلك، عاقد العزم على إرساء مبادئ العدل والحق والحرية والمبادئ الاجتماعية وإزالة كل أشكال الفساد والظلم والتمييز

I will work with you at every moment of my presidential mandate to keep the national fabric coherent and strong, and most of the supreme interests of the nation will be determined to establish the principles of justice, rights, freedom and social principles, and to remove all forms of corruption, injustice and discrimination.

(Morsi's speech, 29 June 2012)

Apart from reconciliation and national interest, there is constant reference to the principles of 'justice, freedom and liberty', as well as 'combating discrimination, corruption and injustices'. These principles and values are in line with the values of democracy, but what is striking about Morsi's speeches is his attempt to ground these principles in Islam. For instance, his talk about injustices and discrimination was supported by a paraphrased verse from the Quran. Similar to Al-Nahda, Morsi sought to show a modern face of the MB, ensuring that the democratic process had been safeguarded. However, in contrast to Al-Nahda, Morsi made heavy use of religion to support his argument and often grounded democratic concepts in Islam, considering them part of Islamic values, suggesting therefore the compatibility of Islam and democracy.

While the religious register remains a noticeable element of Morsi's discourse, the call for unity was also loud and clear. His reference to *miṣr* (Egypt) on numerous occasions shows his sense of responsibility towards the nation and its people. By using the word *miṣr*, Morsi sought to divert attention from himself as president, with a clear focus on the homeland, nation and country, as the following example illustrates.

Example 16

إن مصر في حاجة الآن إلى توحيد الصفوف وجمع الكلمة حتى يجني هذا الشعب العظيم الصابر ثمار تضحياته في العيش الكريم والعدالة الاجتماعية والحرية والكرامة الانسانية، وهي الشعارات الاساسية والاهداف الاساسية التي انطلقت بها حناجر الثوار في كل ميادين مصر في 25 يناير 2011 ، والتي لا تزال هذه الحناجر تعلنها قوية في كل مشاهد الثورة

Egypt, which impressed the world with its queues of voters, now needs to close ranks, unite the word, so that the patient, great Egyptian people can reap the fruit of their sacrifices in a better life, achieve social justice, freedom and human dignity, which are the basic slogans or the main goals that the throats of the revolutionaries kept repeating in all Egyptian squares on 25 January 2011, and which revolutionaries still repeat loudly in all the squares of the revolution, which is still ongoing.

(Morsi's speech, 29 June 2012)

The Use of Legitimacy

Similar to Al-Ghannouchi's discourse, Morsi has repeatedly referred to الشرعية *ashshar'iyya* 'legitimacy' and 'democracy', in an attempt to highlight the importance of the people's voice and the democratic process which crowned him President of Egypt. By reiterating the concept of legitimacy, he sought to remind the nation, including the opposition, that he is the democratically elected president and that the people's decision should be respected. It was also designed to remind the people of his popularity as an elected president in open, fair and transparent elections.

Example 17

جئت اليكم لأنكم مصدر السلطة والشرعية التي تعلوا على الجميع، لا مكان لأحد ولا لمؤسسة ولا هيئة ولا جهة فوق هذه الإرادة. الأمة مصدر السلطات جميعها.
وتتبلور اليوم على شكل إرادة واضحة إرادة الشعب المصري بأجمعه برئيس منتخب للبلاد

I came to talk to you today because I believe that you are the source of power and legitimacy. There is no person, party, institution or authority over or above the will of the people. The nation is the source of all power.

The will of the Egyptian people as a whole is crystallised by an elected president.

رسالتي إليكم جميعًا: متمسك بالشرعية وأقف حاميًا لها، وإلى المؤيدين من كل التيارات الذين يحبون الديمقراطية وتقدم الاقتصاد والقضاء على الفساد، حافظوا على مصر والثورة

My message to all of you is that I am sticking to legitimacy and safeguarding it, and to the supporters of all parties who love democracy, judiciary and economic development and elimination of corruption, safeguard Egypt and the revolution.

(Extracts from Morsi's speech, 29 June 2012)

What is striking about the above examples is the similarity in the discourse of Morsi and Al-Ghannouchi, in relation to the issue of democracy and legitimacy. They both seem to share an awareness of the significance of the people's voice in the democratic process and the importance of adhering and respecting this process.

Realising the challenges their new democracies encountered, both leaders resorted to reminding their people of the importance of democracy and the legitimacy of leaders and governments in governing their nations. They also highlighted the importance of people's power and their right to choose their elected leaders. Morsi acknowledged quite firmly that democracy as manifested in the voice of the people is the ultimate goal and that nothing should come before it. 'The will of people', as he calls it, has collectively led to the election of a new president. This discourse of legitimacy and democracy is new in the MB discourse. What is striking is the absence of religious concepts and terminologies such as '*khilāfa*', '*sharʿ Allah*', *Sharīʿah*', '*shūrā*', and this is very revealing as it shows the willingness of the FJP to get fully involved in the democratic process, leaving behind any reference to *Sharīʿah*. The association of people with democracy and legitimacy is also a new discourse phenomenon in the MB register, where the Islamic concepts of '*khilāfa*', '*Sharīʿah*', '*taṭbīq sharʿ Allah*' have given way to a new discourse. Such a transition in discourse could be interpreted as a change in strategy, where commitment to the democratic process is placed front and centre. It has deviated from the power of the few to the collective responsibility of the people and the elected. This is clearly evident in Morsi's emphasis on inclusivity, collectivism and working together to make a difference, as demonstrated in the following examples.

Example 18

سأعمل معكم في كل لحظة من أجل تحقيق كافة أهداف الثورة ولا اتهاون في أي من حقوقها أو حقوق شهدائها دماء الشهداء والجرحى.

وسأعمل معكم في كل لحظة من ولايتي الرئاسية على بقاء النسيج الوطني متماسك قوي، وسوف أغلب مصالح الوطن العليا على كل ما دون ذلك، عاقد العزم علي إرساء مبادئ العدل والحق والحرية والمبادئ الاجتماعية، وإزالة كل أشكال الفساد والظلم.

I will work with you at every moment in order to achieve all the objectives of the revolution and not to disregard any of its rights or the rights of its martyrs, the blood of the martyrs and the wounded.

I will work with you at every moment of my presidential mandate to keep the national fabric coherent and strong and most of the supreme interests of the nation will be determined to establish the principles of justice, rights, freedom and social principles and to remove all forms of corruption, injustice and discrimination.

سأعمل معكم علي نهضة الاقتصاد المصري ورفع المعاناة عن كاهل ملايين المصريين من أجل حياة كريمة واجتماعية، وهي هدف كل مؤسسات الدولة.

I will work with you on the renaissance of the Egyptian economy and lift the suffering from the burden of millions of Egyptians for a decent and social life which is the goal of all state institutions.

(Extracts from Morsi's speech, 29 June 2012)

As can be noted from the above examples, Morsi repeatedly used the sentence سأعمل معكم *Sa'a'malu ma'akum* (I will work with you), and this could have been designed to show that he is an ordinary citizen who sought to work with everyone, highlighting the inclusive and collective nature of his governance. This sense of collective responsibility is new to the discourse of FJP, which, again, emphasises its appreciation of democracy and recognition of the citizen's role in Egyptian society. While Morsi's selection of lexis shows his desire for collective action, others may question his choice of 'I will work with you' as it strips him of his authority and responsibility as a leader who is supposed to lead and set the direction of travel.

Morsi's choice of lexis also shows his desire to be seen as collaborative and a team player who can motivate, incentivise and energise the people around him to make the ultimate impact on citizens and the country. This level of equality and egalitarianism reflects the shift in Arabic discourse, where citizens have become partners and active contributors, rather than passive recipients of orders and instructions. This level of trust in the people and their ability to participate in and contribute to the development of their societies is prevalent in Morsi's discourse. In expressing his willingness to work collectively with citizens, Morsi has resorted to the use of the active form where the doer of the action 'I' is very explicit. The following section will dwell on the use of the active form in Morsi's discourse.

The Use of the Active Form

Morsi's desire for a collective endeavour is evident in his use of language. However, what is noticeable about Morsi's speeches is his use of the active form, where the agent/doer of the action is visible. In most cases, the agent is used to emphasise the role played by the president, the people and the *Waṭan* (nation). By using the active form, Morsi has shown an explicit approach in terms of the action to be taken, which could be attributed to the following reasons: (1) to claim responsibility for the action, (2) to show that he is the one leading and planning the future of the country. What is striking here, however, is that the active form is used in the context of the negative representation of the other. In the diplomatic sector, leaders often exercise caution in their statements and discourses, allowing a space for flexibility, and they often adopt the passive form in order to conceal the agent of discourse and remain ambiguous, without being associated with certain actions and statements.

In his speeches, for instance, Morsi repeatedly pointed to his role as the leader responsible for leading and developing Egypt. The use of 'I' made the agent very explicit and rendered sentences into the active form, where the responsibility for actions is made clear.

Example 19

سأعمل معكم على عودة مصر رائدة في ابداعها وثقافتها وإعلامها وتعليمها وبحثها وعلمها.

سأعمل معكم علي نهضة الاقتصاد المصري ورفع المعاناة عن كاهل ملايين المصريين من أجل حياة كريمة واجتماعية.

وسأعمل معكم في كل لحظة من ولايتي الرئاسية على بقاء النسيج الوطني متماسك قوي.

I will work with you to return Egypt, a pioneer in its creativeness, culture, information, education, research and science.
I will work with you to rejuvenate the Egyptian economy and lift the suffering from the burden of millions of Egyptians for a decent and social life.
I will work with you at every moment of my presidential mandate to keep the national fabric strong and coherent.

(Morsi's speech, 29 June 2012)

The use of 'I' in the above examples is designed to show leadership and authority, where the doer of the action (Morsi) is explicit. While this could be regarded as a good thing, showing the president's commitment to leading from the front, others may argue that the use of 'I' is obsolete and Morsi should have emphasised the collective nature of governance, as this would reflect his role as president.

The use of the active form, coupled with the discourse of inclusiveness, shows Morsi's desire to position himself as a fair, democratic and transparent leader, who does not hold grudges against the people who have opposed him. This also suggests that there is a break away from the discourse of retribution and authoritarianship to a discourse of reconciliation and inclusiveness, although some may argue that Morsi used this to mask his power, dominance and hegemony. This is epitomised by the extensive use of the first singular pronoun 'I', which will be discussed in detail later on in this chapter.

Sentence Structure

Apart from the use of the active form in his speeches, one cannot help but notice that some of Morsi's sentences are quite long and repetitive. This could be attributed to his desire to provide more information and details at the level of the sentence, making some of them very long, with condensed clauses. The length of his sentences could spring from his willingness to be persuasive in his speeches by providing as much information as possible. However, this could also pose challenges to the reader and listener in understanding, grasping the detail and following the argument.

Morsi's sentence structure seems to flout the traditional norms of Arabic political speeches, where clarity and succinctness are key to having an impact on the audience. Short, clear sentences could have delivered the message in a very persuasive manner. His long sentences not only prolonged his speeches, but made some of them incoherent in their argument. Some of the sentences are as long as a paragraph, with many clauses, some of which serve as a supplementary information to the main topic. Take for instance, the following sentence.

Example 20

ها أنا أقف أمامكم أيها الشعب المصري العظيم قبل أي جهة أخرى وقبل أي إجراءات أخرى وأقول أيها الشعب المصري العظيم أيها الواقفون في كل الميادين أو المشاهدون في كل البيوت يا من انتخبتموني، ويا من عارضتموني وما زلتم، أنا لكم جميعاً في مكان واحد وعلى مسافة واحدة، ولن ينتقص حق من حقوقه من قالوا لي لا كما لا ينتقص حق من حقوق من قالوا نعم هذه هي الديمقراطية

I stand here with you, O great people of Egypt, before the usual formal proceedings, and I say to all honourable Egyptians – those who elected me and those who did not – I'm for all of you, at the same distance from all. I will never subtract from the rights of those who told me 'No', nor will I subtract from the rights of those who said to me 'Yes'. This is democracy.

(Morsi's speech, 29 June 2012)

The violation of the structural norms of political discourse rendered Morsi's speeches incoherent, which had some repercussions on the persuasive power of his speeches. Despite the use of a religious register to support his argument, Morsi's long sentences made some of his arguments too general and unpersuasive, as key messages were lost in the details.

While the nature of his speeches shows his attention to detail, the length of his speeches may undermine the persuasive nature of some of them. In seeking to attract the audience's attention, Morsi addressed his audience directly, as will be discussed in the following section.

Addressing the Audience

What is striking about Morsi's speeches is his direct address to the audience, trying to fully engage them, alluring them to his plans and actions. It could be argued that Morsi's strategy here is designed to value the audience and make them active participants in delivering his plans. By focusing on the audience it could be interpreted that Morsi showed his willingness to serve his people. The use of plural in addressing the audience and nation often shows the addresser's desire to get the addressee on his side.

Example 21

أقف اليوم في ميدان الحرية معكم وميادين أخري في كل مدن مصر لأن هذا الميدان على وجه الخصوص شهد ميلادا جديدا لمصر الحرية والكرامة والإرادة والتغيير والنهضة والحقوق

أيها الشعب العظيم جئت إليكم اليوم لأنني مؤمن تماما بأنكم مصدر السلطة والشرعية. أنتم أهل السلطة ومصدرها، وأنتم الشرعية وأقوي ما فيها. من يحتمي بغيركم يخسر، ومن يسير مع إرادتكم ينجح، ونريد لوطننا النجاح

I stand today in Liberty Square with you and others in all the cities of Egypt because this square in particular has witnessed a new era of Egypt's freedom, dignity, will, change, renaissance and rights.

O great people, I came to you today because I am fully convinced that you are the source of power, authority and legitimacy. Those of you who are protected by others, lose, and those of you who follow your will, succeed, and we want our country to succeed.

(Morsi's speech, 29 June 2012)

As can be seen from the above example, the use of the second plural pronoun to address the people and nation shows Morsi's strategy of being direct, and showing his humility and desire to serve his people. His recognition of the people's power and legitimacy is reiterated several times in his speeches and this is intended again to remind his opposition of the power of the people and their voice.

The use of extensive glorifying terminologies and lexis when addressing the people is a new phenomenon when compared to past speeches. It is customary in Arabic political speeches for praise and recognition to be given, often in the introductory phase of the speech. However, Morsi broke this convention and used extensive gratifying expressions throughout his speeches, which suggest, as discussed above, his intention to recognise the power of the people, their legitimacy and their services to their own country. Others may consider this a strategy for winning Egyptians' hearts and minds in the face of growing opposition to Morsi's rule. The following is a clear example of this.

Example 22

أيها الشعب العظيم، جئت إليكم اليوم لأنني مؤمن تماما بأنكم مصدر السلطة والشرعية. أنتم أهل السلطة ومصدرها، وأنتم الشرعية وأقوى ما فيها، من يحتمي بغيركم يخسر ومن يسير مع إرادتكم ينجح، ونريد لوطننا النجاح

O great people, I came to you today because I am fully convinced that you are the source of power, authority and legitimacy. Those of you who are protected by others, lose, and those of you who follow your will, succeed, and we want our country to succeed.

(Morsi's speech, 29 June 2012)

The above example demonstrates Morsi's main focus on the power and legitimacy of the people, and the need to serve them. It confirms Morsi's belief that the legitimacy of the people is the sole protection from those who may wish harm to the democratic process, or who may wish to depose him and his government. However, this legitimacy and the power of the people collapsed when the military deposed Morsi and took control of the country. By placing so much emphasis on the legitimacy of the people and alienating other parties and stakeholders, including international actors, Morsi and his colleagues created adversaries who saw them as a threat. Such concerns mobilised the opposition and contributed to the overthrow of Morsi and his government.

The Discourse of Humility

What is striking about Morsi's discourse is the use of the phrase 'I came to you', which pays no heed to the Arabic culture and tradition that leaders are respected and recognised for their leadership and authority. But the use of this expression suggests a remarkable change/shift in the use of discourse, where the leader has gone against the norms by showing humility, breaching the social distance and acknowledging the power of the people. The use of pronouns is also very revealing in that the first singular pronoun is used by the president while the second plural pronoun is used to address the crowd, magnifying the level of politeness to the people and emphasising the modesty and humility of the president.

But this is not the only time that Morsi has shown this level of modesty and humility; his discourse about 'working closely' with the people is another type of shift in discourse. The old discourse, where the authority and command of the president are very distinct, appears to have been replaced with one that is more flexible and reflective of the people's power. It should be noted here that this type of discourse is used in times of conflict, when power and authority are threatened or when the speaker is insecure. What is certain in Morsi's speech is that it occurred during a period of transition, marred with so many issues, including conflicts and tensions between different rival groups and parties.

Morsi's discourse of appealing to the electorate and his supporters is a clear recognition of their power in the democratic process. This appeal is visible in the discourse produced by the president, which features expressions of appeal, calls for support and the empowerment of citizens, marking a clear shift in the speeches of political leaders. Example 22 is a good one to cite here, where Morsi addressed Egyptians and considered them to be the source of 'authority, legitimacy and success'.

The conclusion from the above discussion is that when conflicts arise and when opposition to leaders intensifies, there is a moderation process by which the discourse of humility is used to mitigate any discourse of power and authority. By conceding to the people through the mitigation of their discourse, leaders usually seek support, ask for repentance and acknowledge the people's power and authority as citizens. But it could also be used to show that they are democrats who respect people and the democratic process, as Morsi has reiterated several times in his speeches.

Direct Pronoun – First Singular Pronoun 'I'
Arabic political speeches often avoid the use of first singular pronoun, using 'we' instead to reflect the status and authority of the speaker. It also reflects the collective nature of the governance as it presents leaders as representatives of their respective nations. Morsi's speeches tend to emphasise the individual nature of the action. It could well be that he wishes to emphasise his own responsibility towards his people by using the first pronoun 'I'. What is different in Morsi's speeches is his display of modesty and approachableness as a president.

While the use of 'I' could be intended to show modesty and humiliation, it could also be interpreted as a sign of authoritarianism, where authority rests with one person, disregarding the concept of collectivism where actions are taken and acted upon collectively.

From the above examples, it is apparent that Arabic political discourse has undergone some changes, some of which are pertinent to the structure of these speeches, while others are linked to the genre of discourse. The discourse has become less formal and displays elements of individuality where the use of 'I' becomes more prevalent, compared to the use of 'we', which expresses command and the authority of the speaker. The extensive praise of the audience is another new phenomenon in Arabic political discourse, where the audience has been recognised for their power, legitimacy and voice. This has bridged the hierarchical divide between leaders and citizens by granting people more power and authority. Another remark to be made while examining Morsi's speeches is the gentle tone of its discourse, compared to what others may consider to be the aggressive discourse pre Arab Spring. This gentle and often soft approach is evident in the choice of lexis employed, such as 'brothers and sisters', 'friends', 'generous citizens', 'heroes', etc. While this type of discourse reflects the modesty of the speaker, it is intended to establish a rapport between the speaker and the wider society, adopting therefore the notion of extended family where each member of the family has responsibility for the others. This concept, which is new to the Arabic political discourse, could be said to have been designed to bridge the hierarchical structure between the people and their rulers.

The other change that can be noted here is that while the religious register frequently features in Morsi's speeches, it is not as prevalent as pre Arab Spring. What is remarkable here is that a Western political register has been used in the form of democratic concepts, which are widely utilised in the Western context. This bears some similarity to Al-Nahda's speeches, which adopt a similar approach.

The most striking feature of these speeches is the recognition of the audience and their power and legitimacy in the democratic process, a new phenomenon in the discourse of these leaders. The empowerment of the audience/public through the recognition of their power and legitimacy could also be regarded as a new discursive feature, departing from the traditional norm of considering citizens to be passive recipients and participants in the democratic process and decision-making.

This transition in discourse reflects the transition in the political and social landscape post Arab revolutions in Egypt and Tunisia. The shift in political discourse is a result of the change in the political landscape and also in the mindset of the political leaders, who sought to project a new image of championing democracy through the values of freedom, liberty and justice. Another change that has engulfed the political discourse is what I call *the discourse of humility*, as reflected in different linguistic features employed by leaders, some of which include the use of phrases such as 'servant' and 'citizen', as well as attributes that show the modesty and humiliation of some of these leaders. The empowerment of citizens as key stakeholders is another new phenomenon in the new Arabic political discourse. It marks a break with the norms of Arabic political discourse, where citizens have been regarded as passive recipients of information and instructions.

The extensive acknowledgement of the electorate as key partners and participants in the electoral process and governance is a new phenomenon in the Arabic political discourse. While this is an essential ingredient of democracy in other contexts, in the Arab world this marks a great transition in the political discourse.

Attribution Strategies

The recognition of the public as key contributors to the democratic process and to the development of their nation is very evident in the type and nature of Morsi's attribution to the Egyptian people and to the nation as a whole. The extensive use of praise and commendation is mirrored in the genre of attributions bestowed upon nations and citizens. This positive attribution constitutes a new discourse practice and political culture, where citizens and nations have been praised for their key contributions to the democratic process. The following examples illustrate this point clearly.

Example 23

ها أنا أقف أمامكم أيها الشعب المصري العظيم

I stand before you O great Egyptian people.

كل التحية لشعب مصر العظيم، وجيش مصر خير اجناد الأرض، والقوات المسلحة بكل ابنائها اينما وجدوا، تحية خالصة من قلبي لهم وحب لا يعلمه في قلبي إلا الله سبحانه وتعالى. وأنا أحب هؤلاء وأقدر دورهم، وأحرص على تقويتهم والحفاظ عليهم وعلى المؤسسة العريقة التي نحبها ونقدرها جميعا.

I salute the great Egyptian people, and salute the army, the best soldiers on earth, our armed forces, wherever they are. I offer my heartfelt greetings and love to them. I value their role and I am keen to strengthen and secure them and their esteemed institution which we all love and value.

(Morsi's speech, 24 June 2012)

The attribution of 'great people', 'sincere people', 'the best soldiers on earth' are designed to show the president's admiration for his people and military, and this admiration has been reflected in the selected lexis, which is very positive and upbeat, such as 'we all love and value' them.

While the public and citizens have been depicted in a good light, the remains of the old regime have been criticised for their gross failure in the management of the country, as the following example demonstrates.

قبل الثورة كان فيه فساد وتزوير الانتخابات وظلم وعدوان على الإنسان وكرامته، وتأخرت مصر كثيرًا بسبب النظام السابق، الذي أجرم في هذا الوطن

Before the revolution, there was corruption, vote-rigging, injustice and violation of human dignity. Egypt remained undeveloped because of the former regime that committed crimes in this country.

(Morsi's speech, 3 July 2013)

As the above example illustrates, the opposition and remains of the old regime were portrayed in a negative light. They were described as 'corrupts', 'unjust', 'cheats', 'criminals', etc. They were held responsible for the poor economic situation in the country and for the corruption and lack of progress and development. This negative attribution of 'Them' is very revealing indeed. It reveals the existing tension between the new and old guard, and the determination of Morsi and his people to continue to remind the public of the old guard and their unsatisfactory record. Apart from its negative portrayal of the old regime, there is a continued mention of democracy and the democratic process, as well as the legitimacy of the people and the elected president. The shift of power and hierarchy have changed, and more power has been passed on to the people, as reflected in Morsi's speeches. His discourse considers people to be the real governing body; they have the legitimacy and power to elect and deselect whoever they wish.

Discourse of National Interest

The MB has often been criticised for its affiliation with international organisations, which raises doubt about its commitment to national causes. However, the FJP and MB have refuted this claim and asserted that their work is clear evidence of their commitment to the security and prosperity of the nation. The late Egyptian president, Morsi, made this clear in his speeches, in which he displayed his patriotism and eagerness, as well as his desire to improve and develop Egypt. He referred to the Egyptian military as the sole defender of the country and urged people to get behind it. He also praised the security forces and apparatus and called upon citizens to respect them as they are the ones who safeguard their country from external forces.

By referring to the national security, the military and the security apparatus, Morsi wished to demonstrate patriotism and loyalty to his own country, responding therefore to those who questioned his loyalty to the country in which he had been democratically elected as president.

Example 24

اعهد الله واعهدكم يا شعب مصر و يا جماهير مصر

I pledge to God and I pledge to you, the people of Egypt.

كل التحية لشعب مصر العظيم وجيش مصر ، خير اجناد الأرض، والقوات المسلحة بكل ابنائها اينما وجدوا ، تحية خالصة من قلبي لهم وحب لا يعلمه في قلبي إلا الله سبحانه وتعالى، وأنا احب هؤلاء واقدر دورهم واحرص على تقويتهم والحفاظ عليهم وعلى المؤسسة العريقة التي نحبها ونقدرها جميعا

I salute the great people of Egypt, and the army of Egypt, the best soldiers on Earth, the armed forces and all their members, wherever they may be. I salute them sincerely, from the bottom of my heart, and I send them the love reserved in my heart for Allah. Indeed, I love them, I value their role, and I am committed to strengthening them, and to protecting them and the deep-rooted [military] institution that we all love and cherish.

(Morsi's speech, 24 June 2012)

The fact that Morsi swore allegiance to his people and country to safeguard and protect Egypt is very revealing in many ways. It could have been designed to reassure those who casted doubt on his sincerity and sense of belonging. He also sought to reassure the military that he was on their side and ready to defend and protect the army and the security apparatus.

The Use of Vocatives in FJP Leaders' Discourse

Daniel and Spencer (2009: 626) define vocatives as forms 'used for calling out and attracting or maintaining the addressee's attention'. In the same vein, Zwicky (1974: 787), cited in Sonnenhauser and Hanna (2013: 13), distinguished between two types of vocatives, namely, calls and addressees; 'calls are designed to catch the addressee's attention, addresses to maintain or emphasize contact between the speaker and the addressee'. By attracting the attention, the speaker is seeking 'to establish or maintain a relationship between this addressee and some proposition' (Lambrecht 1996: 267).

Apart from establishing a good relationship with the addressee, vocatives can be very instrumental in showing whether this relationship is based on 'respect, formality, endearment, salience, intimacy, power, solidarity, etc.' (Shormani and Qarabesh 2018: 4).

The use of vocatives is prevalent in Morsi's speeches. They are often used in the context of calling for supporters and the public to rally behind their leader, and to show their support and sympathy. Vocatives are also used to acknowledge and recognise citizens' work and their contribution to the country. As the definition indicates, vocatives in Morsi's speeches have been used to attract the addressee's attention and to establish a good rapport with them. In the Arabic context this can be regarded as a sign of modesty. Vocatives have also been used in this context to show the legitimacy and power of the addressee as well as their closeness to the speaker. This extensive use of vocatives could be interpreted as a strategy to gain more help and support, and influence the addressee in times of tension and conflict. In the case of Morsi, as protests against his rule increased and there was a military ultimatum for him to resolve the tension, he used vocatives to attract the public's attention to his own cause in an attempt to gain their support and sympathy. What is striking about the use of vocatives in Morsi's speeches is that the addressee often receives praise and commendation, as the following examples demonstrate: 'oh great Egyptian people', 'oh people of the revolution', 'oh people of 25 January revolution'.

Example 25

أيها الشعب المصري العظيم، يا صاحب ثورة 25 يناير، أخاطبكم، وأنا أعرف وأرى وأنتم تنتظرون كلمة بتوضيح الموقف، ولتعرفوا بلادنا فيه إيه (. . .) يا رجال الثورة الصامتين

Oh Egyptian people of 25 January revolution, I address you, knowing that you are awaiting clarification on what is happening in our country (. . .) oh silent people of the revolution.

(Morsi's speech, 3 July 2013)

The use of attributes such as 'oh great Egyptian people', 'people of revolution', 'great people' . . . is very indicative of the speaker's sentiments, and are often used to cement the bond between the speaker and the addressee. In this case, the speaker sought to establish a firm tie with the revolutionaries who had overthrown the former president and elected Morsi as president. This new discourse of seeking support and sympathy from the public is new to the Arabic discourse, as previous political discourses would not go to this length to acknowledge supporters' power and revolutionary action, but it could be said here that the change to the political landscape has led to a change in the discourse itself of both speakers and recipients.

A New Approach to Studying Shifts in the Discourse of Islamic Parties

In previous sections we have discussed the discourse of Islamic parties such as Al-Nahda and the FJP during the Arab Spring. We have closely examined their discourses and strategies during the conflict and beyond. Our analysis has indicated that there is a shift from a very conservative discourse to a more moderate one. This transition in discourse shapes and is shaped by different political and social changes that have occurred in different Arab states, including Egypt and Tunisia, the case studies of this chapter. Such a shift is evident in the content and structure of discourse of these parties. The framework shown in Figure 7.1 summarises and elucidates this shift.

Figure 7.1 shows a shift in discourse of Islamic parties during different stages of the conflict. The pre-conflict discourse demonstrates a conservative discourse embedded in a religious register, which displays these parties' religious affiliation and values. This type of discourse is often supported by religious texts and linguistic features engrained in the religious register.

During the conflict, however, the religious discourse was replaced with a discourse of unity and togetherness. This type of discourse is designed to appeal to different stakeholders and unite different perspectives away from the religious discourse. This gave way to a discourse of emancipation, liberation and empowerment, where freedom, liberty and democracy have been emphasised. This phase is orchestrated to unite different voices against the regime by offering a popular discourse of emancipation and liberation, aimed at drumming up support and maximising the impact of the uprising. This is evident in different linguistic features such as the binary Us vs Them, nominalisation, personification, etc. (see Chapter 5, micro-analysis).

The last phase of this framework, what we label post-conflict discourse, is when these parties hold power and become part of the establishment.

In order to appeal to domestic and external audiences, they adopt a moderated discourse, which includes features of equality, liberty and freedom of expression. The national interest, reconciliation and unity emerge to form a united front against the opposition. Adopting a liberal discourse could be said to have been used to appeal to a wider section of society, and to reassure the external audience that Islam and democracy are compatible and that Islam, as Al-Ghannouchi argued, embodies values of equality, liberty and freedom.

While the framework shown in Figure 7.1 reflects the shift in the discourse of Islamic parties during different phases of the conflict, this model could be applied to other settings and contexts where different actors, stakeholders and parties go through a similar transition. The basic argument here is that perspectives and stances can be moderated during different stages of conflicts or actions, as the pressing need for this moderation of discourse became apparent. Different governments and organisations have shifted their positions to accommodate the majority of views and appeal to a wider audience. This shift is often captured and manifested in the discursive practices of these actors. New linguistic features and registers emerge to show this transition of discourse and the agility of its producers. Al-Nahda and FJP have

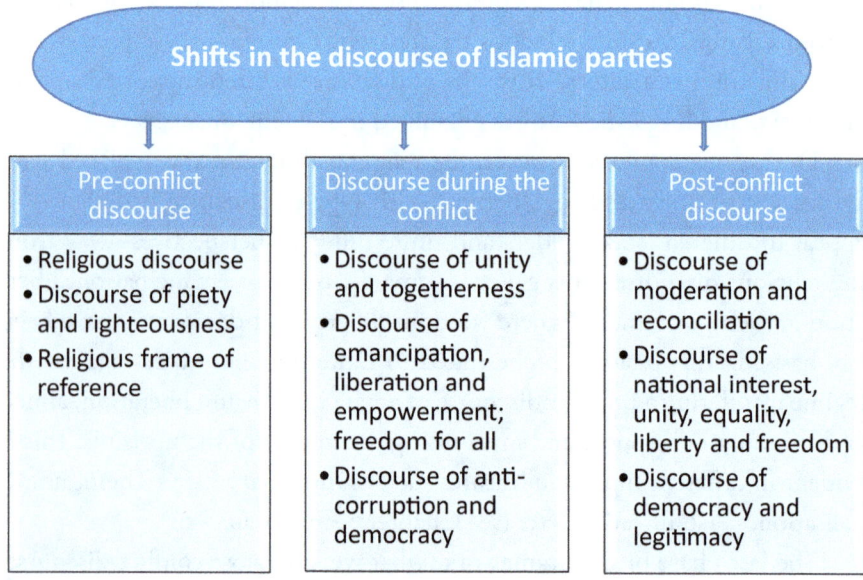

Figure 7.1 Shifts in the discourse of Islamic parties

shown some agility in discourse and its transition as we moved through different stages of the conflict.

Conclusion

This chapter has offered an insight into the main discourses of Al-Nahda and FJP post Arab Spring. It has examined the nature and genre of discourses delivered, concluding that there have been major shifts, and that the discourse of '*khilāfa*', '*Sharī'ah*' has been replaced with one of democracy, liberty, freedom and human rights. This new discourse has led to a shift in the discourse of addressing citizens and recipients, who have been empowered and recognised for their participation in and contribution to the democratic process. This recognition is often mirrored in the language used and attributions employed to describe citizens. Another shift in the Islamists' discourse post Arab Spring is the dearth of religious register in their political discourse. While there has been some use of this register in the form of quotations from the Quran to support their arguments, their speeches witnessed a surge in the use of democratic terminologies such as freedom, liberty, equality, human rights, legitimacy, democracy, etc. Such terminologies have been embedded in these parties' visions and strategies, although some differences can be noted when comparing Al-Nahda and the FJP. The former has extensively used these concepts, while the FJP has used some of them, but in the Islamic context, providing an Islamic justification for their inclusion.

Another emerging feature in these discourses is that of unity, national interest and homeland. This is a dominant theme and it could be interpreted as having been used to reassure the public that these parties are committed to safeguarding the national interest and maintaining the security of their respective countries.

Their discourses present Al-Nahda and the FJP as positive, democratic and progressive parties, whose aim is to defend the national interest, unify the country and safeguard its democratic gains as exemplified in the post Arab Spring elections. Both parties have also resorted to the discourse of inclusiveness where supporters and the opposition have been included in their speeches. However, some argue that the MB's downfall could be attributed to its exclusive approach, in contrast to Al-Nahda's approach which has been widely praised for its flexibility.

The FJP's and Al-Nahda's discourses reflect two main strategies. The first of these is that while Al-Nahda has shown some agility in its approach when dealing with different stakeholders post Arab Spring, the FJP rigidly implemented the election outcome, which handed the party a majority of seats, putting the FJP in the driving seat. Its decision to go it alone without the involvement of other stakeholders has been a source of contention. While Al-Nahda considered this period very crucial to Tunisia's political history and recognised the diversity of political perspectives, which had for so long been governed by 'undemocratically elected government', the MB felt that it had received the mandate to govern on its own. This decision was unpopular with the opposition who felt that they had been marginalised and this triggered the type of contention we witnessed during Morsi's rule.

The second different strategy is FJP's continued criticism of the old regime, as has been exemplified in their language and discourse. They have made the old regime and its remains their enemy number one, exacerbating the situation further and prompting the latter to show animosity to the president and his people.

To sum up, the analysis of Al-Nahda's and the MB's speeches and strategies suggest a shift in their discourse; the traditional discourse of Islam and *Sharī'ah*, as fundamental pillars of governance, has been replaced with liberal democratic discourse, placing the democratic process front and centre. The discourse of empowerment of citizens as active partners is another shift in discourse of these two parties. The discourse of full commitment to the democratic process could also be regarded as a clear shift in the discourse of these two parties. However, the opponents of Al-Nahda and FJP stipulate that this shift does not reflect the genuine change in these parties, but is a tactic adopted to show to the international community that these parties are committed to the democratic process.

Conclusion and Findings

In the course of this book many approaches to discourse, notions and concepts have been introduced, discussed and debated and their relevance to this project has been clarified. While these concepts, theories and approaches remain vital to this project, three key concepts constitute the argument of this book: discourse, framing and conflict. The analysis of discourse and its contextualisation in different contexts and at different stages of the conflict have enabled us not only to account for different voices and stakeholders, but have also allowed us an insight into the new discourse and the emerging discursive practices. By examining discourses of different actors and stakeholders we have managed to fully understand the reality of the tensions and conflict. The dialectical relationship between discourse and society has enabled us to understand how discourses shape and are shaped by events on the ground. In the context of this book, the focus has been on Arab leaders and the Arab public discourses, with a view to understanding the nature of relationship between the two through their own discourse and practice.

What is striking about the findings of this analysis is the polarisation of views and perspectives when considering key issues such as demonstrations, and social and political change. The analysis has revealed that different discourses have been produced at different stages of the conflict by same actors. For instance, in the early stages of the conflict, a discourse of authority and command was displayed by officials and leaders, ensuring full control of the situation. This was exemplified by rejecting outright the demonstrations and blaming it on a minority of bad apples, who were under the pay of foreign agents. However, this discourse shifted in later stages of the conflict when the balance of power changed and protests gained more momentum. The discourse of authority gave way to a discourse of concession and negotiation. This shift in discourse and strategy was evident in the type and nature of language and linguistic features used, most of which offer an insight into the attitudes, responses and reactions of the Arab leaders to protests.

On the other hand, as protests grew, the protesters' discourse shifted too, along with a gradual increase in demands. In early stages of the conflict, demands were confined to the economic situation, with protesters calling for a better standards of living, but as their confidence grew their demands were upgraded and became political, calling for the departure of their leaders. The type of language and linguistic features used, such as imperatives, negative attributions, etc., made this very explicit.

As briefly mentioned above, the analysis of discourse and its transition would not have happened were it not for the availability of the data that has been collected from different online platforms. However, in order to make sense of this complex data, CDA has been applied to cater for shifts in discourse and examine different perspectives and ideologies that shape and are shaped by discourse. While CDA has been a useful tool in identifying the type and nature of discourse used by different stakeholders, it offered little when considering strategies and shifts in discourse at different stages of the conflict. This has induced us to develop a new model to cater for the dynamics and changes of strategies and discourses in times of conflict. The *shift of strategy model* (Figure 5.4) is designed to measure responses to conflicts at different stages. These responses mirror and are mirrored by the production of discourse and the specific language and linguistic features employed to verbalise these strategies. In the context of this study, the strategy shifts of leaders and the public have been analysed in relation to the conflict (i.e. the Arab Spring). A framework for analysing Arabic discourse strategies and representation of the self and other has been developed to accommodate these shifts across the different stages of conflict.

The analysis of shifts in discourse focuses on different themes distributed across different chapters. The first two chapters introduced key approaches to discourse analysis, notably CDA, and the notion of framing and positioning in discourse. The latter were very useful in helping examine how key actors position and represent themselves vis-à-vis each other. It gives the reader an insight into the main strategies employed in discourse. Other chapters have delved into the analysis of different discourses generated by Arab leaders and producers. Chapter 4, for instance, provided a step-by-step textual analysis of some of the data. It has allowed readers to gain a good understanding of the type of language and linguistic features used in the analysis. Chapter 5 examined macro aspects of discourse and analysed Arab leaders' strategies and discourses in response to the Arab Spring. It offered a good understanding of the strategies used in shifts in discourse of both Arab leaders and the public, contextualising these shifts in discourse within their social and political background. This chapter introduced the reader to a new model for the analysis of Arabic discourse in the context of conflict. Chapter 6, however, studied the shift of discourse from a politeness perspective. It examined politeness strategies in different speeches, slogans and statements and contextualised them within the Arabic culture and established norms. The analysis indicated that there is a shift in discourse and that the well-established norms of politeness have been replaced with impolite discourse, where the discourse of loyalty and respect have given way to one of reprimand and accountability, suggesting not only a shift in discourse but in the social and cultural norms.

The last chapter introduced the reader to the Arabic Islamic political discourse by analysing the discourse of Al-Nahda and FJP following their victory in the elections that followed revolutions in Egypt and Tunisia. The analysis suggested that the two parties adopted different discourse strategies in addressing local and international audiences. Contrary to what was expected, there was a shift in the use of terminologies by deviating from the traditional use of Islamic concepts such as *'khilāfa'*, *Sharī'ah*, and adopting liberal democratic terminologies.

The analysis of Arabic political discourse has shown us that discourses shape and are shaped by the context of their production, and that their shift and transition is governed by the circumstances generating them. We have also understood that in the context of conflict discourses are hybrid in terms of their substance and linguistic features. The gist of our analysis and findings suggest that a wide range of strategies has been adopted during the Arab

Spring, and these strategic shifts were designed to accommodate the development of events on the ground. What is striking is that discourses mirror the reality, which explains the reason why some Arab leaders were agile in their approach when trying to defuse the heightened tension with demonstrators. Discourse therefore becomes a product of this interaction between different actors, and as the situation on the ground changes the discourse shifts too. The discourse also shifts as the power dynamics change. Arab leaders, for instance, adopted a discourse of moderation and concession as protests gained momentum. On the other hand, the protesters' voices became louder.

To capture these shifts in Arabic political discourse at a time of conflict, a model has been developed, suggesting that Arabic political discourse changes as the situation on the ground changes (see Chapter 5).

References

Abdul-Raof, H. (2006) *Arabic Rhetoric: A Pragmatic Analysis*. London and New York: Routledge.

Abou El Fadl, K. (2013) 'The Praetorian State in the Arab Spring', <https://www.law.upenn.edu/live/files/2056-abouelfadl34upajintll3052012pdf> (last accessed 8 April 2021).

Abu Hatab, W. (2013) 'Arab Spring Presidential Speeches and New Social Identities: A Critical Discourse Analysis Study'. *The European Conference on Arts & Humanities: Official Conference Proceedings*.

Aday, S., H. Farrell, M. Lynch, J. Sides and D. Freelon (2012) *New Media and Conflict After the Arab Spring*. Washington, DC: United State Institute for Peace.

Achard, M. (1998) *Representation of cognitive Structures: Syntax and Semantics of French Sentential Complements*. Berlin: Mouton de Gruyter.

Achugar, M. (2007) 'Between remembering and forgetting: Uruguayan military discourse about human rights (1976–2004)', *Discourse & Society* 18(5), 521–47.

Ahearn, L. M. (2012) *Living Language: An Introduction to Linguistic Anthropology*. Oxford: Wiley-Blackwell.

Al-Hejin, B. (2012) *Covering Muslim women: A corpus-based critical discourse analysis of the BBC and Arab News*. PhD thesis, Lancaster University.

Al-Jenaibi, B. (2014) 'The nature of Arab public discourse: Social media and the "Arab Spring"', *Journal of Applied Journalism & Media Studies* 3(2), 241–60.

Althusser, L. (1971) 'Ideology and ideological state apparatuses', in L. Althusser (ed.), *Lenin and Philosophy and Other Essays*. New York Monthly Review Press.

Althusser, L. (2014) *On the Reproduction of Capitalism: Ideology and Ideological State Apparatuses*. London and New York: Verso.

Amin, S. (2012) 'The Arab revolutions: a year after', *A Journal for and about Social Movements* 4(1), 33–42.

Atton, C. (2004) *An Alternative Internet: Radical Media, Politics and Creativity*. Edinburgh: Edinburgh University Press.

Bardici, M. V. (2012) *A Discourse Analysis of the Media Representation of Social Media for Social Change – The Case of Egyptian Revolution and Political Change*, <http://muep.mau.se/handle/2043/14121> (last accessed 8 April 2021).

Berkowitz, L. (1993) Aggression: Its Causes, Consequences, and Control. New York: McGraw-Hill Book Company.

Bernstein, B. (1990) *The Structure of Pedagogic Discourse*. London: Routledge.

Blommaert, J. (2005) *Discourse. A Critical Introduction*. Cambridge: Cambridge University Press.

Blum-Kulka, S. and M. Hamo (2011) 'Explanations in naturally occurring peer talk: Conversational emergence and functions, thematic scope, and contribution to the development of discursive skills', *First Language* 30(3–4), 440–60.

Brown, G. and G. Yule (1983) *Discourse Analysis*. Cambridge: Cambridge University Press.

Butler, J. (1990) *Gender Trouble: Feminism and the Subversion of Identity*. New York: Routledge.

Cavatorta, F. (2018) 'The Complexity of Tunisian Islamism: Conflicts and Rivalries over the Role of Religion in Politics', in H. Kraetzschmar and P. Rivetti (eds), *Islamists and the Politics of the Arab Uprisings: Governance, Pluralisation and Contention*. Edinburgh: Edinburgh University Press.

Chaiklin, S. and J. Lave (eds) (1993) *Understanding Practice: Perspectives on Activity and Context*. Cambridge: Cambridge University Press.

Chilton, P. (2004) *Analysing Political Discourse: Theory and Practice*. London and New York: Routledge.

Chilton, P. and C. Schäffner (2011) 'Discourse and politics', in T. A. Van Dijk (ed.), *Discourse Studies: A Multidisciplinary Introduction* (2nd edn, pp. 303–30). London: SAGE.

Chouliaraki, L. and N. Fairclough, N. (1999) *Discourse in Late Modernity: Rethinking Critical Discourse Analysis*. Edinburgh: Edinburgh University Press.

Comninos, A. (2011) 'Twitter revolutions and cyber crackdowns', Association for Progressive Communications (APC).

Covatorta, F. and F. Merone (2015) 'Post-Islamism, ideological evolution and "la tunisianité" of the Tunisian Islamist party al-Nahda', *Journal of Political Ideologies* 20(1), 27–42.

Dalacoura, K. (2018) *Islamism, secularization, secularity: the Muslim Brotherhood in Egypt as a phenomenon of a secular age*. Economy and Society. ISSN 0308–5147.

Daniel, M. and A. Spencer (2009) 'The vocative - an outlier case', in A. Malchukov and A. Spencer (eds), *The Oxford Handbook of Case. Oxford Handbooks in Linguistics*. Oxford: Oxford University Press, pp. 626–34.

Daniels, H. (2007) 'Discourse and Identity in Cultural-Historical Activity Theory: A response', *International Journal of Educational Research* 46, 94–9.

Davies, B. and R. Harré (1990) 'Positionings: The discursive production of selves', in B. Davies (ed.), *A Body of Writing*. New York: AltaMira Press, pp. 87–106.

De Fina, A. (2011) *Discourse and Identity*, in T. A. Van Dijk (ed.), *Discourse Studies. A Multidisciplinary Introduction*. London: SAGE.

De Saussure, F. (1959) *Course in General Linguistics*, trans. Wade Baskin. New York: McGraw-Hill.

Drevon, J. (2018) 'The Reconfiguration of the Egyptian Islamist Social Movement Family after Two Political Transitions', in P. Rivetti and H. Kraetzschmar, *Islamists and the Politics of the Arab Uprisings: Governance, Pluralisation and Contention*, Edinburgh: Edinburgh University Press, pp. 258–73.

Entman, R. M. (2004) *Projections of Power: Framing News, Public Opinion, and U.S. Foreign Policy*. Chicago: University of Chicago Press.

Erikson, E. (1980) *Identity and the Life Cycle*. New York and London: Norton.

Fairclough, N. (1989) *Language and Power*. London: Longman.

Fairclough, N. (1992) *Discourse and Social Change*. Cambridge: Polity Press.

Fairclough, N. (1995a) *Critical Discourse Analysis*. London: Longman.

Fairclough, N. (1995b) *Media Discourse*. London: Arnold.

Fairclough, N. (2000) *New Labour, New Language*. London: Routledge.

Fairclough, N. (2001) *Language and Power*, 2nd edn. London: Pearson Education.

Fairclough, I. and N. Fairclough (2013) *Political Discourse Analysis: A Method for Advanced Students*. London and New York: Routledge.

Faris, D. (2010) 'Amplified voices for the voiceless', *Arab Media and Society* 11.

Fasold, R. (1990) *The Sociolinguistics of Language*. Oxford: Basil Blackwell.

Forgas, J. P. and K. Fiedler (1996) 'Us and them: Mood effects on intergroup discrimination', *Journal of Personality and Social Psychology* 70, 28–40.

Fowler, R., B. Hodge, G. Kress and T. Trew (1979) *Language and Control*. London: Routledge and Kegan Paul.

Fraser, B. (1975) 'The concept of politeness'. Paper Presented at the 1975 *NWAVE*.

Gallagher, S. (1998) *An Intercultural Reading and Critical Analysis of the Discipline of educational Psychology*. Unpublished PhD thesis. Loyola University Chicago.

Gholami, S., I. Montashery and M. Khorrami (2016) 'Metaphors in Arabic and English texts: A case study of translation of metaphors in the English versions of Al-Sahifah Al-Sajjadiyyah', in A. Giddens (1984) *The Constitution of Society*. Cambridge: Polity Press.

Gilmore, N. and M. A. Somerville (1994) 'Stigmatization, scapegoating and discrimination in sexually transmitted diseases: Overcoming "them" and "us"', *Social Science & Medicine* 39(9), 1339–58.

Gitlin, T. (1980) *The Whole World Is Watching: Mass Media in the Making and Unmaking of the New Left*. Berkeley: University of California Press.

Goffman, E. (1974) *Frame Analysis: An Essay on the Organization of Experience*. Cambridge, MA: Harvard University Press.

Gottlieb, R. (1987) *History and Subjectivity: The Transformation of Marxist Theory*. London: Humanities Press.

Halliday, M. A. K. (1973) *Explorations in the Function of Language*. London: Arnold.

Halliday, M. A. K. (1985) *Introduction to Functional Grammar*. London: Arnold.

Halliday, M. A. K. and R. Hasan (1976) *Cohesion in English*. London: Longman.

Hasan, R. (2001) 'Wherefore context? The place of context in the system and process of language', in *Grammar and Discourse: Proceedings of the International Conference on Discourse Analysis*, ed. S. Ren, W. Guthrie, and I. W. R. Fong. Macau: University of Macau.

Heritage, J. (1984) 'A change-of-state token and aspects of its sequential placement', in *Structures of Social Action: Studies in Conversation Analysis*, ed. J. Maxwell Atkinson and J. Heritage. Cambridge: Cambridge University Press, pp. 299–345.

Holland, D., W. Lachiocotte, D. Skinner and C. Cain (1998) *Identity and Agency in Cultural Worlds*. Cambridge, MA: Harvard University Press.

Hutchby, I. (1992) 'Confrontation talk: Aspects of "interruption" in argument sequences on talk radio', *Text* 12(3), 343–71.

Iskander, E. (2011) 'Connecting the National and the Virtual: Can Facebook Activism Remain Relevant After Egypt's January 25 Uprising?', *International Journal of Communication* 5(1), 1225–37.

Jackson, N. B. (1996) 'Arab Americans: Middle East conflicts hit home', in P. M. Lester (ed.), *Images that injure: Pictorial stereotypes in the media*. Westport, CT: Praeger, pp. 63–6.

Jarraya, S. (2013) 'Persuasion in Political Discourse: Tunisian President Ben Ali's Last Speech as a Case Study', *Theses – ALL*. 4, <https://surface.syr.edu/thesis/4> (last accessed 9 April 2021).

Johnstone, B. (1991) *Repetition in Arabic Discourse: Paradigms, Syntagms, and the Ecology of Language*. Amsterdam: John Benjamins.

Joya, A. (2018) 'Is Islamism Accommodating Neo-liberalism? The Case of Egypt's Muslim Brotherhood', in H. Kraetzschmar and P. Rivetti (eds), *Islamists and the Politics of the Arab Uprisings: Governance, Pluralisation and Contention*. Edinburgh: Edinburgh University Press.

Jakubowicz, K. (2007) *Rude awakening: Social and media change in Central and Eastern Europe*. Cresskill, NJ: Hampton Press, Inc.

Keating, E. and A. Duranti (2011) 'Discourse and culture', in T. A. Van Dijk (ed.), *Discourse Studies: A Multidisciplinary Introduction*. Thousand Oaks, CA: SAGE, pp. 331–56.

Khamis, S. (2011) 'The Transformative Egyptian Media Landscape: Changes, Challenges and Comparative Perspectives', *International Journal of Communication* 5, 1159–77.

Khamis, S. and K. Vaughn (2011) 'Cyberactivism in the Egyptian revolution: How civic engagement and citizen journalism tilted the balance', *Arab Media and Society* 14.

Khamis, S. and K. Vaughn (2013) 'Cyberactivism or Cyberbalkanization? Dialectical Tensions in an Online Social Movement', *Journal of Social Media Studies* 2(2), 65–74.

Kinder, D. R. and L. M. Sanders (1990) 'Mimicking political debate with survey questions: The case of White opinion on affirmative action for Blacks', *Social Cognition* 8(1), 73–103.

Kintsch, W. and T. A. Van Dijk (1978) 'Toward a model of text comprehension and production', *Psychological Review* 85, 363–94.

Kress G., R. Leite-Garcia and T. van Leeuwen (2011) 'Discourse semiotics', *Discourse studies: A multidisciplinary introduction* (ed. T. A. Van Dijk), 2nd edn. London, SAGE, pp. 107–25.

Lahlali, E. M. (2007) *Critical Discourse Analysis and Classroom Discourse Practices*. Munich: Lincom Studies.

Lahlali, E. M. (2011) 'The Arab Spring and the discourse of desperation: shifting from an authoritarian discourse into a "democratic" one', *Journal of Arab Media and Society* (13).

Lahlali, E. M. (2012) 'Repetition and Ideology in Naserallah's Political Speeches', *Journal of Arab Media and Society* (15).

Lahlali, E. M. (2014) 'The Discourse of Egyptian Slogans: from "Long Live Sir" to "Down with the Dictator"', *Journal of Arab Media and Society* 19 (Fall).

Lakoff, G. (2004) *Don't Think of an Elephant! Know your Values and Frame the Debate*. White River Junction, VT: Chelsea Green.

Lambrecht, K. (1996) *Information Structure and Sentence Form: Topic, Focus, and the Mental Representations of discourse referents*. Cambridge: Cambridge University Press.

Lasswell, H. D. (1995) 'Propaganda', in R. Jackall (ed.), *Propaganda*. New York: New York University Press, pp. 13–25.

Lave, J. and E. Wenger (1991) *Learning in doing: Social, cognitive, and computational perspectives. Situated learning: Legitimate peripheral participation*. Cambridge: Cambridge University Press.

Leech, G. (1981) *Semantics: The Study of Meaning*. London: Penguin Books.

Leech, G. (1983) *Principles of Pragmatics*. London: Longman.

Leontiev, A. N. (1978) *Activity Consciousness and Personality*. Englewood Cliffs, NJ: Prentice-Hall.

Leudar, I., V. Marsland and J. Nekvapil (2004) 'On Membership Categorization: "Us", "Them" and "Doing Violence" in Political Discourse', *Discourse and Society* 15(2–3), 243–66.

Lopez, A. M. R. (2002) 'Applying Frame Semantics to Translation: A Practical Example', *Meta* 47(3), 312.

Machiavelli, N. (1985) *The Prince*, trans. H. C. Mansfield. London: University of Chicago Press.

Machin, D. and A. Mayr (2012) *How to Do Critical Discourse Analysis: A Multimodal Introduction*. London: SAGE.

Marshall, G. (1994) 'Leading Change: Leadership, Organization, and Social Movements', in N. Nitin and K. Rakesh, *Handbook of Leadership Theory and Practice: A Harvard Business School Centennial Colloquium*. Boston: Harvard Business Press.

Masbah, M. (2018) 'Rise and Endurance: Moderate Islamists and Electoral Politics in the Aftermath of the 'Moroccan Spring', in H. Kraetzschmar and P. Rivetti (eds), *Islamists and the Politics of the Arab Uprisings: Governance, Pluralisation and Contention*. Edinburgh: Edinburgh University Press.

Mautner, G. (2009) 'Corpora and critical discourse analysis', in P. Baker (ed.), *Contemporary Corpus Linguistics*. London: Continuum, pp. 32–46).

Mazraani, N. (1993) *Aspects of Language Variation in Arabic Political Speech Making*, unpublished PhD thesis, University of Cambridge.

Merskin, D. (2004) 'The Construction of Arabs as Enemies: Post-September 11 Discourse of George W. Bush', *Mass Communication & Society* 7(2), 157–75.

Meyer, M. (2001) 'Between Theory, Method, and Politics: Positioning of the Approaches of CDA', in R. Wodak and M. Meyer (eds), *Methods of Critical Discourse Analysis*. London: SAGE, pp. 14–32.

Moaddel, M. (1992) 'Shi'i political discourse and class mobilization in the tobacco movement of 1890–1892', *Sociological Forum* 7(3), 447–68.

Moaddel, M. (2015) 'The Arab Spring and Egyptian Revolution Makers: Predictors of Participation', *Journal of Education and Practice* 6(14).

Moghaddam, F. and R. Harré (eds) (2010) 'Words, conflicts and political processes', *Words of Conflict, Words of War: How the language we use in political processes sparks fighting*. Santa Barbara, CA: Praeger.

Nabavi, N. (2012) 'The "Arab Spring" as Seen through the Prism of the 1979 Iranian Revolution', *International Journal of Middle East Studies* 44(1), 153–5.

Newmeyer, Frederick J. (1983) *Grammatical Theory, its Limits and its Possibilities*. Chicago: University of Chicago Press.

Oddo, J. (2011) 'War legitimation discourse: Representing "Us" and "Them" in four US presidential addresses', *Discourse & Society* 22(3), 287–314.

Oktar, L. (2001) 'The ideological organization of representational processes in the presentation of us and them', *Discourse & Society* 12(3), 313–46.

Olsen, M. and L. G. Harvey (1988) 'Computers in Intellectual History: Lexical Statistics and the Analysis of Political Discourse', *Journal of Interdisciplinary History* 18, 449–64.

Palmer, F. R. (1983) *Semantics*, 2nd edn. Cambridge: Cambridge University Press.

Papaioannou, T. and H. E. Olivos, (2013) 'Cultural Identity and Social Media in the Arab Spring: Collective Goals in the Use of Facebook in the Libyan Context', *Journal of Arab & Muslim Media Research* 6 (2–3), 99–144.

Pecheux, M. (1982) *Language, Semantics and Ideology*. London: Macmillan.

Reese, S. (2001) 'Framing public life: A bridging model for media research', in S. Reese, O. Gandy and A. Grant (eds), *Framing Public Life*. Mahwah, NJ: Erlbaum, pp. 7–31.

Reisigl, M. (2008) 'Rhetoric of Political Speeches', in R. Wodak and V. Koller (eds) (2008) *Communication in the Public Sphere (Handbook of Applied Linguistics* 4) Berlin: De Gruyter.

Reynolds, D. W. (1995) 'Repetition in Non-native Speaker Writing', *SSLA* 17, 185–209.

Richardson, J. E. (2007) *Analysing Newspapers*. London: Macmillan.

Rieschild, V. R. (2006) *Emphatic Repetition in Spoken Arabic*, <https://core.ac.uk/download/pdf/41229479.pdf> (last accessed 9 April 2021).

Rosiny, S. (2012) *The Arab Spring: Triggers, Dynamics and Prospects* (GIGA Focus International Edition 1). Hamburg: GIGA German Institute for Global and Area Studies.

Ryan, Y. (2011) 'How Tunisia's revolution began', *Al Jazeera,* 26 January, <https://www.aljazeera.com/features/2011/1/26/how-tunisias-revolution-began> (last accessed 9 April 2021).

Sacks, H. (1992) *Lectures on Conversation*. 2 vols. Oxford: Blackwell.

Sacks, H., E. A. Schegloff and G. Jefferson (1974) 'A simplest systematic for the organization of turn-taking for conversation', *Language* 50(4), 696–735.

Schiffrin, D. (1994) *Approaches to Discourse*. Oxford: Blackwell.

Scollon, R. (1998) *Mediated Discourse as Social Interaction*. London: Longman.

Seeberg, P. and M. Shteiwi (2014) 'European Narratives on the "Arab Spring" – from Democracy to Security'. DJUCO Joint Publications.

Sewell, W. H. Jr (1985) 'Ideologies and Social Revolutions: Reflections on the French Case', *The Journal of Modern History* 57(1), 57–85.

Shamul, A. B. (1996) 'Debating about Identity in Malaysia: A Discourse Analysis', *Southeast Asian Studies* 34(3).

Shormani, M. and A. Qarabesh (2018) 'Vocatives: correlating the syntax and discourse at the interface', *Cogent Arts & Humanities* 5(1).

Simpson, P. and A. Mayr (2010) *Language and Power: A resource Book for Students*. London: Routledge.

Sonnenhauser, B. and P. N. Hanna (2013) *Vocative! : addressing between system and performance*. Berlin and Boston: Mouton de Gruyter.

Spillman, K. R. and K. Spillmann (1997) 'Some sociobiological and psychological aspects of "Images of the Enemy"', in R. Fiebig-von Has and U. Lehmkuhl (eds), *Enemy Images in American History*. Providence, RI: Berghahn, pp. 43–64.

Stubbs, M. (1983) *Discourse Analysis: the Sociolinguistic Analysis of Natural Language*. Oxford: Blackwell.

Tajfel, H. (1970) 'Experiments in intergroup discrimination', *Scientific American* 223, 96-102.

Tajfel, H. and J. P. Forgas (1981) 'Social Categorization: Cognition, Values and Groups', in Forgas, J. (ed.) *Social Cognition: Perspectives on Everyday Understanding*. London: Academic Press.

Teo, P. (2000) 'Racism in the news: A critical discourse analysis of news reporting in two Australian newspapers', *Discourse and Society* 11, 7–49.

Thorne, S. E., S. R. Kirkham and A. Henderson (1999) 'Ideological implications of the paradigm discourse', *Nursing Inquiry* 4, 1–2.

Tienari, J., E. Vaara and I. Björkman (2003) 'Global capitalism meets national spirit: Discourses in media texts on a cross-border acquisition', *Journal of Management Inquiry* 12(4), 377–93.

Van Dijk, T. A. (ed.) (1985) *Handbook of Discourse Analysis*, 4 vols. London and New York: Academic Press.

Van Dijk, T. A. (1991) *Racism and the Press*. London: Routledge.

Van Dijk, T. A. (1995a) 'Discourse semantics and ideology', *Discourse and Society* 6, 243–89.

Van Dijk, T. A. (1995b) 'Discourse Analysis as Ideology Analysis', in C. Schäffne and A. L. Wenden *Language and Peace*. Aldershot: Dartmouth Publishing.

Van Dijk, T. A. (1996) 'Discourse as interaction in society', in T. A. Van Dijk (ed.) *Discourse as Social Interaction*, vol. 2. London: SAGE, pp. 1–37.

Van Dijk, T. A. (ed.) (1997) *Discourse Studies: A Multidisciplinary Introduction*, 2 vols. London: SAGE.

Van Dijk, T. A. (2000) 'Parliamentary Debates', in R. Wodack and T. A. Van Dijk (eds), *Racism at the Top. Parliamentary Discourses on Ethnic Issues in Six European States*. Klagenfurt: Drava Verlag, pp. 45–78.

Van Dijk, T. A. (2001) 'Critical discourse analysis', in D. Tannen, D. Schiffrin and H. Hamilton (eds), *Handbook of Discourse Analysis*. Oxford: Blackwell, pp. 352–71.

Van Dijk, T. A. (2005) *Racism and discourse in Spain and Latin America*. Amsterdam: Benjamins.

Van Dijk, T. A. (2006) 'Discourse and Manipulation', *Discourse & Society* 17(2): 359–83.

Van Dijk, T. A. (2009) *Society and Discourse: How Context Controls Text and Talk*. Cambridge: Cambridge University Press.

Van Dijk, T. A. (2011a) *Discourse Studies: A Multidisciplinary Introduction*, 2nd edn. London: SAGE.

Van Dijk, T. A. (2011b) 'Discourse and Ideology', in T. A. Van Dijk, *Discourse Studies: A Multidisciplinary Introduction*, 2nd edn. London: SAGE.

Van Dijk, T. A. (2015) 'Critical Discourse Studies: A Sociocognitive Approach', in R. Wodak and M. Meyer, *Methods of Critical Discourse Studies*. London: SAGE.

Van Dijk, T. A. (2016) 'Sociocognitive Discourse Studies', in J. Richardson and J. Flowerdew (eds), *Handbook of Discourse Analysis*. London: Routledge, pp. 26–43.

Van Dijk, T. A. and W. Kintsch (1983) *Strategies of Discourse Comprehension*. New York: Academic Press.

Van Leeuwen, T. (2008) *Discourse and Practice: New Tools for Discourse Analysis*. Oxford: Oxford University Press.

Wertsch, J. V. (1991) 'Sociocultural approach to socially shared cognition', in L. B. Resnick, J. M. Levine and S. D. Teasley (eds), *Perspectives on Socially Shared Cognition*. American Psychological Association, pp. 85–100.

Wertsch, J. V. (1994) 'The primacy of mediated action in sociocultural studies', *Mind, Culture, and Activity* 1(4), 202–8.

Weyland, K. (2012) 'The Arab Spring: Why the Surprising Similarities with the Revolutionary Wave of 1848?', *Perspectives on Politics* 10(4), 917–34.

Widdowson, H. G. (1998) 'The theory and practice of Critical Discourse Analysis', *Applied Linguistics* 19(1), 1.

Weiss, G. and R. Wodak (2003) 'Introduction: Theory, Interdisciplinarity and Critical Discourse Analysis', in G. Weiss and R. Wodak (eds), *Critical Discourse Analysis: Theory and Interdisciplinarity*. Basingstoke: Palgrave Macmillan, pp. 1–34.

Wilson, A. (2005) *Ukraine's Orange Revolution*. New Haven, CT: Yale University Press.

Wilson, J. (1990) *Politically Speaking: The Pragmatic Analysis of Political Language*. Oxford: Basil Blackwell.

Wodak, R. (2001) 'The discourse-historical approach', in R. Wodak and M. Meyer (eds), *Methods of Critical Discourse Analysis*. London: SAGE, pp. 87–122.

Wodak, R. (2007) 'Language and Ideology – Language in Ideology', *Journal of Language and Politics* 6(1).

Wodak, R. (2009) *The Discourse of Politics in Action: Politics as Usual*. Palgrave Macmillan.

Wodak R. and M. Meyer (2015) *Methods of Critical Discourse Analysis*. London: SAGE.

Wood, L. A. and R. O. Kroger (2000) *Doing Discourse Analysis: Methods for studying Action in Talk and Context*. Thousand Oaks, CA: SAGE.

Worth, R. F. (2002) 'A nation defines itself by its evil enemies', *New York Times*, 24 February, Sec. 4, p. 1.

Wuthnow, R. (1989) *Communities of Discourse: Ideology and social structure in the Reformation, the Enlightenment, and European socialism*. Cambridge, MA: Harvard university Press.

Zherebkin, M. (2009) 'In search of a theoretical approach to the analysis of the "Colour revolutions": Transition studies and discourse theory', *Communist and Post-Communist Studies* 42(2), 199–216.

Zollner, B. (2018) 'Does participation lead to moderation? Understanding changes in Egyptian Islamist parties post-Arab Spring', in H. Kraetzschmar and P. Rivetti (eds), *Islamists and the Politics of the Arab Uprisings: Governance, Pluralisation and Contention*. Edinburgh: Edinburgh University Press.

Zwicky, A. (1974) 'Hey, whatsyourname!', in papers from the Tenth Regional Meeting of the Chicago Linguistic Society, ed. Michael La Galy, Robert Fox and Arnold Bruck, pp. 787–80.

Additional References

Abdullah Y. S. (2015) 'Politeness in Arabic Culture', *Theory and Practice in Language Studies* 5(10).

Al-Jabr, A.M. (1987) *Cohesion in Text Differentiation: A Study of English and Arabic*, Unpublished PhD dissertation, University of Aston, Birmingham.

Al-Khafaji, R. (2005) 'Variation and Recurrence in the Lexical Chains of Arabic and English texts', *Poznan Studies in Contemporary Linguistics* 40, 5–25.

Al-Momani, K. (2016) 'Discourse change in a changing society: a critical discourse analysis of political advertisement in Jordan before and after the Arab Spring', *Círculo de Lingüística Aplicada a la Comunicación* 65, 3–43.

Aouragh, M. (2012) 'Framing the Internet in the Arab Revolutions: Myth Meets Modernity', *Cinema Journal* 52(1), 148–56.

Aulich, J. and M. Sylvestrova (1999). *Political Posters in Central and Eastern Europe 1945–95*. Manchester and New York: Manchester University Press.

Avery, S. and D. Roland (2001) 'Styles of Journalism', in R. Stott and S. Avery (eds), *Writing with Style*. London: Longman, pp. 105–26.

Badawi, E., M. G. Carter and A. Gully (2004) *Modern Written Arabic: A Comprehensive Grammar*. London and New York: Routledge.

Barton, E. l. (1999) 'Informational and Interactional Functions of Slogans and Sayings in the Discourse of a Support Group', *Discourse and Society* 10(4), 461–86.

Beard, A. (2000) *The Language of Politics*. London. Routledge.

Bell, A. (1991) *The Language of News Media*. Oxford: Basil Blackwell.

Bielsa, E. and S. Bassnett (2009) *Translation in Global News*. London: Routledge.

Blackedge, A. (2000) *Literacy, Power and Social Justice*. Stoke on Trent: Trentham Books.

Bourdieu, P. (1977) *Outline of a Theory of Practice*. Cambridge: Cambridge University Press.

Burgess, R. (1994) *In the Field: An Introduction to Field Research*, 4th edn. London: Routledge.

Charteris-Black, J. (2004) *Corpus Approaches to Critical Metaphor Analysis*. New York: Palgrave Macmillan.

Chilton, P. (1996) *Security metaphors: Cold War Discourse from Containment to Common House*. New York: Peter Lang.

Chouliaraki, L. (1996) 'Teacher–Pupil talk', *Discourse & Society* 9(1).

Clifton, C. J. and Vaidya (2004) 'New Media at the BBC Service', in C. Paterson and A. Streberny (eds), *International News in the Twenty-first Century*. Luton: University of Luton Press, pp. 79–94.

Coulthard, M. (1985) *An Introduction to Discourse Analysis*. London: Longman.

Danuta, R. (2002) *The Language of Newspapers*. London and New York: Routledge.

Davis, K. (1988) *Power Under the Microscope: Toward a Grounded Theory of Gender Relations in Medical Encounters*. Dordrecht: Foris.

De Fina (2011) 'Researcher and Informant Roles in Narrative Interactions: Constructions of Belonging and Foreign-ness', in A. De Fina and S. Perrino (eds), 'Narratives in Interviews, Interviews in Narrative Studies'. Special Issue: *Language in Society* 40(1), 27–38.

Denton, R. (1980) 'The Rhetorical Functions of Slogans: Classifications and Characteristics', *Communication Quarterly* (28), 10–18.

Fairclough, N. (1992) *Critical Language Awareness*. London: Longman.

Fairclough, N. (1996) 'Border crossings: discourse and social change in contemporary societies', in Hywel Coleman and Lynne Cameron (eds), *Change and Language*, Clevedon: British Association for Applied Lingusitics in Association with Multilingual Matters, pp. 3–17.

Fairclough, N. and R. Wodak (1997) 'Critical discourse analysis', in T. A. van Dijk (1997) *Discourse as Social Interaction*, London: SAGE, pp. 258–84.

Foucault, M. (1980) *Power/Knowledge. Selected Interviews 1972–1977*, ed. C. Gordon. New York: Pantheon.

Fuertes-Olivera, P. A., M. Velasco-Sacristan, A. Arribas-Bano and E. Samaniego-Fernandez (2001) 'Persuasion and advertising English: Metadiscourse in slogans and headlines', *Journal of Pragmatics* 33, 1291–307.

Goffman, E. (1972) *Interaction Ritual: Essays on Face-Face Behaviour*. London: Allen Lane.

Graham, P., T. Keenan and A. Dowd (2004) 'A Call to Arms at the End of History: A Discourse- historical Analysis of George W. Bush's Declaration of War on Terror', *Discourse & Society* 15(2–3): 199–221.

Grice, H. P. (1975) 'Logic and Conversation', in: P. Cole and J. Morgan (eds), *Syntax and Semantics*, vol. 3. New York: Academic Press, pp. 41–58.

Gumperz, J. (1982) *Discourse Strategies*. Cambridge: Cambridge University Press.

Gumperz, J. (1982) *Language and Social Identity*. Cambridge: Cambridge University Press.

Halliday, M. A. K. (1994) *Introduction to Functional Grammar*, 2nd edn. London: Arnold.

Harris, R. (1980) *The Language Makers*. London: Duckworth.

Hatim, B. (2000) *Communication Across Culture: Translation Theory and Contrastive Texts Linguistics*. Exeter: Short Run Press Ltd.

Hatim, B. and I. Mason (1990) *Discourse and the Translator*. London: Longman.

Heath, S. B. (1983) *Ways with Words*. Cambridge: Cambridge University Press.

Hoey, M. (1983) *On the Surface of Discourse*. London: George Allen and Unwin.

Hoey, M. (1991) *Patterns of Lexis in Text*. Oxford: Oxford University Press.

Hoey, M. (2001) *Textual Interaction: An Introduction to Written Discourse Analysis*. London: Routledge.

Holland, D. and W. Lachicotte (2007) 'Vygotsky, Mead, and the new sociocultural studies of identity', in H. Daniels, M. Cole, and J. V. Wertsch (eds), *The Cambridge Companion to Vygotsky*. Cambridge: Cambridge University Press, pp. 101–35.

Hutchby, I. (1996) *Confrontation Talk: Arguments, Asymmetries, and Power on Talk Radio*. New York and London: Routledge.

Johnstone, B. (1994) 'Repetition in discourse: a dialogue', in B. Johnstone (ed), *Repetition in Discourse: Interdisciplinary Perspectives*. Norwood, NJ: Ablex, pp. 2–23.

Khalil, A. M. (1996) *A Contrastive Grammar of English and Arabic*. Jerusalem: Al-Isra' Press.

Kintsch, W. (1998) *Comprehension: A Paradigm for Cognition*. Cambridge: Cambridge University Press.

Kirkman, J. (1999) *Full Marks: Advice on Punctuation for Scientific and Technical Writing*, 3rd edn. Ramsbury: Ramsbury Books.

Kramsch, C. (1998) *Language and Culture*. Oxford: Oxford University Press.

Kress, G. and R. Hodge, R. (1979) *Language as Ideology*. London: Routledge.
Kress, G. and R. Hodge (1988) *Social Semiotics*. Cambridge: Polity.
Kulo, L. (2009) *Linguistic Features in Political Speeches*. Bachelor thesis. Lulea University of Technology.
Kushner, S. A. and A. R. Gershkoff (2004) 'The 9/11–Iraq Connection: How the Bush Administration's Rhetoric in the Iraq Conflict Shifted Public Opinion', paper presented at the Annual Meeting of The Midwest Political Science Association, Palmer House Hilton, Chicago, April.
Lahlali, E. M. (2011) 'Arab Media Discourse: Breaking Taboos', *International Journal of Afro-Asiatic Studies* (13/14).
Lahlali, E. M. (2011) *Contemporary Arab Broadcast Media*. Edinburgh: Edinburgh University Press.
Lazar, A. and M. Lazar (2004) 'The Discourse of the New World Order: "Out-Casting" the Double Face of Threat', *Discourse & Society*, 15 (2–3), 223–42.
Lemke, J. (1995) 'Intertextuality and Text Semantics', in P. H. Fries and M. Gregory (eds), *Discourse in Society: Systemic Functional Perspectives*. Norwood, NJ: Ablex, pp. 85–114.
Leudar, I., V. Marsland and J. Nekvapil (2004) 'On Membership Categorization: "Us", "Them" and "Doing Violence" in Political Discourse', *Discourse & Society* 15(2–3): 243–66.
Levinson, S. C. (1979) 'Activity types and language', *Linguistics* 17, 365–99.
Levinson, S. C. (1983) *Pragmatics*. Cambridge: Cambridge University Press.
Lu, X. (1999) 'An Ideological/Cultural Analysis of Political Slogans in Communist China', *Discourse and Society* 10(4), 487–508.
Malmkjaer, K. (2005) *Linguistics and the Language of Translation* (Edinburgh Textbooks in Applied Linguistics). Edinburgh: Edinburgh University Press.
Martin, J. R. R. and P. R. R. White (2005) *The Language of Evaluation: Appraisal in English*. New York: Palgrave Macmillan.
Mautner, G. (2015) 'Checks and balances: How corpus linguistics can contribute to CDA', in R. Wodak and M. Meyer, *Methods of Critical Discourse Studies*. London: SAGE.
Mills, S. (1997) *Discourse*. Routledge: London.
Mullany, L. (1999) 'Linguistic Politeness and Sex Differences in BBC Radio 4', *Multilingua* 8(2/3), 223–48.
Mumby, D. K. (1989) 'Ideological & the Social Construction of Meaning: A Communication Perspective', *Communication Quarterly* 37, 291–304.

Mumby, D. K. and R. P. Clair (1996) 'Organizational Discourse', in T. A. Van Dijk and N. E. Collinge (eds), *An Encyclopedia of Language*. London: Routledge, pp. 173–206.

Palmer, F. R. (1986) *Semantics*. Cambridge: Cambridge University Press.

Ryan, Y. (2011) 'The tragic life of a street vendor, *Al Jazeera*, 20 January, <https://www.aljazeera.com/features/2011/1/20/the-tragic-life-of-a-street-vendor> (last accessed 9 April 2021).

Sewell, W. H. Jr (1985) 'Ideologies and Social Revolutions: Reflections on the French Case', *The Journal of Modern History* 57(1), 57–85.

Schiffrin, D. (1987) *Approaches to Discourse Analysis*. Oxford: Blackwell.

Silverman, P. (1987) *Communication and Medical Practice: Social Relations*. London: SAGE.

Sinclair, J. (1981) *The Structure of Discourse*. Cambridge. Cambridge University Press.

Stewart, C., C. A. Smith and R. Denton Jr (1995) 'The Persuasive Functions of Slogans', in Robert Jackall (ed.) *Propaganda*, pp. 400–22. New York: New York University Press.

Suchan, J. (2010) 'Toward an understanding of Arabic persuasion', Proceedings of the 75th Annual Convention of the Association for Business Communication. 27–30 October, Chicago.

Thomas, J. (1995) *Meaning in Interaction: An Introduction to Pragmatics*. London: Longman.

Van Dijk, T. A. (1984) *Prejudice in Discourse*. Amsterdam: Benjamins.

Van Dijk, T. A (1988) *News Analysis*. Hillsdale, NJ: Earlbaum.

Van Dijk, T. A. (1993) 'Principles of critical discourse analysis', *Discourse and Society* 4(2), 249–83.

Van Dijk, T. A. (1998) 'Opinions and ideologies in the press', in A. Bell and P. Garrett (eds), *Approaches to Media Discourse*. Oxford: Blackwell, pp. 21–63.

Van Dijk, T. A. (2006) 'Ideology and discourse analysis', *Journal of Political Ideologies* 11(2), 115–40.

Van Leeuwen, T. (2007) 'Legitimation in Discourse and Communication', *Discourse & Communication* 1(1), 91–112.

Wagner, A. (1993) *Literacy, Culture and Development*. Cambridge: Cambridge University Press.

Wang, Shih-ping (2005) 'Corpus-based approaches and discourse analysis in relation to reduplication and repetition', *Journal of Pragmatics* 37(4): 505–40.

White, D. Y. (2003) 'Promoting productive mathematical classroom discourse with diverse students', *The Journal of Mathematical Behaviour* 22(1), 37–53.

Wodak, R. and V. Koller (eds) (2008) *Communication in the Public Sphere* (*Handbook of Applied Linguistics*, vol. 4). Berlin: De Gruyter.

Wodak, R., R. de Cillia, M. Reisigl and K. Liebhart (1999) *The Discursive Construction of National Identity*. Edinburgh: Edinburgh University Press.

Wolf, A. (2018) 'Secular Forms of Politicised Islam in Tunisia: The Constitutional Democratic Rally and Nida' Tunis', in H. Kraetzschmar and P. Rivetti (eds), *Islamists and the Politics of the Arab Uprisings: Governance, Pluralisation and Contention*. Edinburgh: Edinburgh University Press.

Wragg, E. and G. Brown (1993) *Explaining*. London: Routledge.

Wuthnow, R. (1985) 'State Structures and Ideo-logical Outcomes', *American Sociological Review* 50,799–821.

Young, R. (1992) *Critical Theory and Classroom Talk*. Bristol: Longdunn Press.

Yule, G. (1996) *Pragmatics*. Oxford: Oxford University Press.

Index

Note: **bold** indicates figures

'Abduh, Muhammad, 61
Abdul-Raof, H., 47, 48
Abou El Fadl, K., 66
abṭāl (heroes), 161, 199
accountability, 112–13, 139
Achugar, M., 63
action, 21, 41, 76
  grammatical positioning of, 44–5
  and nominalisation, 45–6
active form, 245–7
Aday, S. H., 65–6
adjectives, 61–2
affection, 183–5
Afghanistan, 53, 163, 165–6
agency/agents, 37, 90, 118–21
Ahearn, L. M., 118
Ajdādnā' (ancestors), 161
Akit, 78–9
Al-Jazeera Mubashir, 72
al-muṣālaḥa (reconciliation), 218, 219
Al-Nahda, 2, 5, 134, 204, 205, 259–60, 263
  calls for reconciliation, 218–20
  criticisms of, 232–3
  democratic values, 214–16, 220, 223–4, 225, 230–1
  discourse of, 212–14
  historical background, 207–11
  inclusiveness and exclusiveness in discourse, 226–9
  national interest and unity, 209, 216–18, 220, 222, 223, 225–6, 228, 230, 235–6
  otherness, 229–31

  progressive and tactical nature of discourse, 221–3
  religious register, 223–4, 225
  repetition, 224–6
  representation of the self, 228, 231–2
  speeches, analysis of, 221–33, 235–6
  violence, denunciation of, 220–1
Al-Qaeda, 50, 52–3, 54, 138, 160, 166
Al-ṣaḥwa al-Islāmiyya (Islamic revival), 61
al-wasaṭiyya, 208
Al-waṭan ya'lū wa lā yu'lā 'alayhi (the homeland is above all), 116–17
Algeria, 202
allegory, 48
Althusser, L., 13, 23, 25
'ām (general), 117
anā (I), 121, 146–7, 158
anāniya (selfishness), 121
anonymisation, 131–3
antonyms, 201–2
April 6 movement, 72
Arab Spring, 1, 3–4, 29, 30, 56
  Arab leaders' strategy and discourse shifts, 144–6, **145**, 156–7, 172–4, **173**, 174–9, **178**, **179**
  and the beliefs of discourse producers, 84–5
  causes, 56–8, 59, 66, 69, 72, 85–7
  changes in public discourse, 88–90, 124–5, 170–1, 177–9, **178**, **179**, 194–6
  discourse against rulers and leaders, 91–4
  and identity, 33
  ideology, 60

282

leadership, 58, 63–5
limitation and constrainment strategies, 81–2
multilingualism, 108–9, **109**
national flags as a symbol of identity, 106–7, **106**
religion, role of, 60–3
representation of Arab leaders in images, 101–6, **102**, **104**, **105**
semiotics of, 100–1
and social media, 67–73
success of, 64, 69–70
transnational Arab media vs social media, 65–7, 68–9
vocabulary, 61–2
see also Islamic political discourse/Islamic parties
argumentation, 22, 137–9
shifts in argument, 174–9, **178**, **179**
ashshar'iyya (legitimacy), 237
asymmetry, 75
Atton, C, 72
attribution strategies, 253–4
audience strategies, 248–50, 251–2, 255–7
awlādnā (our children), 165

backgrounding, 4, 122–3, *125*
Bardici, M. V., 71
basmala, 237
Ben Ali, Zine El Abidine, 56, 104–6, **105**, 107, 198–9
conciliatory approach, 169
heroism discourse, 154
mental state, 181–3, 184, 185, 185–6
scaremongering, 163–4, 165
self-identification with history, 150, 160
speeches, 95–6, 112–13, 114, 115–17, 121, 122–4, 126, 127–8, 130, 131, 132, 133–4, 138–9, 140, 142–3, 148–50, 154, 158, 163–4, 165, 168, 172, 175–6, 177, 181–2, 184, 185
Berkowitz, L., 83
Bernstein, B., 32, 55
Bin Laden, Osama, 82, 166
Blair, Tony, 55–6, 82
blame, 139–46
Blommaert, J., 29
Blum-Kulka, S., 187
Bouazizi, Mohammed, 56, 87, 123, 158, 183
Bourqiba, Habib, 150, 151, 154
Brown, G., 9
Bush Jr., George, 50, 52–3, 54–5, 76
'call to arms' speeches, 79–81, 82
Butler, J., 31

Chilton, P., 21–2
Chouliaraki, L., 14, 20
clauses, 25–6
cognition, 9, 21
affection in leaders' discourse, 183–5
mental process and expressions of perception, 185–6
mental processes in political speeches, 181–3
social-cognitive model (Van Dijk), 15–16, 34, 78
socio-cognitive structures, 38
cohesion and coherence, 4, 135, 169–70
local coherence relations and ideology, 25–6
collectivisation, 43–4, 75, 121–2, 125–7, 245
command, 167–71
common enemy concept, 50–3, 55–6, 76
Comninos, A., 70
concession, 172–4, **173**, 176–7
context, 8, 19, 21, 28, 40
conversational analysis (CA), 10–12
counter public theory, 67
Covatorta, F., 209
critical discourse analysis (CDA), 2, 3, 5, 6, 34, 37–8, 75, 204, 207, 262, 263
criticism of, 19–20
definitions, 14–15
and language, 9–10
and power, 26–9
culture, 31–4, 40, 42–3
Cumhuriyet, 78–9

Daniel, M., 255
Daniels, H., 55
defiance, 146–8
democracy, 47, 58, 129, 220, 230–1, 243–4
and Islamic values, 214–16, 223–4
denial, 139–46
discourse, 1–2
conversational analysis, 10–12
critical linguistics, 12–13
definitions, 6–10
dialectical relationship with society, 60, 261
discursive change, 29
formalist/functionalist divide, 7–8
and identity and culture, 31–4
ideological structures of, 75–87
and ideology, 23–5, 28–9
Islamic discourse, 60–1
language use, 9–10
local coherence relations and ideology, 25–6
mediated discourse, 23, 27, 28
order of, 29
political discourse analysis, 20–3
as a political practice, 17
and power, 26–9
practice of, 18–19
of revolutions, 56–65
social-cognitive model (Van Dijk), 15–16, 34
social component, 78
social practice, 19–20
social theory of (Fairclough's model), 16–17, **18**, 34
as text, 18
discrimination, 82–3, 84, 241–2, 244

domination, 28–9
Duranti, A., 40

Egypt, 2, 5, 29, 56, 88, 218
    clampdown on protesters, 61–2
    ICT access, 70, 71–2
    images of Mubarak, 101–3, **102**
    Islamic parties, 205–7, 210–11
    media, 54
    military coup 2013, 205–6, 210, 230
    Mubarak's speeches, 112, 114, 118, 126,
        129–32, 138–9, 143, 149–50, 153, 155,
        164, 172–3, 175, 176, 177, 182, 184, 185
    religion, 159
    revolution, aspects of, 64–5
    slogans against Mubarak, 91–3, 190, 193–4,
        193, 195
    social media, 65–6
    see also Freedom and Justice Party (FJP);
        Islamic political discourse/Islamic parties
emotion, 115–16, 123–5, 182–3, 185–6
emphasis, 114
Erikson, E., 31
ethnomethodology, 10–11

face-to-face discourse, 27, 28
Facebook, 70, 73
fahimtukum (I understand you), 115–16
Fairclough, I., 21, 22–3, 121
Fairclough, N., 2, 5, 6, 9, 10, 11, 13, 14,
    18–19, 21, 22–3, 24, 25, 40, 41–2, 44,
    60, 121
    CDA approach, 19–20, 204, 207
    discursive change, 29
    intertextuality, 30–1
    power and discourse, 26–8
    social model, 16–17, **18**, 34
Falklands War, 52
Faluja, 138
Faris, D., 67
Fasold, R., 9
feminism, 84
Fiedler, K., 82–3
Fina, A. De, 31, 33–4, 39–40
foregrounding, 4, 122–3
    and remorse, 123–5, *125*
foreign actors, 95–100, 138–9, 141, 161–2,
    166, 169, 239–40
Forgas, J. P., 82–3
Foucault, M., 14, 16
Fowler, R., 12–13, 74, 75
framing, 2, 3, 36, 38–9, 111–13, 263
Fraser, B., 187
Freedom and Justice Party (FJP), 2, 5, 204, 205,
    210–11, 218, 233–57, 259–60, 263
    active form, use of, 245–7
    attribution strategies, 253–4
    audience strategies, 248–50, 255–7
    direct pronouns, use of, 251–3

    discursive practices, 236–57
    humility discourse, 250–1
    legitimacy, use of, 243–5, 249–50, 252
    national interest discourse, 254–5
    otherness, 237–40
    reconciliation and unity, 240–2
    religious register, 236–7, 242
    sentence structure, 247–8
    vocatives in leaders' speeches, 255–7
French Revolution, 58

Gaddafi, Muammar, 138, 186, 203
    antonyms, use of, 202
    command discourse, 168–9
    defiant discourse, 146–8
    heroism discourse, 155–6
    images of, 103–4, **104**, **191**
    lack of cohesion in speeches, 169–70
    politeness strategies, 197–8
    recognition of tribes, 199–201
    religious discourse, 159–60
    scaremongering, 163, 166
    self-identification with history, 150–2,
        161–2, 169
    slogans against, 190–1, **191**
    speeches, 96–100, 107–8, 117–18, 122, 131,
        134, 135, 138, 147, 159–60, 161–2, 163,
        166, 168–9, 174, 189, 197–8,
        199–200
Gallagher, S., 19–20
Al-Ghannouchi, Rachid, 209, 215–16, 217,
    219, 220–1, 225, 227–8, 229–30, 231,
    236, 243, 258
Garfinkel, Harold, 10
Gilmore, N., 83
Gitlin, T., 38
Goffman, E., 38–9
Gottlieb, R., 19
grammar, 13, 17, 41, 111–13
    grammatical positioning and persuasion in
        speeches, 113–18
    and positioning of actions, 44–5
greatness, 148–50

Hadith, 212, 223–4
Halliday, M. A. K., 13, 17
Hamo, M., 187
Harré, R., 39
Hasan, R., 32
hedging, 31, 48–9
hegemony, 26
heroism discourse, 154–7
ḥiwār (dialogue), 90
Ḥizb al-Ḥurriyya wa al-'Adāla *see* Freedom and
    Justice Party (FJP)
Holland, D., 32
humility, 250–1, 252
Hussein, Saddam, 50–1, 55–6, 80–1
Hutchby, I., 12

identity, 16–17, 19, 35–7, 75–6
  constraint of, 39–40
  and culture, 31–4, 40
  definitions, 31–2
  national flags as a symbol of identity, 106–7
  processes, 33–4
  of protesters, 94–5, 132–3
  types of, 33
ideology, 23–5, 28–9, 42, 75–87
  definitions, 60
  ideological communication, 78
  ideological square, 76, 78
  ideological structures of discourse, 75–87
  and local coherence relations, 25–6
  of protesters, 85–7
  revolutionary ideology, 59
Idris I, King of Libya, 151, 161
images *see* semiotics
immigration, 77–8
imperative, use of, 88, 89, 93, 167–71, 188
inclusivity, 75, 112, 121–2, 165–7, 226–9, 244
indexicality, 33–4
individualisation, 43–4, 125–7
inna (indeed, verily), 114, 122, 153
inqilābiyūn (coupists), 230
intafiḍ (rise up against/protest), 141
interests, 76–7
intertextual analysis/intertextuality, 18–19, 30–1, 160–3, 199
Iranian Revolution, 59–61, 62–4
Iraq, 50–1, 80–1, 165–6
irḥal (leave), 88–90, 109, 146, 158, 171, 173, 190, 194
Irḥal yā chayṭān (leave oh devil), 89
Iskander, E., 71
Islamic political discourse/Islamic parties, 2, 5, 58, 204–60
  active form, use of, 245–7
  Al-Nahda's historical background, 207–11
  Al-Nahda's speeches, analysis of, 221–33, 235–6
  Arab Spring and Islamic parties, 205–7
  attribution strategies, 253–4
  audience strategies, 248–50, 251–2
  criticisms of, 232–3, 235
  democratic values, 214–16, 220, 223–4, 225, 230–1, 243–4
  direct pronouns, use of, 251–3
  Freedom and Justice Party (FJP), Egypt, 233–57
  humility discourse, 250–1, 252
  inclusiveness and exclusiveness in discourse, 226–9, 244
  legitimacy, use of, 237, 243–5, 249–50, 252
  national interest and unity, 216–18, 220, 222, 223, 225–6, 230, 235–6, 240, 254–5
  otherness, 229–31, 237–40
  progressive and tactical nature of discourse, 221–3
  reconciliation, 218–20, 240–2
  religious register in discourse, 221–3, 223–4, 225, 236–7, 257, 259
  secularisation, 211, 212–13
  and sentence structure, 247–8
  shifts in the discourse of, 257–9, **258**
  speeches of Al-Nahda's leaders, 212–14
  violence, denunciation of, 216, 220–1
istaqil (resign), 158

Jackson, N. B., 50
Jamal Uddin 'al-Afghani,' Sayyid', 61
Jarraya, S., 118, 121
Jefferson, Gail, 10
Al-Jenaibi, B., 66–7, 67–9
Joya, A., 210, 233
Justice and Development Party (PJD), 205, 210, 211

Keating, E., 40
Khamis, S., 64–5, 71–2
Khan, Sayyid Ahmad, 61
khāṣ (specific), 117
khawana (traitors), 90
khiṭāb al-qā'id (the speech of the leader), 197–8
Khomeini, Ayatollah Ruhollah, 59, 60, 62, 63–4
Kinder, D. R., 38
Kintsch, W., 15–16
Kress, G., 8
kul (all), 117
Kulunā (we are all), 87

labelling, 4
  semantic labelling, 42–3
Lahlali, E. M., 91, 114, 140, 144, 150, 171
Lakoff, G., 38
language, 5, 63
  critical linguistics, 12–13
  formalist/functionalist divide, 7–8
  linguistic analysis, 18
  multilingualism, 108–9, **109**, 192–6, **193**
  and politics, 21, 55–6
  use of, 9–10, 16–17
laqad, 114
Lasswell, H. D., 51
Lebanon, 202
Leech, G., 7, 42
legitimacy, 237, 243–5, 249–50, 252
Leontiev, A. N., 55
Leudar, I., 82
lexis, 22, 36–7, 39, 41, 43, 239, 245
  overlexicalisation, 49–56, 114–18, 135, 158
Libya, 2, 29, 56, 72–3, 206
  Gaddafi's defiance, 146–8
  Gaddafi's speeches, 96–100, 107–8, 117–18, 122, 131, 134, 135, 138, 147, 159–60, 161–2, 163, 166, 168–9, 174, 189, 197–8, 199–200

Libya (cont.)
  images of Gaddafi, 103–4, **104**
  political system, 107
  tribes, 199–201

Machiavelli, N., 118
Machin, D., 35–8, 45, 46, 47, 94, 101, 114–15, 129, 181
macro-analysis of political discourse, 137–86
  affection in leaders' discourse, 183–5
  argumentation, 137–9, 174–9, **178**, **179**
  blame and denial strategy, 139–46
  cognition in political discourse, 181–6
  concession discourse, 172–4, **173**, 176–7
  defiance discourse, 146–8
  heroism discourse, 154–7
  inclusivity, 165–7
  intertextuality and persuasion in leaders' speeches, 160–3
  leaders' strategy shift, 144–6, **144**
  mental process and expressions of perception, 185–6
  mental processes in political speeches, 181–3
  model for analysing discursive strategy shifts, **178**, **179**, 180–1, 262
  positioning through history, 150–4, 160–3, 199
  reconciliation and command discourses, 167–71
  regime self-praise and glorification, 148–50
  religious discourse, 159–60
  scaremongering, 144, 163–5, 166
  syntax as power of persuasion, 157–8
madsūsīn (agents), 90
Marshall, G., 83
martyrdom, 147–8, 161
Masbah, M., 211
maṭlabunā wāḥid (we have shared demands), 141
Mautner, G., 9
Mayr, A., 35–8, 45, 46, 47, 94, 101, 114–15, 129, 181
media *see* news and media
mediated discourse, 23, 27, 28
Merone, F., 209
Merskin, D., 49, 52–3, 53
metonymy, 46–7
Meyer, M., 15
microanalysis of political discourse, 111–36
  agency, 118–21
  anonymisation, 131–3
  cohesion and coherence, 135
  deictic pronouns, 121–2
  foregrounding and backgrounding in speeches, 122–3
  foregrounding and remorse, 123–5, **125**
  framing/positioning and grammar, 111–13
  grammatical positioning and persuasion in speeches, 113–18

individualisation vs collectivisation, 125–7
modality in leaders' speeches, 127–9
personification in speeches, 129–31
presupposition in speeches, 133–4
Moaddel, M., 59, 60–1, 63
modality, 127–9
Modern Standard Arabic, 183, 193, **193**
Moghaddam, F., 39
mood effects, 82–3
Morocco, 205, 210, 211
Morsi, Mohamed, 205–6, 210, 218, 230, 233, 234
  active form, use of, 245–7
  attribution strategies, 253–4
  audience strategies, 248–50, 251–2, 255–7
  direct pronouns, use of, 251–3
  gentle nature of discourse, 251–2
  humility discourse, 250–1, 252
  legitimacy, use of, 243–5, 249–50, 252
  national interest discourse, 254–5
  otherness, 237–40
  reconciliation, 240–2
  religious register, 236–7
  sentence structure, 247–8
  speeches, 236–57
  vocatives, use of, 255–7
Mubarak, Hosni, 54, 96, 101–3, **102**, 107, 140, 171, 190, 210, 239
  conciliatory approach, 169
  heroism discourse, 155
  mental state, 182–3, 184, 185–6
  scaremongering, 164
  self-identification with history, 150, 153, 160
  slogans against, 91–3, 190, 193–4, **193**, 195
  speeches, 112, 114, 118, 126, 129–32, 138–9, 143, 149–50, 153, 155, 164, 172–3, 175, 176, 177, 182, 184, 185
muḍāharāt silmiyya (peaceful demonstrations), 90
mukharibūn (vandals), 90
Mukhtar, Omar, 151–2, 155, 161, 163, 200
munāwi'ūna ma'jūrūna (hostile elements in the pay of foreigners), 144
musālaḥa (reconciliation), 90, 241
Muslim Brotherhood (MB), 65, 159, 207, 208, 210, 218, 230, 236
  democratic values, 243–4
  international relations strategy, 239–40
  national interest and unity, 240–1
  tension with the state, 233–5
muwāṭinūn (citizens), 237

nā (we, prefix), 165
Nabavi, N., 63–4
nafdīk, 87–8
nahḍawiyūn/nahḍawiyat, 226–7, 228
naḥnu (we), 121, 226
Nasser, Gamal Abdel, 118, 147, 152, 155, 234
National Coalition for Change, 72

national interest, 52, 81, 101, 209, 216–18, 220, 222, 223, 225–6, 228, 230, 235–6, 240
Newmeyer, Frederick J., 7
news and media, 15–16, 39, 43–4, 83
  attitude to protesters, 85–6
  news frames, 36
  and reality, 53–6
  representation of others, 49–53
  social media and the Arab Spring, 67–73
  transnational Arab media vs social media, 65–7, 68–9
  Turkish media, 78–9
nominalisation, 4, 45–6
norms, 76
nouns, 44
nukalimmukum (I/we address you), 115–16

objectification, 47–8
Oddo, J., 79–81
Oktar, L., 78–9
Olivos, H. E., 72–3
Orange Revolution, Ukraine, 57–8
Osborne, Darren, 49–50
otherness, 36, 49–53, 75, *125*, 229–31, 237–40
  negative other in political discourse, 94–107
  negative other in public discourse, 91–4
  representation of protesters (them) in political speeches, 94–5

Palmer, F. R., 201
Papaioannou, T., 72–3
patriotism, 115–17, 129–31, 163
Pecheux, M., 13
perception, 185–6
personification, 47–8, 129–31
persuasion, 4–5, 114, 160–3
  syntax as power of persuasion, 157–8
phir'awn (pharoah), 171
polarisation, 75, 79, 81, 86, 202, 228, 261–2
politeness, 2, 5, 187–203, 263
  and Arabic discourse, 187–92
  breaking social and cultural taboos, 194–6
  in leaders' speeches, 196–9
  and multilingual slogans, 192–6, **193**
  slur in Arabic culture, 189–92, **191**, **192**
  strategies, 188–9, 201
  and tribes, 199–201
political discourse
  analysis of, 20–3
  homogeneity and heterogeneity of, 107–8
  and multilingualism, 108–9, **109**
  national flags as a symbol of identity, 106–7, **106**
  positive self and negative other in political discourse, 94–107
  representation of Arab leaders in images, 101–6, **102**, **104**, **105**
  representation of foreign actors in political speeches, 95–100

representation of protesters (them) in political speeches, 94–5
and semiotic representation, 100–7
see also Islamic political discourse/Islamic parties; macroanalysis of political discourse; microanalysis of political discourse
positioning, 3–4, 32, 39–40, 41, 55, 111–13, 263
  grammatical positioning and persuasion in speeches, 113–18
  grammatical positioning of actions, 44–5
  and history, 150–4
power, 12, 17, 21
  and discourse, 26–9, 75, 76–7, 78, 85
presupposition, 4, 133–4
pronouns, 44, 75, 250
  deictic pronouns, 121–2
  direct pronouns, 251–3
public discourse, 87–94, 158
  imperative, use of, 88, 89, 93
  negative other, 91–4
  retribution and vengeance against regimes, 87–8
  shahīd and *nafdīk*, 87–8
  shifts in discourse strategies, 124–5, 170–1, 177–9, **178**, **179**, 194–6
  transition from regimes to protesters, 88–90

qad, 153
qātil (murderer/assassin), 91
Quran, 212, 223–4, 237, 259

racism, 75, 77
Reagan, Ronald, 51
reality, 9, 23, 31–2, 53–6
reconciliation, 142–3, 167–71, 218–20, 240–2
Reese, S., 39
Reisigl, M., 114
religion, 36, 60–1, 82, 147, 159–60
  see also Islamic political discourse/Islamic parties
remorse, 123–5, *125*
repetition, 114–18, 135, 158, 182, 224–6
representation, 2, 3–4, 16
  of Arab leaders in images, 101–6, **102**, **104**, **105**
  discourse representation, 41–5
  of foreign actors in political speeches, 95–100
  hedging, 48–9
  metonymy, 46–7
  nominalisation, 45–6
  overlexicalisation, 49–56
  personification/objectification, 47–8
  of protesters (them) in political speeches, 94–5
  revolutions, discourse of, 56–65
  of the self, 228, 231–2
  semiotic representation and political discourse, 100–7

representation (cont.)
    strategies, 35–40
    see also macroanalysis of political discourse; microanalysis of political discourse
revolutions, 56–65
    causes, 56–8
    clampdown on protesters, 62–3
    discursive strategies, 59–60
    ideology, 59
    leadership, 58, 63–5
    religion, role of, 60–3
    social revolutions, 58–9
    vocabulary, 61–2
Richardson, J. E., 44
Rieschild, V. R., 114
Roosevelt, Franklin D., 79–80
Rosiny, S., 69

Sa'āmalu ma'akum (I will work with you), 245
Sacks, Harvey, 10, 11, 12
Saleh, Abdullah, 192, **192**
Sanders, L. M., 38
Saussure, F. De, 16
scaremongering, 144, 163–5, 166
Schäffner, C., 21–2
Schegloff, Emanuel, 10
Schiffrin, D., 7
Scollon, R, 23
self-descriptions/over descriptions, 76
self-praise, 148–50
semantics
    engineering, 42
    labelling, 42–3
semiotics
    of the Arab Spring, 100–1
    national flags as a symbol of identity, 106–7, **106**
    representation of Arab leaders in images, 101–6, **102**, **104**, **105**
sentences, 25–6, 44–5, 247–8
Sewell, W. H., 58
shahīd (martyrdom), 87
Shamul, A. B., 31–2
shuhadā' (martyrs), 161, 199
silmiyya (peaceful), 90–1, 141
simile, 48
slogans, 58, 59, 63, 87, 108, 141, 170–1, 188, 192, **192**
    against Gaddafi, 190–1, **191**
    against Mubarak, 91–3, 190, 193–5, **193**
    multilingualism, 108–9, **109**, 192–6, **193**
    see also public discourse
slur, 189–92, **191**, **192**
social change, 2, 5
    and discourse, 6–34
    and social movement, 83–7
social media see news and media
Somerville, M. A., 83

speeches, 23
    affection in leaders' discourse, 183–5
    anonymisation, 131–3
    antonyms and politeness in leaders' speeches, 201–2
    argumentation, 137–9, 174–9, **178**, **179**
    blame and denial strategy, 139–46
    'call to arms' speeches, 79–81, 82
    cohesion and coherence, 135
    concession discourse, 172–4, **173**, 176–7
    deictic pronouns, 121–2
    foregrounding and backgrounding in speeches, 122–3
    framing/positioning and grammar, 111–13
    grammatical positioning and persuasion, 113–18
    heroism discourse, 154–7
    individualisation vs collectivisation, 125–7
    leaders' strategy shift, 144–6, **145**
    mental process and expressions of perception, 185–6
    mental processes in political speeches, 181–3
    modality, 127–9
    personification, 129–31
    politeness in leaders' speeches, 196–9
    positioning through history, 150–4, 160–3
    presupposition, 133–4
    reconciliation and command discourses, 167–71
    repetition, 114–18, 135
    representation of foreign actors in political speeches, 95–100
    representation of protesters (them) in political speeches, 94–5
    revolutionary speeches, 107–8, 117
    rhetorical speeches, 47–8
    scaremongering, 144, 163–5
    speech reportage, 42
    syntax as power of persuasion, 157–8
    see also Islamic political discourse/Islamic parties
Spencer, A., 255
Spillmann, K. R and K., 52
stereotyping, 49–50, 53, 83
strategic function, 22–3
Stubbs, M., 7
subjectivity, 42
Sudan, 202
syntax, 22
    as power of persuasion, 157–8

tāghūt (dictator), 91, 171
Tajfel, H., 83
Taliban, 50, 54
ta'mīm (generalisation), 145
tashārukiyya (partnership), 220
tawkīd (emphasis), 114
Teo, P., 114

texts
  and context, 19
  discourse as text, 18
  indexicality, 33–4
  intertextual analysis/intertextuality, 18–19, 30–1, 160–3, 199
  news texts, 15–16, 39, 43–4
  textual analysis, 42
Thatcher, Margaret, 52
thawrī (revolution), 117, 150–1
Tienari, J. E., 54–5
tribes, 199–201
Tunisia, 2, 5, 29, 56–7, 70, 72, 73
  Ben Ali's speeches, 95–6, 112–13, 115–17, 121, 122–4, 126, 127–8, 130, 131, 132, 133–4, 138–9, 140, 142–3, 148–50, 154, 158, 163–4, 165, 168, 172, 175–6, 177, 181–2, 184, 185
  images of Ben Ali, 104–6, **105**
  see also Islamic political discourse/Islamic parties
Turkey, 78–9
turn-taking, 11–12, 28

UK Independence Party (UKIP), 77–8
Us vs Them notion, 2, 3–4, 44, 53, 74–5, 141, 191–2, **192**, 228, 257
  and agency, 118–21
  and the beliefs of discourse producers, 84
  'call to arms' speeches, 79–81, 82
  mood effects on intergroup discrimination, 82–3
  and polarisation, 75, 79, 81
  in slogans, 91–2

  social component in discourse, 78–9
  in UKIP's discourse

Van Dijk, T. A., 7–8, 9, 14, 24–5, 26, 37, 42–3, 44–5, 74, 75–7, 84–5, 86
  social-cognitive model, 15–16, 34, 78
Vaughn, K., 71
vocabulary, 13, 41–2, 61–2
vocatives, 255–7

warā'ahā ayādin (at the instigation of parties), 144–5
waṭan (nation), 106, 245
'We are all Khalid Said,' 72
weekdays
  as adjectives, 61–2
  Fridays, 61–2, 66, 108
Weiss, G., 26
Widdowson, H. G., 19
Wilson, A., 56
Wilson, J., 121
Wodack, R., 14–15, 22, 24, 26, 30
Wolf, A., 211
Worth, R. F., 52
Wuthnow, R., 60

yajib, lābuda (should), 128
yasquṭi al-ṭāghūt (down with the tyrant), 158
Yemen, 192, **192**
Yule, G., 9

ẓālim (oppressor), 91
Zollner, B., 211
Zwicky, A., 255

EU representative:
Easy Access System Europe
Mustamäe tee 50, 10621 Tallinn, Estonia
Gpsr.requests@easproject.com

www.ingramcontent.com/pod-product-compliance
Lightning Source LLC
Chambersburg PA
CBHW052046220426
43663CB00012B/2462